The Specter of the Indian

The Specter of the Indian

Race, Gender, and Ghosts
in American Séances,
1848–1890

Kathryn Troy

Published by State University of New York Press, Albany

© 2017 State University of New York

All rights reserved

Printed in the United States of America

No part of this book may be used or reproduced in any manner whatsoever without written permission. No part of this book may be stored in a retrieval system or transmitted in any form or by any means including electronic, electrostatic, magnetic tape, mechanical, photocopying, recording, or otherwise without the prior permission in writing of the publisher.

For information, contact State University of New York Press, Albany, NY
www.sunypress.edu

Production, Ryan Morris
Marketing, Fran Keneseton

Library of Congress Cataloging-in-Publication Data

Names: Troy, Kathryn, 1984- author.
Title: The specter of the Indian : race, gender, and ghosts in American séances, 1848-1890 / Kathryn Troy.
Description: Albany : State University of New York Press, [2017] | Includes bibliographical references and index. | Description based on print version record and CIP data provided by publisher; resource not viewed.
Identifiers: LCCN 2016040641 (print) | LCCN 2017019430 (ebook) | ISBN 9781438466101 (e-book) | ISBN 9781438466095 (hardcover : alk. paper) | ISBN 9781438466088 (paperback : alk. paper)
Subjects: LCSH: Indians of North America—Religion. | Seances—United States—History—19th century. | Spiritualism—United States—History—19th century.
Classification: LCC E98.R3 (ebook) | LCC E98.R3 T76 2017 (print) | DDC 299.7--dc23
LC record available at https://lccn.loc.gov/2016040641

10 9 8 7 6 5 4 3 2 1

For Annabelle Harker and Adrian Belmont

Contents

	Acknowledgments	ix
	Introduction	xi
ONE	Uncanny Indians	1
TWO	Chief Spirit: The Appearance of Black Hawk as Case Study	21
THREE	Spirit Council: The Mission of Dead Chiefs	55
FOUR	Spectral Romance: Sympathy for the Indian Maidens	91
FIVE	Race and Reform Among Spiritualists	115
	Conclusion	151
	Notes	153
	Bibliography	181
	Index	199

Acknowledgments

This book was made possible by many helping hands. First and foremost, the stalwart souls of the Special Collections departments of the American Antiquarian Society, The University of Rochester Library, the Utica Historical Society, and the Boston Athenaeum. God bless that woman working the Houdini Collection at the Library of Congress, and the Interlibrary Loan clerk who processed pile after pile of books, always with a keen interest and good conversation. Special thanks are also deserved by Praeger Publishing, who printed an earlier portion of the analysis on Black Hawk presented here while the longer work was still in progress. A deep, hearty thank you is merited by teachers and mentors for their encouragement over my academic career: Michael D'Innocenzo, Mario Ruiz, Edwin Burrows, and especially Louis Kern, whose willingness to help me go beyond standard course offerings and into independent study planted the germ for the pages that follow. This book is written in loving memory of Edward Solosky, whose bright character and engaging storytelling rang true in my head many years after I left his class, pulling me out of law school and guiding me to my proper place, and my dearly missed grandfather, Louis Sabatella, who made history at Anzio, Italy, who shined with constant laughter, and who encouraged my passion as a way to make friends, rather than enemies. My deepest thanks and unending love to my husband Andy—my sorely overworked, overtraveled, and underpaid research assistant, who scanned and photographed countless pages, held innumerable brainstorming and counseling sessions, and all without question or complaint. In the many brilliant works of his yet to come, I vow to return the favor.

Introduction

The Vanished Return

In her 1885 book *Life and Labor in the Spirit World*, Mary Shelhamer, the sitting medium for the primary Spiritualist journal the *Banner of Light*, recounted her visit to the ghostly realm. "Beyond [a] rolling river," she wrote, "there is a deeply-wooded country. Here you are up high among the mountains; this is the red man's home … it is a refuge for the poor, hunted and despised Indian, who, fleeing from mortal chains, finds therein rest and peace."[1] Her description of Indians as figures in flight, as members of a dying race, was by the late nineteenth century a common one. For many white Americans, Indians were, for the most part, already a thing of the past. They appeared constantly in popular culture as figures of legend and literature, but real Indians were primarily perceived as living relics—faint reminders of a vanished people. But to nineteenth-century Spiritualists, Indians had never completely gone; the ghosts of Indian dead walked among them. The proclaimed presence of Indian spirits in American séances challenged the dominant discourse of Indians as vanished, and had a profound impact not only on the Spiritualist movement, but also on some of the most important debates of the day—those on race, gender, civilization, and the development of an American national character.

This book explores the spectral appearances of Indians in late-nineteenth-century American séances in relation to those national debates, and analyzes the importance of such apparitions on several levels—racial, gendered, religious, and political. It demonstrates the overwhelming pervasiveness of this sorely understudied phenomenon as a central social element of the

Spiritualist movement. The project establishes how the witnessing of Indian spirits affected American minds and the reception of federal Indian policy by influencing concepts of racial difference and sociopolitical hierarchy.

The heart of my analysis examines the racial elements unique to the spiritual manifestations of Indians, as well as how American Spiritualists utilized the Indian spirits they claimed to encounter as sources of political empowerment—as agents of peace between whites and Indians, as models of sexual difference, and as guides to spiritual progression for both races. Spiritualists understood Indian ghosts to appear in séances with a mission to fulfill: to help ensure the inner illumination of Spiritualists, to support white attempts at social reform, and to serve as sources of strength to the female mediums they possessed. They acted as mediators between the material and spiritual realms, providing essential information about the condition and means of progression through the several spiritual spheres, and communicating the temperament and will of the supreme deity commonly referred to as the Great Spirit. Through Indian spirit appearances, Spiritualists were apprised of the Great Spirit's attitude regarding social and political issues, such as the actions to be taken regarding Indian nations, political equality for women, or the correct position on congressional policies. The presence, strength, and support of Indian ghosts were recognized as contributing to the efforts and accomplishments of Spiritualists to create a "heaven on earth" that reflected the enlightened position of spirits.

These spirits did not manifest predominantly as nostalgic symbols of a vanishing race. They appeared frequently in the 1860s to 1880s, when the United States was almost constantly at war with Indian nations, when debates about what to do with Indians raged, and when the future of the North American West was anything but certain. They did not simply appear as Indians who were better off dead in the Happy Hunting Ground, assuaging white guilt about conquests and an imagined vanishing, as has been suggested by many historians—such as Alan Trachtenberg in his writing of fictionalized Indians, Jared Farmer in his discussion of legends representing Indians as ghostly, and most pointedly Molly McGarry in her chapter on Indian spirits.[2] Indian spirits were also not categorized on the whole as being from the distant past and thus safely nonthreatening.[3]

Spiritualists saw Indian ghosts as awakening public outrage and inciting political opposition against the wars waged by the United States on Indians, causing Spiritualists to question government objectives in the West. Spiritualist publications vehemently denounced the Sand Creek Massacre of 1864,

Introduction

George Custer's invasion of the Black Hills, and the duplicity and corruption of American Indian policy, as exemplified in the Ponca Affair of the 1870s and multiple reports on dismal reservation conditions. Spiritualists recognized the support of Indian ghosts for peace policies and political equality, and the efforts of Spiritualists to restore what they felt their country, allegedly superior in religion and civilization, had lost—its sense of honor. They were not simply utilized as servants of the mediums who conjured them; they were praised as guides and instructors, helping to ensure the nation's spiritual future. When Spiritualists closely followed the development of the Indian Peace Commission in 1867, the rise and decline of Ulysses S. Grant's Peace Policy, the success of "civilized" tribes such as the Cherokee, the Carlisle and Hampton Institutes, and the implementation of the Dawes Severalty Act in 1887, they believed they were both heeding ghostly warnings and working to rebuild the pride of their nation. These major events in American/Indian relations are linked in this project to the intensity of Indian spectral appearances and their centrality to the Spiritualist movement's contemporary development, serving as the basis for the powerful trope of the "Indian spirit guide," which persists today.

A deeper analysis than those by previous scholars of the manifestations themselves reveals the complex and sometimes conflicting nature of such phenomena. Scrutiny of the methods, acknowledgments, and purposes of Indian manifestations opens wide a door to a much richer understanding of how the intellectual and professional classes that comprised the foundation of the Spiritualist Movement constantly redefined and integrated the concept of "Indian" into a society structured by racial and sexual difference. The notion of Indianness that emerged from Spiritualist séances advocated a politically nonracial society, whereby Indians could and should become American citizens, and incorporated gender models that undermined contemporary definitions of manliness as positively linked to violence.

In using such terms as "Indian spirits," I refer to manifestations witnessed by Spiritualists in which they claimed to see Indians, including cases of specifically named Indians, as well as those whose "Indianness" derived solely from Spiritualist identification. The ways in which Indian celebrities were authenticated and nameless "Indians" were recognized both reflected how "Indianness" as a scientific racial category was understood and constructed in the Spiritualist arena and, I posit, were reflective of broader American cultural attitudes. The actual presence of Indian spirits at nineteenth-century séances is neither accepted nor denied in this book. It is only relevant that

Spiritualists accepted their experiences as truth. To assert at the onset that all Spiritualists were knowing frauds is risky and counterproductive. Such evaluations invite statements like those of Lisa Lenker, who in her research connected her discussion of Spiritualism with Manifest Destiny rhetoric as supporting the ethnic cleansing of the American continent. Lenker asserted that all Indian ghosts were simply and happily dead (not undead, as the term *ghost* suggests).[4] The ghosts of Indians will often be described throughout this book from the perspective of the Spiritualists themselves—as distinct historical actors. To believers, these specters spoke, made claims, and issued warnings. Writing about their alleged activity in such a way allows this book to delve into the responses and reactions of Spiritualists who believed these apparitions to be intelligent, active agencies. This approach to describing spectral activity is offset by the simultaneous focus on specific individuals deeply involved with Indian apparitions, including the mediums Jennie Lord, Mary Shelhamer, Fannie Conant, and Cora Tappan.

Placing Spiritualist manifestations at the center of this project, essentially shifting the focus onto nonentities, is a somewhat unorthodox approach to the study of history, and has not been the practice employed by other scholars of Spiritualism. Yet doing so allows the incorporation of a body of literature on ghostliness and hauntings that is central to this project. Such scholarship has to this point been absent from Spiritualist studies, strangely so given that the movement, at its core, was about communicating with the dead. Rather than referring to these manifestations only as spirits from the celestial realm or as the products of an American imagination, I abstain from judgment on their existence. By using the labels that Spiritualists themselves did—ghosts of the dead returned to life—I employ a lexicon of definitions that are critical to understanding the full significance of Spiritualist encounters with such phenomena. "Ghosts" are undead—uncanny, temporal disruptions that appear in specific ways at specific times to deliver a message. Communication by such entities conveys information about an obscured past occurrence. To the witness of such phenomena, the presence of the ghost is made clear through a distinct sensory experience, its disruption of logical time remedied only by listening to what the ghost wants and providing it with satisfaction. It is with these terms in mind, originating predominantly in fictive, psychological, and paranormal studies, that I look upon séance activities of nineteenth-century America. In his work on literary hauntings of America during the first half of the century (the period of federally sanctioned Indian removal), Renee Bergland rightly suggested that representations of Indian

Introduction

ghosts simultaneously established and questioned an intangible American nationality, as well as racial and sexual classifications.[5] Examining how the Indian spirits of séances contributed to changing definitions of race and gender is the main thrust of this project.

Organized by theme rather than time, the chapters included in this book cover the nature of Spiritualist hauntings marked as specifically Indian, and the questioning and redefinition of masculinity, femininity, and morality as linked to national progress that took place within séance circles beginning in the 1850s and continuing throughout the 1880s. This time frame will be repeated in each chapter as different aspects of Indian hauntings are visited. A majority of works on Spiritualism have chosen to narrow their scope to the earlier, formative years of the movement. Studies about the Fox Sisters or Andrew Jackson Davis, for example, emphasize the Spiritualism of the 1850s as definitive of the entire movement. Bret Carroll highlighted the 1850s as an emergent period, as did Howard Kerr.[6] Such an approach is not appropriate here. The frequency with which Indian manifestations were recorded was fairly comparable from the 1850s through the 1880s, peaking during the 1860s and 1870s. The decline that Burton Brown said occurred in the 1870s is not borne out by the increased frequency of Indian apparitions.[7] The seemingly consistent presence of Indian ghosts at séances serves in part to bolster my argument that Indian ghosts were a defining characteristic of Spiritualist practice from its inception, and makes discussion of the movement through the course of the century imperative to my efforts. Both Indian policy and Spiritualism evolved in the twentieth century, and continue to do so, but analysis of such changes is beyond the scope of this book. My intention is to demonstrate how spiritual tropes of Indianness developed on the crest of Spiritualism in tandem with a dramatic change in Indian visibility in the public eye.

My focus on recorded instances of Indian specters also determines to a large degree the emphasis on certain sources at the expense of others. While myriad articles, pamphlets, treatises, and monographs by Spiritualists provide this project with a contextual foundation for their beliefs, as well as Indian manifestations, the recording of Indian ghosts emerged predominantly in certain forms of Spiritualist print—namely, their periodicals. Newspapers played a critical role in the development and dispersion of representations of Indians that saturated nineteenth-century American culture and continue to do so.[8] The majority of writing on such phenomena appeared in the *Religio-Philosophical Journal* and *Banner of Light*; these sources are therefore dominant forces in this project. My use of the *Banner of Light* in this book works somewhat as a centralizing force in a movement which had none, and provides a modicum of order to the cacophony of Spiritualist voices. *Banner of Light* takes on an added significance in my research because of its extensive coverage of Indian affairs. The development of the Indian Peace Commission, the Modoc War, the Ponca Affair, and the violation of the 1868 Treaty of Fort Laramie were all covered and editorialized in the weekly journal, receiving consistent attention in a periodical ostensibly dedicated to matters of the spirit. The amount of space accorded to such news should not continue to be overlooked in the analysis of Spiritualist print. The longevity of the *Banner of Light*, enjoying an approximately fifty-year run, speaks once again to the pervasiveness within Spiritualism of this very specific racial phenomenon.[9]

Geographically speaking, this project views Spiritualism as a national movement in a broad sense, with loci of activity in New York and Boston. As the sites of some of the first violent contests with Indian nations, the northeastern states have a well-developed "penchant for hauntedness," as Judith Richardson claimed, "alongside a more enduring popular interest in ghosts and the supernatural."[10] Local variations of Spiritualism did not seem to have a significant impact on Indian spectrality, and so have been omitted from this project. The one exception to that is the Spiritual culture of New Orleans. The connection between this city's history and the spirit of Black Hawk will be discussed in chapter 2. Likewise, while there are many significant connections to be made with contemporary Spiritualist movements across the globe, this project's focus is on American Indian ghosts within American Spiritualism, and the resulting effect on American society. This intention, juxtaposed with the virtual absence of similar phenomena in Europe, justifies the exclusion of such a discussion in this work. The references to Britain's literary gothic tradition are brief, and useful only in demonstrating Spiritualism's place among the gothic tradition of the Western world. European Spiritualism is beyond the scope of this book. Additionally, this project is not about Indian spirituality in its own right, as there were no significant efforts on the part of Spiritualists to understand or incorporate Indian religions into their own belief system. Their interest in native spirituality extended to generalized ideas about animism and a natural Romanticism, which will be addressed in chapter 4.

The remainder of this introduction will serve several functions. It provides a background on aspects of Spiritualist theology that are essential to understanding the arguments made in this project, a discussion of Spiritualism and Indian hauntings in context with changes in federal

Indian policy, a brief summary of the key goals and themes of each chapter, and a few words about the bodies of scholarship most directly engaged and built upon in this book.

The Specter of the Indian

As a consequence of their strong presence in the Spiritualist Movement, American Indian spirits were also the most clearly defined apparitions, even if those definitions were at times inconsistent. In some instances, prominent Indian figures such as Black Hawk appeared to Spiritualists; in a great many others, the "Indians" that appeared in séance rooms did not have proclaimed affiliations to any tribe. The spirit was instead the synthesis of images, characteristics, and behaviors that New England and Midwestern Spiritualists had come to associate with "Indianness" through their exposure to white representations of Indians in popular and scientific media. The presence of Indians in myriad cultural and intellectual forms has been well studied by many, Berkhofer, Trachtenberg, Farmer, and Deloria included. But the study of ghostly Indians in a historical sense, which was built to some degree on Indian figures of folklore and fiction, has been largely ignored as an avenue for studying American perceptions of "Indianness."

Elizabeth Bird rightly argued that imagery of Indians is both profuse and self-reflexive in American culture, yet is also ever-changing.[11] It is for that reason that Spiritualist conjurings of Indians should not be lumped together with literary representations of natives, ghostly or otherwise. Their apparitions exhibited a variety of characteristics of so-called Indianness—savagery, simplicity, nobility, mysticism, and so on. The complexity of Indian manifestations deserves to be analyzed in its own right, with more attention to depth and detail than has been previously attempted by scholars of Spiritualism or of the reappropriation of Indian cultures. My endeavor to do so here is meant to demonstrate how Spiritualists, as a particular segment of American society, built upon legendary and literary imagery while deviating from the justification of Indian death common to those narratives. The literal haunting of America, unlike its literary haunting, caused Spiritualists to see Indian ghosts in a new light that cast moral doubt upon the conquest of the American West. The focus in American literature on Indians as ghosts made their vanishing more finite and complete; as Trachtenberg observed, it absolved guilt over a national virtue built upon violence against Indians.[12] But ghosts, by definition, are more than dead. They are undead, which, when unfettered by the fixed nature of fiction, complicates that absolution of vanishing Indians and reveals a more complex meaning behind representations of Indians as ghostly than literary analyses have to this point suggested.

Scholars of Spiritualism have rarely emphasized the personalities of the apparitions who allegedly appeared at séances. The ghosts under scrutiny in Brown's work are described either as the founding fathers, especially Benjamin Franklin, or as dead relatives of séance sitters. Who the spirits were, how they appeared, or most importantly, what they said, was not discussed in detail. His focus on specific mediums comes at the expense of the broader-based cultural phenomena that are of greater interest to this book. As Carroll argues in "Unfree Spirits," examining the specters as distinct actors, even if they are imagined, is essential to a fuller comprehension of Spiritualism.[13] But while he contends that investigating spirits as actors is essential to understanding Spiritualist theology, he does not engage with spectral manifestations, or recognize the racial and sexual differences among them, except to mention the ghosts of American celebrities such as Thomas Paine or Benjamin Franklin. Carroll argued that spiritual celebrity and authentication were necessary to assert an authority outside the self, which he cited as one of the major appeals of Spiritualism. In my analysis, I connect the particular appearance of a spirit with the desire to prove that such phenomena did not emanate from within the medium. This outward projection in turn changed how Spiritualists perceived living Indians in relation to their spectral counterparts. Given the prevalence of Indian spirits and their status as figures of authority, it is especially important that they be looked at with a critical eye toward how they represented Indianness and how witnessing their apparitions affected the American political climate.

In Carroll's understanding, that also means that this project is more focused on what he called the "popular" or "phenomenal" aspect of the movement, moreso than the "philosophical." While he is correct in arguing that the phenomenal experiences of Spiritualists are meaningless if they do not act as expressions of their philosophy, a submersion into Spiritualist practices, the séance especially, is necessary to access Spiritualist philosophy on its deepest levels.[14] It also corrects the confusion Morita claims is caused by historians' dismissal of the sensational aspects of Spiritualism as unworthy subjects of research.[15] Delving deeper into the details of the séance also distinguishes Spiritualism as unique from mainline Protestantism and other

Introduction   xix

religious minorities of the nineteenth century, hence the exclusive focus in this project on Indian ghosts as they appeared in Spiritualism.[16]

The methods of authenticating Indianness were found in how spirits looked, dressed, sounded, spoke, and moved. Each occurrence under analysis here is thoroughly probed in an effort to trace the ethnic markers and essential elements of racialized and gendered manifestations. Those markers were paramount in Spiritualist attempts to authenticate and legitimate the presence of Indian ghosts in their sitting rooms and spirit cabinets to Americans who, through cultural exposure, had come to see such traits as definitive of Indianness. The simultaneous use of high and low imagery reflects the period's ambiguous definition of "Indian" as a seemingly crystallized set of tropes, though very clearly still in flux.

Similar to the attempted legitimization of Spiritualist beliefs, nineteenth-century concepts of race were also based in science, with physical traits being positively connected to racial difference and hierarchy. My analytical approach to Indian manifestations reflects the empirical modes through which Spiritualists themselves understood the phenomena they claimed to witness, in order to explain the processes of identification, sensory authentication, and construction of racial hierarchies that took place within nineteenth-century séances. This approach on the part of Spiritualists justifies my analysis of these spirits in positivistic ways to identify markers of racial and sexual difference.[17] It also coincides with my treatment of Indian manifestations as literal ghosts, based in sensory realities that are at once similar to and different from the ways in which we perceive the living. Spiritualists heard and saw Indian ghosts, but not in the same way that they heard and saw the people sitting next to them at the séance table. Sensory perception and empiricism are thus doubly important to the analysis of Spiritualist manifestation records.

Chapter 1 provides the groundwork for connecting Spiritualist beliefs and practices with nineteenth-century Indian policy. It also explains in detail my description of Spiritualist experiences in this work as literal hauntings. Chapter 2 focuses on the spectrality of Black Hawk's ghost as a case study, and begins my discussion of several important elements central to the materialization of Indian ghosts. Among these are an analysis of the perceived commonalities in speech patterns, general behavior, and cultural performance that were necessary to the Spiritualist establishment of the identity of Indian spirits. In this way, generalizations and stereotypes were often perpetuated in spectral appearances. Celebrity on the part of Indian spirits therefore took on an added significance. The more details known about the individual, through public speeches or, in the case of Black Hawk, a widely read autobiography, the easier it became to authenticate the spiritual performance. The more accurate and specific the connection between the dead figure and the manifesting spirit, the more credibility Spiritualists gained for their methods, beliefs, and goals for society. Although gone from this world, Indian specters were just that—*Indian* spirits. Many Spiritualists believed they retained all their characteristic traits acquired while on the earth.[18] And yet, Indian spirits did undergo changes—they were described as peaceful and helpful, and oftentimes the spirits themselves acknowledged the postmortem change in their temperament. This transition in image that accompanied the transition to the spirit world is highlighted in the case of Black Hawk. His earlier manifestations through the medium Jennie Lord in the 1850s and 1860s were predominantly descriptive; by the 1880s, Mary Shelhamer's manifestations of Black Hawk's spirit indicated his progression through a change in style and purpose, focusing more strongly on advocating racial peace. In her analysis of Black Hawk's autobiography, Susan Scheckel described Black Hawk, as he appeared in the text, as a constructed figure in an ongoing struggle to be included in the American historical narrative. Yet he no longer fought for a place for Indians living a physical reality.[19] As a spiritual manifestation, Black Hawk continued to appear to the American public on behalf of real Indians. His spirit had one of the most extended presences within Spiritualism, spanning almost the entire movement from his first appearance in 1857 to his last recorded manifestation in 1886. The longevity of Black Hawk's ghostly career makes him an ideal candidate to introduce both the practice of defining Indianness in spiritual bodies characteristic of earlier séances of the 1850s and 1860s and the growing emphasis on spiritual and moral improvement among Indian ghosts more common to later manifestations of the 1870s and 1880s.

It is of great importance that the spirits of Indian males—those of Black Hawk, Logan, Powhatan, King Philip, and Red Jacket, to name a few, were recognized not only as Indians, but as chiefs. Chapter 3 extends the analysis of Indian spirits in positivistic terms to uncover gender differences among Indians as written on ghostly bodies. I focus on the significance of Spiritualists' acknowledgment of almost all male apparitions as chiefs. They recognized strong Indian spirits as signaling that living Indians were deserving of political enfranchisement. Additionally, the elevated moral faculty that spirit chiefs exhibited through their communications served as models of masculinity for white males. The manifestations of chiefs represented a blend of competing nineteenth-century definitions of manhood that valued virility and musculature on the one hand, and civility and restraint on the other. Gail Bederman's work on changing gender values in the nineteenth century, most notably her terms of "primitive" and "restrained" manhood to describe simultaneous yet conflicting definitions of masculinity, will be especially useful in this project in delineating Spiritualists' definitions of manliness, which exhibited a less stark contrast in gender norms at the same time that it espoused gender differentiation as the pinnacle of civilization. This preference was displayed in Spiritualists' positions on Indian policy reform in the 1870s and 1880s, which supported the educational agenda of Richard Pratt at the Carlisle Institute, and the tribal severalty of the Dawes Act, which prioritized individualism and private ownership. These efforts were viewed as humane alternatives to the conquest and extermination that was celebrated by Indian removal and ongoing warfare. Throughout the 1860s and 1870s, some of the most prominent American mediums—Cora Tappan, Fannie Conant, and Mary Shelhamer, for example—were almost constantly haunted by spirit chiefs. While some apparitions were recognized as being long dead, such as Powhatan and Philip, more recently deceased Indians like the Dakota Sioux chief Little Crow appeared with more frequency. His ghost encouraged peaceful negotiations between the United States and his former tribe. The forgiveness of whites exhibited by Little Crow and others was seen as demonstrative of the progress Indian spirits had undergone. During the 1880s, evidence of spiritual progression was cited when arguing that living Indians were capable of being educated and deserving of political entitlement.

Chapter 4 contrasts the appearances of spirit chiefs to those of spirit maidens, who asserted a distinctly feminine moral superiority at the séance table. They did not exert authority through their spiritual strength or claims to power as the chiefs did, but instead highlighted the contradictions between American supremacy and moral virtue. Spirit maidens represented a stronger manifestation of Indians as Romantic and admirably simple, contributing to the mission of spirit chiefs by garnering white sympathy and asserting a subtler critique of white civilization and religious institutions. More strongly than spirit chiefs, female ghosts embodied imagery of the "noble savage" and the tragic Indian. In the 1860s and 1870s, Mrs. Conant's control spirit, Winona, spoke of the violent consequences of white contact and detailed life in the spirit world. One of Cora Hatch's closest spirit guides, Ouina, told similarly tragic stories of her life from the 1860s through the 1880s. Mary Shelhamer's female manifestations in the 1870s and 1880s of lesser-known spirits were profuse in their encouragement of white moral progress. Their descriptions of heaven represented both an Indian ideal, a space free of racial difference and warfare, and an American ideal of political equality for all races and both sexes. Female spirit communications espoused a shift away from the virile masculinity toward a manhood rooted more firmly in Christian morality.

The culmination of Indian manifestations and the effect they had on Spiritualists is the focal point of chapter 5. The book concludes with the contested place of Indians within the spiritual hierarchy and Spiritualist attempts to mimic the spirit world by advocating Indian policy reform. This chapter is most strongly connected to the material world that Spiritualists observed and attempted to improve, based on the models provided by their consulting spirits. It details the support of reform geared toward Indian enfranchisement throughout the Spiritualist movement by focusing on the copious amount of Spiritualist writing related to U.S./Indian interactions. Brown wrote about the lack of a reform impulse among Spiritualists, claiming that they did not experience anything that required them to actively seek abolition. He also asserted that the *Banner of Light* was initially reluctant to discuss political issues surrounding the Civil War.[20] This was not the case regarding Indian affairs. Of particular interest to Spiritualists were negotiations with various tribes, government management of Indian affairs, the emergence of the Grant Peace Policy and Indian Peace Commission, and the emergence of Indian advocacy groups such as the Indian Rights Association and the Women's National Indian Association. My goal is to uncover concerns about Indian affairs as a driving social force of Spiritualism. My research also reveals the movement as a significant site of debate about race, gender, and power, by showing the conflicting views reflected in Spiritualist literature that fed on these issues on a national scale. By undermining the honorable position of Indian conquest, Spiritualist activists endorsed a more humanitarian manhood, one invested heavily in men's role as protectors rather than conquerors. The discovery of corruption in the administration of Indian affairs, actions taken by the federal government to improve living conditions for Indians, and the emergence of legislation aimed at educating and enfranchising Indians were of primary concern to Spiritualists in the 1880s, as evidenced by their constant print coverage of Indian-related topics. Their interest in and response to changes in Indian policy at the end of the century form the core of this final chapter.

This project does not intend to suggest that Spiritualism was the sole driving force behind late-century Indian policy reform. Members of the

Indian Peace Commission and Indian policy reformers more broadly used overwhelmingly Christian language to describe their responsibilities to Indian peoples. So too did Spiritualists in describing their political goals. I do not posit that the attitudes toward Indians that emerged from séances were unique to believers. I do, however, seek to determine where and how Spiritualists and their changing ideas of race and gender fit into the broader push for policy reform present in late-nineteenth-century society. By doing so I hope to add another layer to the concept of reformers' motivations to include Indians in America's future, providing a more nuanced depiction of the nineteenth-century conviction in a progressive society and the place of Indian peoples within that society's hierarchical structure. This book intentionally contributes much more to the understanding of Spiritualist politics than it does to the history of Indian policy.[21] It builds upon the works of Braude and the like, which demonstrate the movement's significance to changing gender values, by addressing definitions of manhood in conjunction with womanhood. It adds a racial dimension to Spiritualist studies that accurately depicts the multiple divisions of nineteenth-century society, rather than focusing on an exclusive black/white binary which overemphasizes slavery and emancipation and obscures the role of U.S./Indian relations in developing the national character. Looking at Spiritualism as a specific group within American society, one that had an enormous amount of interaction with Indian spirits, real or otherwise, it details Spiritualist sentiments on the changing political atmosphere for living Indians away from removal and back toward assimilation. Finally, it prioritizes manifestational phenomena over the theological posturing of mediums in order to showcase the core meanings and cultural significance of Spiritualist experience.

Intersecting Race, Gender, and Ghosts

Several separate bodies of historical scholarship—most notably studies of nineteenth-century Spiritualism, Indian policy, and the history of American perceptions of Indians—are brought together by this project. Doing so illuminates the previously neglected role of the Native American ghost as central for Spiritualists. Recent scholarship on Spiritualism has focused on the social and religious goals of its adherents as participants in a movement for reform. Spiritualist efforts have been connected to the struggle for women's rights, a feminized social morality, and abolitionism. As a religious movement, its purpose was to contact the spirits of loved ones separated by death in order to fill an emotional void many felt stemmed from contemporary, overrationalized religious experiences. Yet any discussion of the spirits themselves has been overly cursory and simplistic. The work *Mediums and Spirit Rappers*, for example, cites the 1850s and 1870s as two peaks of the movement, but treats Spiritualism as a historical subject very briefly, dedicating most of its pages to Spiritualism's influence on American literature. The research undertaken here demonstrates that racial and sexual distinctions are insignificant to the understanding of the movement.[22] Of primary concern to Robert Moore's work are the ways in which Spiritualists both adopted and perpetuated scientific language, interest, and values. Yet it addresses the periphery of the séance experience, rather than the séance itself, which is situated at the movement's core. Again, ghosts are treated in his work as collective and homogenous, with no consideration given to sexual or racial difference.

Too few pages have been dedicated to the large presence of Indian spirits in this movement and the broader insights into nineteenth-century society that such an analysis can provide. In her book on Spiritualist campgrounds as feminized Indian space, Bernadino Angelino gave short shrift to the description of the ghosts coming out of the wigwams themselves. She claimed they appeared grand and somber, and that "mirthful" appearances would have been rare.[23] In the larger body of Spiritualist literature, many spirit chiefs, including Black Hawk, and almost all the spirit maidens, exhibited enthusiasm and vivacity as central components of their hauntings. Indian spirits need to be broken down into their constituent categories—celebrity versus generic, male versus female—to fully realize the complexity of their Indianness. Though the white rendition of "Indian" is quickly dismissed by scholars as an overused stereotype, examining the act of stereotyping can itself be useful. Stereotypes have a plurality that can be self-contradictory, and each variation of a stereotype is imbued with distinct meanings that are connected to racial, sexual, and cultural tropes at play both within the Spiritualist movement and American culture. Though Molly McGarry's work *Ghosts of Futures Past* included a chapter dedicated to Indian ghosts and made some observations about militant advocacy among Indian spirits, she did not discuss specific policy advocacy for Indians on the part of Spiritualists, such as their efforts toward education and citizenship rights that culminated in the Dawes Act; nor did she carry her analysis to the end of the nineteenth century to view the comprehensive impact of Indian spirit appearances. The nuances of Indian manifestations, which she herself wrote were "central and particular to the practice of Spiritualism," are the heart of this book.[24]

Likewise, not enough attention has been paid to the spirits of Indian ghosts as a direct source of empowerment for their white, middle-class, predominantly female mediums. Women such as Emma Hardinge Britten, Jennie Lord, and Cora Richmond were among the highest respected mediums at the height of the movement. As such, they were able to reach much larger audiences, and have a more direct impact on American political and social life. Female mediums acquired their strong public voices not simply by "playing Indian"; in fact, pains were constantly taken to demonstrate that Indian spirits, while communicating through their mediums, were physically separate from their mediums. The spirits' voices, statures, and physical shapes were deliberately and meticulously recorded as being impossible for the often frail and petite mediums to mimic. The mediums' source of empowerment came not from a cultural performance alone but from the psychological and emotional support that such an appearance was believed to provide, as well as the speeches and publications that followed. It came from a new and meaningful relationship with Native Americans, even if a relationship entirely in spirit (with the exception of Cora Richmond, who claimed partial Indian ancestry), that provided a new outlook on national designs of expansion. It came from the conviction that the mediums' efforts at peace and social reform reflected a divine will, and that the future of the nation would be one of destruction and heavenly retribution in the absence of their efforts. In essence, the public role that mediums took on, under the guidance of their Indian spirits, became a responsibility of cosmic proportions.

The intimate connection between Spiritualists and the nineteenth-century impulse for social reform has been well studied. In centering on women's rights activists and abolitionists, a direct focus on the voices of Indians (and, for that matter, African Americans) has been largely omitted from Spiritualist scholarship. Just as Braude argues that "the annals of Spiritualism contain the history of another woman's rights movement in addition to the ... women suffrage movement," a heretofore obscured history of the constructed Indian is also accessible.[25]

Important events and shifts in U.S. federal policy also play a pivotal role in this project. The history of changing Indian relations is juxtaposed to important shifts in Spiritualist sentiment and actions happening during the same time. Such events are considered in relation to Spiritualist thought; the materials under analysis in this book are scrutinized not only for Spiritualist reactions to séances they conducted, but also for their responses to reports about violence and negotiation between Americans and various Indian nations, including the Cherokee, Ponca, and Sioux. Both the history of changing interactions between America and Indians and how those interactions were depicted by the nineteenth-century press are therefore essential. The large body of scholarship on U.S./Indian relations is drawn on in this project to help provide a historical context for Spiritualist attitudes and advocacy. More prominent works include those of Prucha, Adams, Hoxie, Berkhofer, and Ostler. The works of Francis Prucha and John Coward in discussing Indian policy and media coverage are invaluable. I incorporate the work of scholars such as David Adams and Ward Churchill in relation to growing American attempts, largely supported by Spiritualists, to assimilate Indians culturally.

Much has been written on how the image of the Indian was constructed by whites at various historical points, but scholars of such phenomena have rarely reached out to Spiritualist sources as an avenue of inquiry. In *History's Shadow*, Steven Conn argues that nineteenth-century racial categories were complicated by the still-strong presence of Native Americans in the white American consciousness, and that only at the beginning of the twentieth century did these categories devolve into the black/white binary so common among historians of race.[26] It is therefore appropriate that Spiritualism, a major social force in the nineteenth century, be examined for evidence of what Conn called a "third" racial category—that of Indians—and American modes of its construction and its impact on white society.

The abundance of scholarship dedicated to studying white representations of Indians has focused primarily on the concept of civilization and the "noble savage." Ter Ellingson and Robert Berkhofer see "savagery" as the most important aspect of Indian representation, without fully acknowledging the impact of the spiritual image of Indians on white imaginations as morally superior. Ellingson goes farther, arguing that images of Indians were constructed to suit white political needs. This project argues that the images of Indian ghosts reveal a complex debate about the "Indian question" through language that sometimes supported vanishing by depicting spiritual appearances as yet another mode of "civilizing" Indians, and at other times deemed imagined Indian lifestyles and religions as socially and morally superior. Showcasing the centrality of Indian spirits puts a new focus on how Spiritualists and their goals are currently understood—placing the previous emphasis on the Spiritualist struggle for women's rights and abolition within a broader social context of how race and gender norms were defined and power was contested. It also demonstrates the growing importance of an imagined Indian spirituality to American culture in the nineteenth century; current scholarship on this phenomenon, such as Philip Jenkins's work, has been almost exclusively focused on the twentieth century, and Indian elements of the New Age.

The appearances of Native Americans in Spiritualist séances should not be oversimplified as yet another form of what Philip Deloria labeled "Indian play."[27] Rayna Green wrote that the act of "playing Indian," as defined by Deloria, is a very particular process, dependent upon the physical and psychological removal of Indians, to the point that Americans must either believe Indians to be dead or kill them off to successfully impersonate them.[28] It is for this reason that spirit manifestations cannot be dismissively lumped into a category that defines them as Indian play. Under analysis here are not just Indians, but Indian ghosts, things that exist by definition simultaneously in the past and the present. In a "physical" sense, Indian spirits were dead, yet materialized (to the satisfaction of séance participants) a spiritual body that was acknowledged by the senses—sound, touch, and, occasionally, sight. Living Indians, seen in continuity with the dead, were not perceived by Spiritualists as vanished. Indians were still publicly visible to them in news reports of military campaigns, peace treaties, published autobiographies, Eastern tours, visits to Washington, and publicized speeches. One of the most direct links between Indians and Indian ghosts were the spirit messages that came addressed specifically to other Indians, as in the case of Red Cloud and Big Eagle, discussed in chapter 3. In a "psychological" sense, Indian spirits were still present through the consistent recognition of markers of "Indianness" on the spiritual body. Indianness as a racial concept, and Indians as racial other, were still present in nineteenth-century séances. Living Indians were also still psychologically present to Spiritualists. The connection between Indian spirits and Indians remained firmly established through the insistence on spiritual Indianness, and the spiritual discourse about conditions for living Indians in need of correction. The issue of what to do with living Indians, and how Indian policy should be reformed, were ongoing questions that remained at the forefront of Spiritualist consciousness. The "removal" or "vanishing" of Indians, especially for Spiritualists and other advocates, was not a completed process. Perhaps Indian populations had drastically declined in the past few decades, and they had been physically removed from certain areas, but the federal policy of removal was one part of an ongoing effort to solve the Indian problem. And while Indian removal certainly helped support imagery of Indians as "vanishing," fictional or otherwise, it was insufficient to cement the figure of the Indian as entirely "vanished" for Spiritualists, who experienced a counterexpression of that vanishing through their hauntings. Indians continued to exist for Americans, as their ghosts haunted Americans both physically and mentally.[29] Therefore, the practice of "playing Indian" as a theoretical construct has a limited usefulness in discussing Indian manifestations. While it focuses on aspects of Indianness recognized by non-Indians through performance, Spiritualist convictions in the truth of their experiences shifts the focus to the haunting aspects of Spiritualism, moreso than an evaluation of deliberate mimicry.

Recent historians have done laudable work in correcting the notion that Spiritualism was a cultural aberration, unworthy of scholarly analysis, by demonstrating its profound social significance. Scholars of fin-de-siècle American culture have also acknowledged the impact of the movement. In his religious survey of America, Sydney Ahlstrom described Spiritualism as "a religious force [that] became a common phenomenon all across the country," which attracted members from a variety of more traditional denominations and sects.[30] Ahlstrom placed Spiritualism within the context of new ways of death, dying, and mourning after the Civil War. For Jackson Lears, Spiritualism was one of many manifestations of turn-of-the-century antimodernism.[31] Yet in many ways, Spiritualists situated themselves as members of a distinctly modern religion. Adherents to Spiritualism wrote of their many influences from alternative religions, both ancient and contemporary. They drew from the theological traditions of Quakers, Shakers, Swedenborgians, Hermetics, and Freemasons. Simultaneously, they aligned themselves with cutting-edge scientific philosophies—psychometry, phrenology, and mesmerism—and praised instances of clairvoyance wherever they were recognized.[32] Albanese describes Spiritualism as a hub that combined "the vernacular practices of whites, Indians, and blacks," and strains of "Hermeticism, Quakerism, Swedenborgianism, Davis's harmonialism, universalism, popularized Transcendentalism, progressivism, social reform and rationalized scientism."[33]

Studying Spiritualism in the context of broader shifts and reactions toward modernity positions the movement at the center of key changes in American life. Yet I agree with Moore's assessment that the majority of the writing on Spiritualism oversimplifies the movement by categorizing it as one more manifestation of social and religious unrest.[34] Looking at Spiritualism solely in the context of other nineteenth-century religious movements does not do it justice, but neither does analyzing Spiritualism only on its edges.

By restricting inquiries into the lives of mediums, and not the ghosts they conjured, our understanding of Spiritualism and its importance will stagnate. To comprehend the movement and its impact on American culture, we must look more closely at their records of séance activity, scrutinizing who and what was being manifested, and to what end. My particular focus on Spiritualist reform initiatives as connected to changes in Indian policy highlights how their ideas about the spiritual realm were expressed in their goals for the material realm.

Several other bodies of literature also support this focus. Putting more of an emphasis on the ghosts themselves facilitates the incorporation of literature on the significance of haunting, and the cultural impact of Indian ghosts as the return of a race commonly perceived as "vanishing." Close attention is paid in this project to the ways in which the ghosts that manifested at séance tables resembled ghosts of legend and literature. The fictive "Indian" served as a central figure of American literature since the 1820s. The "cult of the Vanishing American" was crystallized in James Fenimore Cooper's 1826 novel *The Last of the Mohicans*. The countless tales that succeeded it created a national literature, drawing tension from the characterization of Indians as noble savages, quickly and sadly fading from this world.[35] Their mortality made them highly Romanticized tragic subjects. As Louise Barnett wrote, "concern with the tragedy of the Indians was a legitimate manifestation of nationalism, for from that tragedy, what promised to be the greatest example of Western civilization [came to be ... it] promulgated a more complex attitude about white-Indian relations than the captivity narrative, [contextualizing] the struggle for possession of the continent."[36] Despite the overwhelming success of Henry Wadsworth Longfellow's poem *The Song of Hiawatha* in 1855, by the 1860s, the figure of the Indian as "Noble Savage" was relegated to popular cultural forms.[37] The Romantic tropes of the Noble Savage saturated the American cultural landscape, and informed how Spiritualists reacted to Indians hauntings.

The study of gender in the nineteenth century is also central to my analysis of male and female spirits, their differing appearances and their acceptance by Spiritualists as ideal gender models. The works of Gail Bederman and Amy Greenberg in particular have contributed to this project's understanding of late-nineteenth-century definitions of manliness and womanliness, and how both race and gender figured into a Darwinian concept of sociopolitical hierarchy and a progressive civilization. J. A. Mangan spoke of "manliness" as a fluid term in the nineteenth century; in this book I describe Spiritualism as a site not only of information about female empowerment and women's rights, as Braude points out, but also where nineteenth-century ideas and expressions of manliness, as well as womanliness, can be observed.[38] The models put forth by Indian manifestations were meant to be absorbed and imitated, and were in dialogue with other definitions of sexual difference and moral values being expressed. Ideas about racial difference in relation to the gendered body and political enfranchisement are also reflected in the manifestations of spirit chiefs and maidens, who were touted as ideals of gendered perfection, citizenship, and civic virtue. My intention with this project is to contextualize Spiritualism within these bodies of work by detailing the activities and attitudes of Spiritualists that demonstrated deep concern over the definition of an American identity as powerful yet civilized, and the intimate connection between the understanding of race, gender differentiation, and the national character.

ONE

Uncanny Indians

Spiritualist Belief and Practice

At the center of the loosely defined Spiritualist Movement was the belief that the spirits of the dead could communicate with the living. Seen by many Spiritualists and Spiritualist scholars as beginning with the Fox Sister rappings in New York in 1848, Spiritualism emerged as a widely popular and progressive religious movement, predominantly in the Northeast, but which spread "steadily and rapidly … in the West, and in the Old World as much as the New."[1] Spiritualism as a movement continues to be loosely defined due to its nature; as an outgrowth of Reform Protestantism, Spiritualism was vehemently antiauthoritarian, which made organization of members and the declaration of a common creed nearly impossible.[2] It is likewise difficult to specifically define the demographic composition of such a fluctuating constituency. Several scholars have noted the difficulty of pinpointing a Spiritualist constituency as a result of their own aversion to institutionalization. Brown's research centered around the lack of organization among Spiritualists, the problems that led to disunity and noninstitutionalism, and the difficulty scholars have faced in attempting to impose order and a general definition on Spiritualism that did not exist in its own time.[3] He asserted that attempting demographic coverage would be unproductive and unreliable.[4] The difficulty of defining a body of Spiritualists, and the seemingly small return on such efforts, does not merit my attempting it here.[5]

Spiritualists did make some attempts to quantify their movement in both geographical and numerical terms. In her monograph *Modern American*

Spiritualism, the eminent medium Emma Hardinge Britten categorized the growth of the movement as follows:

> No year in the first epoch of modern Spiritualism [as opposed to the spiritualism of antiquity] has been more fruitful with events of interest than 1850. It was in that year that manifestations of the most violent and astounding character appeared in the family of Dr. Eliakim Phelps, D.D., of Stratford, Connecticut. It was then also that rappings, automatic writing, and other intelligent modes of communing with spirits became familiar in Boston through the mediumship of Mrs. Margaret Cooper, daughter of the eminent lecturer and writer, LeRoy Sunderland.[6]

Only two short years after the spiritual instigation of the Rochester rappings, Britten claimed, Spiritualists in New England began to develop a variety of skills and methods for communicating with the dead. Individual mediums became known by the specific methods they employed, including such things as conducting light or dark séances, automatic writing, trance manifestations, spirit portraiture or photography, or an especial focus on musical séances. Britten went on to explain the geographic reach of the movement, stating that "the soaring spirit of a liberal and progressive community has given so warm and hospitable a reception to the angel visitors of the spheres, that Cincinnati may well be called a royal stronghold of Spiritualism."[7] She noted that "as early as 1852, a paper entitled *Light from the Spirit World* was published in St. Louis, Missouri, and that the first circles conducted there were done so by a Mr. Hedges, who had received guidance on this front during a visit to New York."[8]

The publication of Spiritualist journals was a central activity within the movement, connecting adherents across the country by disseminating their opinions on issues of faith and philosophy. Readers were kept abreast of the stance of Spiritualism toward worldly events and developments, and also read contributors' experiences of spiritual activity and manifestations, as both proof of a progressive afterlife and a source of illumination. The most prominent, prolific, and popularly read of these publications was the *Banner of Light*, a weekly journal published in Boston from 1857 to 1905. This periodical served as the central source of Spiritualist information and thought, republishing correspondence from local papers across the country, and likewise being cited in those smaller journals to more local bodies of readership. Throughout the *Banner of Light*'s pages, correspondence regarding Spiritualist activity came from major cities across the country, including Cincinnati, St. Louis, and San Francisco.

When Emma Hardinge Britten published her history of modern Spiritualism, the movement was still vigorous and ongoing. The proofs of the truth of Spiritualism, she said, "are indeed, still transpiring, and occur constantly in the experience of *eleven millions* of persons in America, whose numbers include authors, editors, doctors, lawyers, clergymen, professors of colleges, magistrates on the bench, statesmen, traders, operatives, and mechanics."[9] In Dr. James M. Peebles's work *Seers of the Ages: Embracing Spiritualism Past and Present*, he referred to the prestigious opinion of the famous Spiritualist Judge Edmonds, described as "a jurist of unimpeachable integrity and keen discernment, [who] estimate[d] the number of Spiritualists in this country at 'eleven millions.'"[10] Historian Robert Cox's work supported a membership in the millions, and Ann Braude wrote of a possible membership range between "a few hundred thousand to eleven million" out of a national population of twenty-five million in 1890.[11]

The relationship between Spiritualism and Christianity is largely ambiguous. Many treatises on the philosophy of Spiritualism were in fact discussions of Christian theology and the intersection between Christian and Spiritualist thought. Some Spiritualist writers described the supernatural events of the Bible as the spiritualism of antiquity, in continuity with contemporary phenomena termed "modern" spiritualism. Spirits were often compared to Biblical angels, lending their communications significant weight.[12] The perceived superiority of spirits in matters of morality elevated spirits and their messages, Indian or otherwise, to a higher position than that afforded to the living, allowing them to serve as models of gender differentiation and racial equality. Many who identified themselves as Spiritualists did not cease to identify as Christians; Universalists, for example, constituted a large part of the Spiritualist Movement because the latter's general ideals coincided with the former's goal of a society in universal harmony.[13] Methodists, Presbyterians and other Protestant sects also filled the ranks of Spiritualism. The morality espoused by Spiritualists in regard to treatment of Indians was itself largely Christian in nature. The difference, Spiritualists argued, was that the tenets of Christianity would be more truthfully followed by those communing with the dead, with a watchful eye on the use of Christian supremacy as a faulty rationalization for Indian disenfranchisement. Ann Taves spoke of Spiritualism as a liberal outgrowth of Protestant opposition to formalism and institutionalization.[14] Their distaste for official churches is pertinent to the notion of the afterlife as Romantic and natural, propounded by the spirit maidens at the center of chapter 4, and it also figures in chapter 5's discussion of their discourse on President Grant's Peace Policy. Others saw demonic forces at work in Spiritualism, rejecting it as a form of Satanic delusion and a false religion. While this project makes claims about Spiritualist ideas and attitudes in a broad sense as expressed in their literature, it is equally important to remember that Spiritualist voices were not always united, and reflected the various opinions of Americans on issues such as race and gender on a national scale. The relationship between Spiritualists' beliefs and their Christian background was likewise individualistic. That fact will be important in considering how Spiritualists related to their largely Christian nation. Spiritualists would frequently call upon Christian sentiments and obligations, for example, in advocating reform in Indian policy, a point developed further in chapter 5.

One of the few practices common among Spiritualists was the definition of spiritual communications in scientific terms of the day—"in terms of magnetism, electricity, and nervous fluid."[15] "Spiritualists," the editor of the periodical *The Present Age* said, "profess to have a scientific religion, and we should therefore, expect among them to find an ardent devotion to science, and a high degree of scientific culture."[16] Throughout Spiritualism's popularity, the debate about how to define the movement—as a new religion, as a new religious sect, or as a new science, was ongoing, and never entirely resolved. Dr. Napoleon Wolfe, for example, declared that "Spiritualism is not a religion in a partisan sense. It is greater than this: *it is a science.* With no church but the universe, with no creed but truth, with no formulated prayer to sustain it, it constructs itself a power to rescue mankind from the sin of ignorance, from the crime of false worship."[17] On the one hand, this passage references the need for quantifiable data and proof able to withstand contemporary scientific scrutiny in the accreditation of recorded phenomena; it also demonstrates the acceptance of Spiritualist interpretations of the meaning and consequences of that spiritual truth. Scientific accountability, in other words, was essential to establishing the legitimacy of Spiritualism, as a religion or otherwise. It demonstrated that Spiritualism defied conventional definitions of religion. It lacked a dogma or organizational structure—in both belief and practice. To a large extent, this is also why the approach of different Christian sects to Spiritualism would become problematic. On the whole, the view of Spiritualism espoused by Wolfe put two major points into perspective:

the obstacles to quantifying a Spiritualist constituency, and the crucial role of contemporary science.

Spiritualism had much in common with its abundant metaphysical contemporaries. In a broad sense, occultism is generally understood to be of a hidden or private nature. But according to religious scholar Mitch Horowitz, American religions with occultist leanings were distinctively open to the public. The practices of American occultists, he argues, emphasized an "ethic of social progress and individual betterment. These religious radicals, living outside the folds of traditional churches and mostly overlooked in the pages of history, transformed a young nation into a launching pad for the revolutions in therapeutic alternative spirituality that swept the earth in the nineteenth and twentieth centuries."[18] Spiritualists' deviation from the furtiveness normally associated with occultism came more from their scientific perspective. As Moore points out, séance attendees were encouraged to repeat their experiences to anyone who would listen. The retelling of the events of a séance acted as a sort of scientific reporting of results, whereby the medium was bound (sometimes literally) to specific conditions which would satisfy her audience of the authenticity of the spirit communication. Yet these retellings were done in a simple manner, requiring neither specialized knowledge nor preparation on the part of the circle.[19] Although many Spiritualists disavowed themselves of religious labels, opting instead to see Spiritualism as a modern science, they still operated within a religious context—they legitimized ancient spiritualisms as much as they panned them. If anything, the battle in print to define Spiritualism by either term only demonstrates this as both an internal and external conflict.

Spiritualism is grounded firmly in metaphysical thought. Catherine Albanese writes that metaphorical movements defined the material world and the spiritual world as mirror images of each other.[20] Spiritualist practitioners borrowed language about altered states of consciousness and the higher faculties of the brain, including clairvoyance, largely from mesmerism and phrenology, both imported from Europe in the 1830s.[21] Self-improvement and social reform were tenets of phrenology, Freemasonry, and radical Quakerism before the famous rappings heard at the Fox household in 1848.[22] Spiritualism was nonconventional and pluralistic by nature. Most importantly, Spiritualism, like other American metaphysics, shined light on occultism, commodifying "what had once been but dimly understood, deeply feared, and described in contradiction to scriptural morality," and made it available for the masses.[23] Though many séances were conducted in the dark, they were far from invisible. Mediums repeatedly extended invitations to the public to experience their mediumship and judge for themselves.[24] It turned discourse that was the traditional purview of theologians into a scientific debate.

The scientific rhetoric of Spiritualism extended to technological innovation—the mode of ghostly communion was commonly referred to as the "spiritual telegraph line."[25] As part of their efforts at legitimacy, Spiritualists defined the phenomena they witnessed and interpreted them through the lens of accepted contemporary sciences. In attempting to define members of the Spiritualist movement, Robert Moore emphasized the relationship between Spiritualist language and contemporary values of empiricism, optimism, evolutionary progress, and reform.[26]

Both nineteenth-century practitioners and contemporary scholars have pointed to the many parallels between Spiritualism and Shakerism. Emma Hardinge Britten described Shakerism as "heralding modern Spiritualism."[27] The most pertinent similarity between the two for the purposes of this book, moreso than the "prominence of women in the facilitation of religious experience" described by Albanese, are the "hordes of Indians" manifested during Shaker ceremonies.[28] Yet Spiritualist manifestations of Indians differed greatly from those of the Shakers, which Albanese called largely "boisterous antics."[29]

The preeminent literature on performance studies, including *Playing Indian*, *Love and Theft*, and *Bodies in Dissent* has a limited usefulness here. So much of the analysis of racial performances rely on the consciousness of the performers and the active negotiation of cultural tropes in the search for "authenticity." In *Bodies in Dissent*, Daphne Brooks describes spirit possession as the "comingling of male Indian bodies with female white ones as a loss of social and cultural categories."[30] She writes about Spiritualism in the context of nineteenth-century showmanship, where the séance is aimed at demonstrating "spectacles of transfiguration" and "the convertibility of the body."[31] This proves problematic because of the Spiritualist claims of agencies outside of the self, and the emphasis of spirit over matter. Working within Brooks's framework would require this book to assume that all nineteenth-century Spiritualists were conscious performers—in other words, that they were all frauds. That is not a claim I am willing to make here—namely, because it would be irrelevant. They were not transparent in their mimicry or an alleged desire to deceive others. If instead we look at these performances as either genuine or unconscious/internalized, only what practitioners believed is relevant, and the mechanics of the construction of racial tropes emerges from an indeterminate agency. Only the results are palpable—that the racial character of these specters was *recognized* as such. The recognition in this case is rather a passive act. It rests upon the satisfaction of the audience, not the action of the medium. Both the medium and the manifestation must rely on established cultural objects, and would have to adhere to them for legitimacy and authenticity. Mediums could not, in essence, break new ground in stereotype construction without first playing upon accepted ones. That is what Indian manifestations within séances exhibit—stereotypes of Indians are framed and interpreted in very specific ways that reflect the complex interplay between race and gender, "Indianness" as related to modernity, and the conflicted sentiment toward Indian peoples and policy.

Albanese places emphasis on Spiritualist reform efforts for women's rights, as argued by Braude, and abolition. Indian rights as an impetus is acknowledged, but minimally. I argue that it was at least as important as these. Given their connection to Quakers, the forerunners of Indian missions, it was ingrained in Spiritualist culture from its inception. The link between Indian appearances and Spiritual political posturing is clearly demonstrable.[32] The main tenets of Spiritualism drew deeply on the society from which it emerged. Due to the previous popularity of scientific-occult movements, as Butler observed, the American middle-class elite easily digested the claim of the Fox sisters.[33] They were also primed to accept Indian ghosts. By 1848, rhetoric of the "vanishing Indian" was also firmly established, and these two driving forces of American culture readily coalesced.

Among the most important strains of Spiritualist thought were the parallels Spiritualists drew between concepts of civilization and racial difference and their understanding of spiritual hierarchies. Drawing on Swedenborgian thought, they generally understood the spirit world to consist of several spheres, each with its own unique character.[34] In the *Religio-Philosophical Journal*, Prentice Mulford described these spheres as "partly located in belts or bands encircling our earth, somewhat as the rings about Saturn and Jupiter."[35] They believed movement occurred between these spheres, but under very specific conditions on the part of the spirit. When traveling between spheres (Earth included), "spirits pass into these new forms in accordance with the same law which in turn decomposes and etherealizes the grain of sand. It is the grand chemistry of Nature."[36] The spheres themselves, and the processes by which spirits move through them, is thus defined as a chemical process. According to Dr. William Ramsey, "there are many circles, probably seven."[37] Seven was the most common number used when defining the spheres, with Earth as the first sphere, and spheres two through seven representing different stages of spiritual progress.

Spiritualists thought that the sphere in which a particular spirit resided was directly connected to their individual state of enlightenment. Passing through one sphere to the next, therefore, required a change in the character of the spirit itself. Just as the firm belief in the inevitability of national and individual progress was a central value in American life, progress and spiritual evolution were key components of the afterlife in the mind of the American Spiritualist. The spirit-driven motivation to evolve and proceed through the spheres served as the primary purpose for spirit interactions with humans. This hierarchical aspect of the spiritual appearance was an integral one to the recognition of racial and spiritual difference. Concerning the quantifiable parameters of the spiritual world, "the Spirit-Land has no particular locality or limit. It is boundless and diffused throughout all space. It is divided into many worlds, or spheres, each corresponding with the degree of development of its inhabitants … it is just as tangible and appears just as real to us [spirits] as earth does to you."[38] The spirit world was described as spatially abstract, yet with a structure firmly based in a sensory reality. In describing the spirit world to the members of séance circles, apparitions consistently emphasized the exacting materialistic nature of the spirit world as a mirror image of Earth, vastly improved:

> [T]he spirit, or Summer-Land, is real and substantial—more substantial to spirits than this earth to mortals … The spiritual is real … so the entranced and clairvoyant of this age behold delightful fields, landscapes, gardens, flowers, fruits, rivers, lakes, fountains, vast assemblages of spirits, musical bands, lyceum gatherings, sportive children, scholars of design, art galleries, magnificent mansions, and architectural abodes of beauty, where loving hearts beat and throb as one.[39]

The reference to the spirit world as the "Summer-Land" was a common one; the description of the world in this seasonal tone was intended to connote the lush verdure, pleasant atmosphere, and Edenic harmony to be found there. The idyllic natural landscape was populated with the best society had to offer, as the reference above to museums and art galleries suggested, but there was a consistent emphasis on the natural character of the Summer Land in multiple descriptions of it. Any departure from that was made relevant by the Romantic tone of the depiction. The spirit of Josephine Bonaparte, for example, explained the parallel between heaven and earth thus: "We have in the Spirit-land all you have in life: birds, fruits, flowers, paintings, books, and whatever else that can charm the taste or improve the understanding. Here all is beautiful, all is harmony and peace."[40] Art and literature continued to be regarded as means of enlightenment and development in the spirit world, alongside a more naturalized setting. As Bonaparte's spirit suggested, the central characteristics of the spirit land were beauty, harmony, and happiness. But there were levels of happiness, and levels of spiritual evolution, that were marked by a journey through all the spheres as a sign of a spirit's ultimate progress. Dr. Peebles claimed that "all spirits were once mortals. All angels were once spirits ... Those in the celestial heavens are termed angels, because they have *advanced* beyond the taints and selfish loves of their mortal existence."[41] According to the Illinois State Spiritualist Association, all spirits fell under one of three major categories:

> FIRST, those who are so bound to earth conditions that they will try to come into contact, and to communicate with it through any avenue they find available; SECOND, those who are naturally attracted to us [mortals] by the ties of relationship and the laws of love. THIRD, those advanced and developed spirits who return from the higher spheres of life in the Spirit World, filled with Holy Love for Humanity, for the purpose of guiding and leading mankind into higher knowledge and Further Light.[42]

Thus, the character of each spirit, and their reasons for appearing in séances, demarcated a specific status for each spirit, integrally connected to their level of progression and the sphere (or state of progress) in which they were purported to reside.

This basic understanding of spiritual difference takes on an added significance when Indian spirits, defined generally as belonging to a separate racial category, are analyzed and categorized according to the accepted hierarchical structure of the universe. Their communication with the living was understood on a basic level as one of the essential pieces of their upward transcendence of the spheres. Carroll argued in his work that acknowledging spirits and their position in the celestial hierarchy was an important element of Spiritualists' search for order.[43] It is unfortunate that his work lacks an in-depth discussion of who spirits purported to be or what they allegedly said, making the important task of determining spirits as authority figures impossible. I attempt to remedy that omission herein. Although not universally accepted, Spiritualists sometimes interpreted the frequency of Indian apparitions as deriving from lower spheres, thus demarcating a lower spiritual status for Indians. They were perceived as more bound to earth, connected still to its inhabitants, and *needing* to help living souls if they hoped to achieve higher planes of existence. This work was the recognized fate of most Indians, because of their wars and perceptions of living Indians as savage. Other Spiritualists argued that Indian spirits, with their lofty aims for humankind, hailed from the highest spheres. This debate will be returned to in chapter 5.

The division of spheres not only dictated the nature of relations between spirits and mortals, but also defined interactions between spirits residing in different spheres, delineating further the distinct divisions and hierarchies among recognized forms of spiritual existence. In *The Revelator*, Abraham Pierce described how "in each circle [spirits] had teachers from higher spheres, who come to instruct them and to assist them to progress. As they progress in knowledge of the great truths, they change in their conditions, and pass onward to a higher circle."[44] The ultimate goal of all spirits, then, was to help less enlightened or "lower" spirits attain further illumination and ultimately pass to heaven, described more as a state of mind, rather than a distinct place, outside of the seven spheres. The way this perfected harmony and progress was achieved was through close interaction and education between the spheres. This method of progress was mirrored by Spiritualists who, in their interactions with nonbelievers and intercessions for the rights of Indians, upheld the value of education—both in explaining what they thought to be the universal truths of Spiritualism, and in their support of initiatives to educate Native Americans (and other unfortunates) about intellectual and morally upright living.

Spiritualists and the Indian Question

The connections Spiritualists drew between empirical science and spiritual appearances, between the evolution of civilization and progression through the spheres, and between the natural laws that ordered the material and spiritual realms, were all understood and discussed in the most literal of tones, and had a real impact on American life. As Andrew Jackson Davis put it in 1863, Spiritualism was a movement that meant to turn the prayer "thy kingdom come, thy will be done on earth, *as it is in heaven*" into a reality.⁴⁵ In the nineteenth century, America's reality was saturated with Indians. An overwhelming concern for many was what to do with Indians in the face of America's growth; this debate was commonly referred to as the "Indian Question" or the "Indian Problem."

There were several attempts to answer this question. Since Europeans' earliest encounters with American Indians, converting them to Christianity was a primary goal of colonization. Beaver points out that "the missionary purpose of colonization was made explicit in the first Virginia charter in 1606."⁴⁶ The sentiment to convert rather than kill the Indians was reinforced in 1610 by the pastor William Crashaw, but Beaver dates the tension between these two objectives as early as 1620.⁴⁷

When Britain's colonies separated, Indian nations retained their sovereign identities. The Constitution granted Congress the power to negotiate treaties. Indian policy was put in the hands of the War Department.⁴⁸ Shortly after Thomas Jefferson authored the foundation of the U.S. government, he expressed his hope for racial blending. In *Notes on the State of Virginia*, published in 1784, Jefferson favored civilization as a means of absorbing Indian cultures to help create an authentically "American" culture. Advocates of Indian "civilization" programs sought the complete political and social absorption of Indians into American life.⁴⁹ A large component in the push for cultural assimilation of Indians was religious education. In the early decades of the nineteenth century, scores of Quakers, Baptists, Methodists, and other missionaries flocked into Indian-inhabited areas to instill Christian principles in the hearts of Indians.⁵⁰ Such missions were still hard at work in 1830, when President Andrew Jackson made removal the federal policy, claiming that the massive relocation of entire populations benefited both natives and Americans. By midcentury, the understanding of Indian nations as sovereign entities largely faded from U.S. federal policy. Through a series of treaty negotiations, many tribes became financially dependent on federal aid, having lost access to key resources, land and food chief among them. By 1849, the administration of Indian policy had been transferred to the newly created Department of the Interior.⁵¹ Indian policy had transformed into a domestic issue, rather than an international one. As Simard has written, "For most Indian communities, treaty negotiations blessed and legitimized their dispossession [and] starting in the late eighteenth century created in rudimentary form the shape of a liberal welfare state in Canada and the U.S."⁵² By the 1850s, a third solution to the Indian Problem was implemented. The U.S. government instituted the reservation system, setting aside large tracts of land, allegedly protected by treaty, meant to keep Indians safe from white encroachment and separate from American society. It echoed Jefferson's concept of an Indian Reserve, which he suggested as a productive use of the Louisiana Purchase of 1803. But rather than safeguard boundaries that Jefferson envisioned as gradually fading, the reservations served to keep Indians effectively separated from the rest of American society, making assimilation in its most well-meaning form a nigh impossible feat. The concept of white supremacy had been a part of the American intellectual landscape since 1735, when Carl von Linnaeus organized human classification on skin color. He described Indians, or *Homo Americanus,* as "reddish, choleric, obstinate, contented, and regulated by customs."[53] American Indians were thus deftly labeled as unchangeable, while white men were conveniently described as being governed by law. In Johann Blumenbach's 1781 treatise *On the Natural Variety of Mankind,* Indians were classified as one of the five races of man. They were racially separate for the American naturalist Samuel George Morton in the 1830s and '40s. Darwin, too, did not dispute the categorization of Indians as racially distinct. By the publication of Darwin's *Origin of Species* in 1859, a majority of Americans were convinced that the racial superiority they asserted over Native Americans was proven as scientific fact. Many tribes resisted the reservation system and its mismanagement, as well as the assumption on the part of many whites that the only effective solution to the "Indian Problem" was extermination.

In the wake of the Civil War, interest in westward expansion and development exploded. Beaver describes the deleterious effects of "repeated removals of the tribes, their difficulty in adjusting to reservation life, nonfulfillment of treaty obligations by the government, the corruption of the Indian service, the Westward rush of settlers with their insatiable appetite for land, and the building of railroads into Indian country."[54] However, a large degree of public sentiment remained in favor not only of ceasing to kill Indians, but in support of integrating them as much as possible into American life. In 1869, Grant's Peace Policy was instituted in response to corruption on reservations. The goal of Grant's program was to ferret out government corruption in the administration of Indian affairs and to subsidize the work of the missions. The intention was twofold: to remove the circumstances that provoked disgruntled tribes to warfare, and to make the imposition of American religion and culture more palatable. Agents and commissioners were handpicked for their personal dedication, placing, as Beaver wrote, "the improvement of the Indians under religious sponsorship and inject[ing] a spiritual dynamic into the process of civilizing the Indians."⁵⁵ Quakers and other favored denominations worked diligently to effect the Indians' voluntary acceptance of the value of individual labor, land ownership, and responsibility. The wholehearted adoption of such concepts was deemed necessary to the overall success of assimilation.⁵⁶ In the 1870s, a growing number of Americans saw Indians as wards of the government, requiring protection and education in the ways of the white man. Advocates of policy reform fought to keep Indian affairs under the auspices of the Department of the Interior, seeing the proposed return to the War Department as a threat to their relatively humane efforts. By 1880, efforts to "civilize" Indians through instruction were largely supported and government-funded. In 1887, the Dawes Severalty Allotment Act made the reservation system obsolete by dealing with natives as individuals rather than tribal entities. This step was intended to encourage self-reliance and industry among American Indians, necessary characteristics of American citizens.

In the last decades of the nineteenth century, the war between these possible solutions to the Indian problem—extermination, assimilation, reservation—still raged. The abundance of Spiritualist writing about this debate indicates their deep concern over how the "Indian Question" would ultimately be answered. They frequently discussed the moral dimensions of America's treatment of Indians, expressing their disgust at the nation's failure to live up to its creed of political equality for all with a foundation in Christian love. When applying their understanding of the cosmos to Indian-related matters, Spiritualists fell largely on the side of interracial peace. They argued that the strides of the "civilized" tribes such as the Cherokee, along with the celestial progress exhibited by their "spirit friends," proved beyond a doubt that Indians were capable of improving themselves. For their part, failure to provide Indians with the support they required was seen as potentially catastrophic for America's reputation and spiritual future.

This project tracks the progression of the Spiritualist movement and the centrality of Indian manifestations to the movement in relation to significant changes in Indian policy. Parallels are drawn between the movement's peak in the 1860s through the 1880s, and the Indian-related events to which Spiritualist journals dedicated their pages. The Sand Creek Massacre of 1864, negotiations and hostilities of the 1870s, the rise and fall of Grant's Peace Policy, the progress of the Carlisle Institute, and the institutionalization of the Dawes Act in 1887 will all be discussed in the context of Spiritualist attempts to fashion their world after the heavenly models presented at séance tables. By the 1890s, such changes to the legal status of Indians were established as federal policy lasting into the twentieth century. Satisfied, the fervor of Spiritualists and other Indian advocates for bettering native circumstances declined as a result. At around the same time, "the Spiritualist connection with social reform was, in effect, dead."[57] Other metaphysical religions that were grounded in Spiritualist influences became more prominent features of the American landscape. Parapsychology became slowly more methodical and respected, and Christian Science, Theosophy, and New Thought gained steam. The temporal focus of this book is centered around the formative years of Spiritualism, from the Rochester rappings in 1848 to the filing of the patent for the Ouija board in 1890, after which Spiritualism became astronomically more commodified.[58] The reappropriation of racialized, imagined religions holds a central place in alternative beliefs to this day; its roots lie in the historical context of Indian relations as it saturated the American consciousness in Spiritualism's foundational years. This deepens the current understanding of the Spiritualist movement's involvement in national debates, expanding on its role in helping to define gender and adding to that Spiritualist positions on racial difference, the nation's character, and how its future would be defined.

Uncanny Indians

Nineteenth-century séances, especially those where Indian specters were present, operated as hauntings in a literal sense. Understanding Spiritualist practices as hauntings is a core precept of this work. The ghostliness of Indian figures has been analyzed as it appears in literature, yet this is only a part of Spiritualism's larger context. The psychical and paranormal research of the twentieth and twenty-first centuries are outgrowths of Spiritualism's empirical nature, with evidence and experience as authenticating factors. Spiritualist historians have yet to marry this aspect of the movement to its other social and religious elements. The hauntedness at the core of Spiritualism should not be kept separate any longer from the cultural persistence of hauntedness that finite and narrow interpretations of the movement have left largely unexplored. Fictive hauntings still contribute, however, to the interpretation of spectral Indians in this work. As Larry Danielson so aptly pointed out, "even when the narrative purports to describe actual paranormal experience, the art of the storyteller is at work [and it] involve[s] a complex interaction between personal experience, traditional lore about the supernatural, and canons of narrative aesthetics."[59] In her book on the ghostly lore of the Hudson

Valley, Judith Richardson wrote of hauntings as the consistent subject of popular interest that demands further scrutiny "because of what they reveal about how senses of the past and of place are apprehended and created."[60] The paranormal experience of being haunted is at the heart of Spiritualism, even as it occurred in expected, controlled conditions rather than in musty attics or on abandoned roads. The aim of this project is to study Spiritualism print records for evidence of the processes of experience and reporting, and how living Indians and their realities were incorporated into the narrative of Indian apparitions. Spectral Indians brought American guilt over their proclaimed vanishing to the fore. They presented the Indian question as unanswered and needing continual attention, rather than emphasizing the ameliorating effect of ghosting/vanishing Indians—when looking at haunting contexts, this uneasiness and disruption is more readily apparent. Only when we stop being haunted can we begin to discuss whether the Indian question has been sufficiently settled. That the end of Indian imagery as ghostly or Romantic appears to be nowhere in sight is a testament to the cultural staying power of this phenomenon and the ongoing ambiguities of claiming these racial spiritual identities. Avery Gordon spoke of haunting as a manner of knowledge production, one in which "abusive systems of power make themselves known and their impact felt in everyday life, especially when they are supposedly over and done with."[61] In this way, Spiritualism served as a forum for the expression of political opposition and the reformatory impulse. Mediums turned haunting into an exacting mode of knowledge by seeking information from ghosts—about their families, the structure of the universe, and the fate of their nation.

The ghosts of Indian chiefs recognized there by Spiritualists were "apparitions out of the past"[62]—representatives of a race that many Anglo-Americans perceived as disappearing from the earth. It is important to remember that the term *ghost* is not synonymous with *dead*; a "ghost" is someone who has returned from the dead. That difference is significant in studying Indian spectral manifestations, yet has been overlooked by those who have studied cultural imagery of Indians as "ghostly" or as "vanishing." Those two terms have frequently been used interchangeably. To do so simplifies such imagery and is incorrect. Depictions of Indians as "vanishing" portray them in the act of disappearing. Describing them as "ghostly," by strict definition, implies the opposite. Spectral representations of Indians undermine the idea of Indians as gone, rather than justifying or celebrating it. It is the reappearance of Indian spirits, and the reentry of the "Indian" into the American consciousness, that lay at the heart of Spiritualist manifestations of them. As Richardson observed, apparitions can act as subversive voices, "serving to affix blame and guilt where courts and official records had failed."[63] Such specters are frightening because they reveal moral iniquities and chastise the unjust.[64] A haunting, she argued, allows the haunted party to renegotiate the past and help shape the present moment. "In many cases," she writes, "the contest is one between different versions of memory and myth which vie over the same place, each with a compelling claim, and each supporting a different view of who or what belongs there."[65] Spiritualist believers saw spirit Indian personalities as evidence to question the logic of the inevitable doom supposedly facing all Indians, and to advocate contemporary programs that promoted education over continual and financially draining warfare. Analyzing such phenomena and their psychological effects on American politics in this way has been overlooked by McGarry, Trachtenberg, and the like, and as such is the primary goal of this book.

According to Terry Castle in her discussion of ghosts and their definition as "uncanny" figures, "the idea that spirits of the dead might come back to haunt murderers, locate stolen objects, enforce the terms of legacies, expose adulterers, and so on, functioned as a kind of implicit social control."[66] As Bridget Bennett explained, a haunting is a disruption of the present by the past—it is not subject to the linear progression of time or logic or institutional power.[67] Spirit chiefs largely fulfilled these commonly understood roles of ghosts as described in literature and folklore. By the nineteenth century, the ideology of progress—on a national, industrial, economic, scientific, and moral scale—was a prevailing intellectual force in America. The majority of Americans viewed natives and native ways of life as counterintuitive to progress. As John Coward pointed out in *The Newspaper Indian*, the majority of Americans were convinced of their nation's destiny for greatness because they believed their Christian and civilized character was superior to those of other nations and races.[68] By adhering to the messages of Indian specters, American Spiritualists sought to combat what they recognized as a political and moral injustice. According to Jared Farmer, "The rhetoric of the Vanishing American—as old as the United States itself—reached its zenith in the fin-de-siècle era when the aggregate native population reached its nadir."[69] The peak of rhetoric regarding Indians as vanished coincided with the peak of Spiritualism and the height of Indian appearances within the movement in particular. Approximately 90 percent of the Indian manifestations recorded in the *Banner of Light* occurred in the years between

1860 and 1890, with roughly 50 percent of those appearing in the 1870s. Communications from spirit chiefs pointed to U.S. generals as murderers of Indian women and children, criticized American society for its deceitfulness and theft of Indian lands, and attempted to enact, through their audiences, a federal Indian policy that would honor its promises. In 1831, Chief Justice John Marshall declared that "Indians were not 'foreign nations' but 'domestic dependent nations': they are in a state of pupilage. Their relation to the United States resembles that of a ward to his guardian."[70] As such, Spiritualists argued, the welfare of Indian peoples was the responsibility of all American citizens, especially those who had been enlightened by spirit communication. The role toward Indians as their protectors was a traditionally masculine one; Spiritualists, along with their ghostly controls, sought to undermine America's masculinity and honor by emphasizing its failure to protect Indian peoples from white predation.

The ability of spirit chief manifestations to act as social controls lay in their uncanny nature. As Julian Wolfreys stated in *Victorian Hauntings*, "The spectral is, strictly speaking, neither alive nor dead."[71] The Indian ghosts were undead, and their race was not entirely vanished, as evidenced to Spiritualists by continuous news coverage of the ongoing interactions between the United States and Indian nations during the mid to late nineteenth century. Sigmund Freud's definition of the uncanny, or *unheimlich,* is particularly useful. The uncanny is the return of something familiar that has been repressed—an intrusion of the past upon the present.[72] The specters of Indian chiefs existed in both the past and present. The narrative of Indian disenfranchisement is as old as the colonization of North America itself. Indian nations were continually repressed, first by Europe, then by America, and relegated to public invisibility and alienated by an arbitrary distinction of vanishing as inevitable. Indians had been depicted for centuries as figments of the past. Indian policies further distanced America's racial reality from its claim to the morally righteous character of a free and equal nation. The concept of the vanished Indian was pervasive and highly romanticized. According to John Coward, their romanticism and the sentiments consequently roused by such figures stemmed from their imminent disappearance, but also celebrated that disappearance.[73] From a Spiritualist perspective, the romantic and sympathetic figure became the source of social disruption.

Spiritualist recordings of Indian ghosts should be interpreted as related to but not the same as Indian ghosts appearing in literature. Though there are a great many similarities, the effects of a literal haunting, as opposed to a literary one, are more profound. The presence of ghosts in séances was recognized by Spiritualists by the same methods described in works of fiction. In traditional ghost stories, ghosts make themselves known to the senses in ways that simultaneously indicated their presence and absence. Take, for example, the archetypal image of the ghost in sheets. Conjure to mind the Ghost of Christmas Yet to Come in Charles Dickens's 1843 tale *A Christmas Carol,* or the figure in the gothic giant M. R. James's "Oh Whistle, and I'll Come to You My Lad" of 1904. The sheet is visible, with its folds and billows suggesting a humanoid form underneath. Yet there is nothing under the sheet, so far as the eye can tell. This kind of seeing/not seeing experience is unsettling, and the source of the fear instilled by such apparitions. It is in this way that both literal and literary ghosts were recognized. Such stories and the Spiritualist publication record under analysis here are being produced so close upon each other that it is not only appropriate but necessary to consider the terms *spirit* and *ghost,* and their connotations, in tandem. Spiritualists' choice of the word *spirits* did not stop them from understanding the ghostly functions of their visions. The ghost of Jacob Marley and the three succeeding spirits (*his* language) of Dickens's traditional novel come to work, in their own words, Ebenezer Scrooge's salvation. Writing of actual paranormal experience, Danielson reports that "over forty percent of the apparitions described in the [collected] accounts are purposeful, most of them involved in helpful missions to the living."[74] That was precisely the reason that Indian spirits, by their own admission, visited Spiritualist circles. That was how séance participants interpreted their presence, amplified by the established trope of Indians as guides. Spiritualist responses to Indian spirits, or any of the specters that illuminated their sitting rooms, cannot be fully understood without first situating the Spiritualist movement in the context of ghostliness to which it so intimately belongs.

The impact of witnessing such phenomena in person would have a markedly different effect on someone than reading a story in which an apparition appears. Though a literary ghost would still be interpreted as a source of social disruption, that disruption would be contained within the fictional work. The haunting would be resolved by the end of the story, as it is for Scrooge on Christmas morning. That is, the spirit's message would most likely be heeded and thus cease to visit the living—and as fiction, its manifestation occurs at a safe distance from the reader. Being haunted in reality, or believing yourself to be haunted, as Spiritualists did, was quite the different experience. The unsettling, frightening experience would be continual without action on the part of the one being haunted. The threat that the ghosts represented would be keenly felt, rather than experienced passively and vicariously by identifying with the fictional protagonist of a ghost story. The literal haunting that Spiritualists claimed to witness demanded a response from them, both in mind and word, in a way that reading about Indian ghosts did not. Their disappearance in the context of the real was not mere staging. It provided an impending sense of imperative action to avoid the wrath of spirits who had long been understood as "extremely vengeful."[75]

The ongoing presence of Indian apparitions in nineteenth-century séances defied the strict categorization of Indians as past. The return of the repressed in ghostly form demanded that Indian apparitions and their living counterparts be considered as ever present. In Freudian terms, "a successful analysis [of the haunting], ostensibly, is a kind of exorcism … the patient [in this case, American Spiritualists and by extension, American society], who have hitherto turned [their] eyes away in terror from [their] own pathological productions, begins to attend to them and obtains a clearer and more detailed view of them."[76] As a result of their encounters with spirit chiefs, Spiritualists became diligent overseers and investigators of Indian policies and enforcing government agencies. Through publications like the *Banner of Light*, they attempted to circulate information about the greed and corruption running rampant in Indian country that tainted the nation's honor, and, as McGarry stated, directed Spiritualists to political action, a point to be discussed at length in chapter 5.[77]

TWO

CHIEF SPIRIT

The Appearance of Black Hawk as Case Study

INTRODUCTION

The spirit of Black Hawk will be used as a case study in this chapter to begin analysis of several aspects of nineteenth-century séances significant to this work. This includes issues of racial recognition and categorization through sound, touch, and sight, the importance of celebrity and popular imagery to spirit authentication, and the physical mechanics of the séance. Black Hawk's spectral appearances through the famed medium Jennie Lord were an early and highly visible model of how to authenticate Indian apparitions through sensory experiences, helping to lay the groundwork for future manifestations of Indian ghosts. His spirit as manifested by Mary Shelhamer in the 1880s served as a clear symbol of the purpose of Indian ghosts in communicating with the living. Over the course of the nineteenth century, his spectral appearances demonstrated the change in relations between whites and Indians that took place between the borders of the material and the spiritual realms. Through the acute popular interest in Black Hawk's person and the mediumship of Lord and Shelhamer, Black Hawk's spirit arguably represented the strongest and most frequent Indian presence in the Spiritualist movement, both as part of the first wave of prominent manifestations in the 1850s and 1860s, and as a regularly reappearing figure in the latter part of the movement in the 1880s.

Born in 1767, Black Hawk became the leader of the Sac nation, inhabiting parts of the Midwest east of the Mississippi. Black Hawk acted as the representative of the Sac in all things, known as "an unyielding traditionalist, honor[ing] old customs and old ways."[1] His traditionalism was one of the many traits Black Hawk possessed that aided whites in labeling him as an "authentic" Indian during his lifetime. His acrimonious relationship with the United States began, according to him, with the shooting of an Indian prisoner in 1804 who was meant to be freed during a treaty.[2] He fought on the side of his British "father"[3] in the War of 1812, and waged the notoriously labeled Black Hawk War in 1832 in defense of traditional lands. Black Hawk ranked high with the federal government among troublesome chiefs because of his uncompromising nature. In 1833, five years before his death, he relayed the story of his life to Antoine LeClaire, the government interpreter at Fort Armstrong, Rock Island.[4] Black Hawk expressed in this work his understanding of his position, his belief in American deception and cruelty, ending with a deep desire for peace.[5]

Through this work, and the huge amount of interest it generated among the American populace, Black Hawk's presence as an Indian celebrity in American culture exceeded that of many of his contemporaries. His celebrity contributed to the ease with which his ghost was recognized by Spiritualists—not only as a specific individual, but as an Indian chief, a category that carried with it a sense of both manhood and power. Further, in the same way that the American public viewed Black Hawk as a model of the traditional Indian man, the manifestations of Black Hawk's spirit can be analyzed to determine the quintessential elements that defined Indians, including Indian spirits, to members of the Spiritualist movement. It will also serve to demonstrate that the Spiritualist movement was yet another important arena in which the concept of the "Indian," which historian Robert Berkhofer described as a white invention, image, and stereotype, was constructed in the nineteenth century.[6] Such an analysis will be the starting point to discussing how Spiritualists sought to define ideal manhood and womanhood, for Indians and whites alike, and how ideas about race and gender circulating in Spiritualist circles colored their positions on Indian policy and concepts of citizenship.

The Life and Death of Black Hawk

By the time his autobiography was published in 1833, Black Hawk was already a prominent public figure. The Ohio newspaper *The Hesperian*[7] published an article upon his death that stated "the compulsory removal of BLACK-HAWK and his adherents to the west side of the Mississippi, are spread upon former pages of this magazine, and have, besides, so recently been the theme of newspaper comment, that their particular repetition here is considered unnecessary."[8] The author here is revealing that a base of knowledge about Black Hawk is assumed on the part of a white readership. He further alludes to Black Hawk's appearance in other widely read publications of the day. A Google NGram reveals that in the nineteenth century, Black Hawk was referenced in print approximately 250,000 times, with more than 90 percent of those references appearing after Black Hawk's death.[9] Black Hawk's popularity stretched beyond the narrow readership of one particular periodical and spilled over into common knowledge through a proliferation of monographs, articles, and news items appearing in local, state, and national papers.

The publication of Black Hawk's autobiography only increased his celebrity. An element of novelty as well as genuine interest was factored in; according to *The Hesperian*, it was "a subject of considerable curiosity and interest, as being, we believe, the first published production of an American Indian."[10] Five editions of the work were distributed within a year of its initial publication, with another reprint appearing in 1882. The publication of the 1882 edition was overseen by John Patterson, who had helped Antoine LeClaire publish the initial version and had sworn to the work's authenticity as Black Hawk's words. This later edition, historian Donald Jackson asserted, contained linguistic changes that portrayed Black Hawk in an even more sympathetic light than the original, which parallels the gradually improved character of Black Hawk's ghost as depicted by Shelhamer.[11] After the book's initial publication, it was reviewed in several general interest periodicals, including the *North American Review*, *American Quarterly Review*, *Hesperian*, and *New-England Magazine*. These elements combined to propel Black Hawk to a considerable state of celebrity. In this context, it seems only appropriate that an Indian of such high renown was manifested in Spiritualist séances and that his presence became a dominant one in this forum, given Spiritualist concerns about authentication.

The mention of Black Hawk in the emerging and vastly significant print culture of the day did not cease upon his death. Decades after his passing, in 1869 Black Hawk appeared in a *Harper's New Monthly Magazine*[12] article entitled "Border Reminiscences." An entire section is devoted to the Black Hawk War, where the author described the same treaty alluded to earlier by Black Hawk as a "treaty, like many others made with the Indians, [that] had been forced upon them by designing agents and rapacious traders, speculators, and interpreters."[13] The popular story of Black Hawk's War and its outcomes was used as a continuing metaphor for ongoing Indian policies and debates. The language of this article adopts a somewhat sympathetic tone toward Indians, critiquing how American removal policies were enforced, if not necessarily the policies themselves. What's important is that this author uses the memory of the Black Hawk War and its particular circumstances to comment on how Indian tribes were dealt with in general, creating a typical example of American-Indian interaction. This critique would have held a continued relevance in the late 1860s-early 1870s, when tensions with the Plains tribes and the Dakota Wars dominated the American consciousness regarding Indian relations. That this connection was made through the Black Hawk War by name demonstrates its continued popularity and its use as a model for understanding Indians and U.S./Indian relations.

Black Hawk's continued appearance in print is a strong indicator of his pervasiveness in American minds. There have been many studies on the impact of print culture on nineteenth-century America, and by "tracing the development of the public sphere in the emerging magazine print culture of the early republic, Carroll Smith-Rosenberg illustrates how these new periodicals interpellated [*sic*] a national subject ... who was white, male, and middle class, against a growing list of 'negative others' that included white women, Native Americans, and African-Americans."[14] Opposite the American subject, Black Hawk and his interactions with the government became an object of great interest and curiosity. Upon the publication of his autobiography, reviews of the work were found in abundance that also referred to Black Hawk as an established, notorious figure: "We have seen Black Hawk in that country, and have *always heard him mentioned* as a dangerous and formidable warrior" (emphasis mine).[15] As Philip Deloria pointed out, "Some of the most popular dying Indian figures ... appeared in everything from popular newspapers and schoolbooks to Jefferson's *Notes*."[16] Speaking of Indian imagery, Bridget Bennett wrote that famous figures were "passing into literary mythologies, [and] were also being reproduced in other popular forms."[17] Black Hawk was no exception to this; his autobiography tapped into an established American interest in literary myths about Indians, and American readers avidly consumed any material related to Black Hawk. Laura Mielke in her work *Moving Encounters* made reference to the emergence of the term *Blackhawkiana* to describe the abundance of print gossip about Black Hawk that was instigated by his national tour. This demand, Mielke argued, factored into Black Hawk's decision to produce a textual account of his life in the first place.[18]

Despite Black Hawk's prominence, his story had always been told from an American perspective. His autobiography garnered huge popularity not only as a novelty, but as a source of new information about an already familiar and widely intriguing topic. According to R. G. Thwaites, the author of an 1886 article on the Black Hawk War appearing in the *Magazine of Western History*, "The force of circumstances caused [Black Hawk] to become a national celebrity in his own day and a prominent figure in Western history for all time."[19] Laura Mielke observed that Indian biographies such as Black Hawk's were intimately tied to nineteenth-century sentimentalism, and indeed Black Hawk's voice as expressed through his autobiography contributed to an increased feeling of American sympathy for Black Hawk and the peoples that Americans believed he represented. As Mielke argued, his death became tragic and his person romantic after the publication of his suffering at the hands of Americans. Susan Scheckel wrote that Black Hawk, as represented in the autobiography, became a literary figure that allowed Americans to reflect upon the moral character of the nation's historical narrative.[20] The autobiography, then, ironically helped to project Black Hawk to a literary, legendary state. Over time, he was increasingly separated from these representations, though Spiritualists insisted on the reality of his presence. His story, as retold by Americans, symbolized the major flaws in federal/Indian relations. Such a sympathetic characterization of Black Hawk was continued in Spiritualist manifestations of him.[21] Interest in Black Hawk and his presence in the public eye expanded past the span of his lifetime, transitioning the image of Black Hawk progressively into one of constructed racial memory, manifesting within Spiritualist circles.

His celebrity was not confined to print culture, but touched upon other arenas of American public life as well. The following is an exemplary demonstration of the scale of his popularity. In June 1833, the imprisoned Black Hawk crossed paths in Baltimore with President Andrew Jackson.[22] This meeting was described as "resulting in 'the attention of the house [being] very equally divided between them.'"[23] This retelling serves to demonstrate two important things—one, that Black Hawk was such a powerful figure, representative of the cultural distance and political tensions between America and Indian nations, that the capture of this one singular man could assert white superiority. The other, that public knowledge of and interest in him ran deep enough to compete with a man currently the president of the United States. This instance was remembered in a review of Black Hawk's autobiography, describing the "eager anxiety" of the American people to look upon the Indian chief, and the consequent rumor that "popular curiosity and admiration was setting so fast in favour of the Indian warrior, that the natural anxiety of those who directed the movements of his illustrious rival, to monopolize the earnest gaze of the people, prompted a sudden separation of the routes of the travelling chiefs."[24] Black Hawk came dangerously close to overshadowing public interest in the president when placed side by side, to the point where both men were referred to by the same title of "chief." The interest in Black Hawk and the gaze that he attracted was described here as natural, uncontrollable, and threatening to the image of the president, famous for his efforts at Indian removal. Scheckel argued that, in his imprisoned state, Black Hawk, and the Indian resistance to expansion he represented, became entirely nonthreatening. Represented as "vanishing," it became safe to gaze upon Indians like Black Hawk.[25] That safety would slowly lead to American sympathy for Indians. When juxtaposed with the nation's praise of its own political, economic, and military progress, the threatening nature of Indians at any point in history would be questioned. This in turn would call into question the labeling of the conquest of Indian peoples as honorable and justified.

An important factor in building credibility for Spiritualist manifestations was authenticating the identity of the specter, which was greatly facilitated by the conjuring of recognizable spirits by name.[26] This was especially true for Indian spirits; spirit authentication and "Indian" recognition, historian Robert Cox asserted, allowed Spiritualists to claim the power to define and interpret the figures that were represented in the séance.[27] Indian manifestations had to be represented in culturally widespread, common terms in order to be deemed legitimate. Spiritualists hoped the recognition of Indian ghosts would lend credence to the position on Indians and Indian policy espoused through those apparitions. Black Hawk's celebrity was, for Spiritualists, a significantly useful aspect of his character in this regard.

The passages relaying Black Hawk's spirituality were of particular interest to American readers, and were referred to as such in multiple reviews of his autobiography. The *American Quarterly* and other reviews even went so far as to reprint large sections of the book in their entirety. Purchase of a copy was thus unnecessary to possess knowledge of Black Hawk's spirituality. Black Hawk's medicine bundle was continually described as going hand in hand with Black Hawk himself, and became a staple in depictions of him. George Catlin, observing Sac ways of life, mentions the medicine bag as well, recalling that it was made with "the skin of a black hawk, from which he had taken his name, and the tail of which made him a fan, which he was *almost constantly using*" (emphasis mine).[28] This portrayal of the medicine bag suggests that the bundle was rarely if ever out of Black Hawk's reach, implying that Black Hawk was ever protective and conscious not only of the physical bundle itself, but all the responsibilities that it signified for him as its owner. As Kerry Trask observed, "That medicine bag for Black Hawk was a magical object—containing or symbolizing the very essence of the Sauk identity,"[29] an identity Black Hawk felt it was his duty to preserve. The effect of this was Black Hawk's resistance to Sac removal and assimilation. The sense of purpose derived from the medicine bag affected how he dealt with the American government, which in turn affected how Black Hawk was portrayed in public discourse about the status of the West and American expansion. Black Hawk's behavior served to label him as authentically Indian, unwilling and unable to accept modern progress.

Many aspects of Black Hawk's public life lent itself easily to spectral transformation, and several links can be made between the living Black Hawk and his ghost. One crucial factor was Black Hawk's renowned spirituality. Black Hawk claimed his authority derived from his possession of a medicine bundle, representing the essence of the Sac. In his autobiography, he described how the bundle was first possessed by his great-grandfather Nanamakee. Through a dream, the Great Spirit convinced the old chief to relinquish the bundle to Nanamakee, who was in turn told that "it is the soul of [the Sac] nation, it has never yet been disgraced and I will expect you to keep it unsullied."[30] The tale's place at the start of the narrative cements Black Hawk's sense of place within his tribe, and a driving motivational force.

Black Hawk was known to be spiritual in other ways. After the death of his father in battle, it was said he "blackened his face with soot, suffered his hair to grow, fasted and prayed, and remained quiet for five years."[31] Reviewers of Black Hawk's story were careful to include information about his spiritual life in their publications, and this kind of behavior on the part of Black Hawk was increasingly seen as having a spiritual purpose, as more information about Indian religious practices traveled from west to east. According to Trask, the point of "fasting and self-purification [was to] experience powerful dreams believed to contain messages from the supernatural forces that governed the world."[32] Nanamakee's story grounded the significance of dreams in Sac life; talk of the medicine bundle and its significance spanned dozens of pages of book reviews and offering a context for his message.[3] The Great Spirit was constantly referred to in the autobiography as a source of guidance, protection, and power.[34]

The strongest example of the Great Spirit's influential power over Black Hawk's thinking is a passage delineating the logic behind his refusal to concede land:

> My reason teaches me that land cannot be sold. The Great Spirit gave it to his children to live upon and cultivate as far as necessary for their subsistence, and so long as they occupy and cultivate it they have a right to the soil, but if they voluntarily leave it, then any other people have a right to settle on it. Nothing can be sold but such things as can be carried away.[35]

Black Hawk's oppositional principles to land sale were not unique to him. The importance of his words lay in their form. The autobiography was not filled with the kind of broken English seen in Lord's spiritual manifestations of Black Hawk's voice, but was instead recorded as possessing a stylistic eloquence. This passage was one of countless speeches that bolstered the perceived power of "noble" speech among Indian chiefs.

Black Hawk's death was widely publicized. In his final years, American journalism acknowledged a marked change in his character. This change served as the foundation for accepting a shift in Black Hawk's spirit from a belligerent Indian to a noble spirit chief who supported white efforts for peace. Elijah Kilbourn, a prisoner of Black Hawk's during the War of 1812, recounted this conversation with the aging chief upon his release in his own narrative, *The Soldier's Cabinet*:

> "When you [Kilbourn] return to your chief I want you to tell him all my words … The Great Spirit has whispered among the tree-tops in the morning and the evening, and says that Black Hawk's days are few, and that he is wanted in the Spirit land. He is half dead, his arm shakes and is no longer strong, and his feet are slow on the warpath. Tell him all this, and tell him too," continued the untutored hero of the forest, "that Black Hawk would have been a friend to the whites, but they would not let him."[36]

This speech, and others with similar allusions to the Great Spirit and Black Hawk's impending journey to the spirit land, was reprinted in multiple articles about Black Hawk's life and reviews of his autobiography.[37] Collectively, such passages portrayed a melancholy Black Hawk who referenced his own spirituality directly. His allusions to the Great Spirit and the Spirit land would have been simple for Spiritualists to incorporate into their own belief system, given that the language utilized was identical. Frank Stevens, author of one of many Black Hawk biographies, also reflected upon the change in Black Hawk's character at the end of his life. He claimed that American sympathy for the chief developed "during the last five or six years of his long life, while he was in a sense a captive, brooding over his fallen estate, while the drapery of an eternal evening was fast falling about him."[38] The shift in discourse over Black Hawk's consciousness toward the next life did not go unnoticed by Spiritualists, and it would become a focal point of Black Hawk's spiritual manifestations.

Discourse about Black Hawk did not cease upon his death. He was memorialized to a limited extent; the Honorable Perry Armstrong, for example, remembered him in his biography of the chief thus:

> Black Hawk was the purest and best of his race and true to his every obligation, and although no "monument" … has been erected to his memory, his noble devotion to the welfare of his nation, coupled with his many virtues and few vices, constitute a monument far more stable and enduring than sculptured marble or beaten brass to him who as good as he was great. We close this sketch by quoting the last sentence of his autobiography: "May the Great Spirit keep our people and the whites always at peace is the sincere wish of Black Hawk."[39]

He was remembered, at the end of his life, as seeking peace and divine guidance. A monument of sorts was eventually recognized at Black Hawk's Tower in Rock Island, Illinois. This site became known by some Spiritualists as an opportune location for communicating with the dead chief.

Black Hawk's body was not at rest after his passing; he was first buried near his home village in Iowa. In 1839, an unknown party robbed Black Hawk's grave of his bones, jewelry, and other grave goods. These were displayed for a brief period in Alton, Illinois. The governor of Iowa then returned Black Hawk's body to his irate sons in 1840. Soon after, the Burlington Geographical and Historical Society in Iowa displayed Black Hawk's body, once again stolen. There it remained until 1855, when a fire destroyed the entire museum and its holdings.[40] This story sparked outrage with the public as much as with Black Hawk's family. Biographer Frank Stevens stated that "if Black Hawk had faults, they were buried with his body, which by all rules of decency should have remained sacred."[41] This passage is one instance of public interest in Black Hawk after his death, and suggested that death could improve Black Hawk's character. His public reputation continued to change for the better throughout his spiritual appearances.

Identifying Black Hawk's Spirit

As a ghost, the specter of Black Hawk continued to represent the quintessential Indian. Authenticating Indian spirits to the satisfaction of Spiritualist observers required the use of racial constructions to achieve an accurate identification. As Bridget Bennett observed of Shaker manifestations, "The codes of performance for white spirits and nonwhite spirits are not the same. The nonwhite spirits tend toward a hyperbolic enactment of racial stereotype that relies on exaggerated gesture, movement, and mime."[42] Likewise, racially specific elements including patterns of speech, behavior, and movement comprised the major components of Spiritualist authentication. How the performance of those tropes was executed relied on generally disseminated knowledge about Black Hawk's person, which historian Kerry Trask described as the "very personification of [his] tribe's authentic collective identity."[43] His spiritual performance strongly reflected past descriptions of Black Hawk as he lived.

The appearance of Black Hawk's spirit was recorded for the first time in 1857 in a local paper in Nashua, New Hampshire, then reprinted in the *Banner of Light*. The unnamed mediums leading these séances were described as "two young ladies from Portland ... One of them is a medium for music. She has two violins, a guitar, a triangle, two accordeons, a tambourine, and two bells, placed under the table, and oftentimes *all* are played upon at once, and the music is said to be very fine."[44] Given the described significance of musical elements in this series of séances, as well as the fact that *two* young ladies were ones conducting the séances, these séances are almost certainly among the debuts of the Lord sisters, Jennie and Annie. Throughout their careers as mediums, they were recognized repeatedly for the fine musicality of their séances, as well as their "strong manifestations," alluded to even in this first article. For three weeks, they "astound[ed] the good citizens of Nashua with manifestations of a most extraordinary character."[45] Jennie Lord and her sister Annie captured American interest in the 1860s. In July 1864, a journal article from Windsor, Connecticut, reported that a two-week engagement brought "nearly two hundred each night [and those] who could not gain seats on the inside of the house remained outside."[46] Jennie Lord covered a great deal of the Eastern Seaboard throughout her mediumship, venturing occasionally to Illinois, but remaining largely in Massachusetts and New York.

The 1857 article recognized the Lords' mediumship as both "extraordinary" and "peculiar," making specific reference to Black Hawk's controlling presence. "At the request of the circle," the article continued, "Black Hawk steps around *on* the table, and places his large moccasined foot in every hand. There it is palpable to the touch, though nothing can be seen."[47] In this first recorded instance of Jennie Lord's séances, several elements that would become characteristic of her séances were already present. These elements presented spirit manifestations of Spiritualist séances as uncanny figures, setting the groundwork for how Spiritualists would sense the haunting presence of ghosts. First and foremost was the presence of music. Several instruments were said to be playing at once. In later manifestations, it would be further clarified that Lord was not physically responsible for the sounds thus produced. The music was described here as "very fine;" in future séances, the quality of the music, and the ability of the instruments to keep perfect time, became worthy of notice. The strong presence of sound at Lord's séances was meant in part to compensate for the absence of light; in dark séances such as the ones Lord conducted, ghosts were primarily heard rather than seen. Sound was used to prove the presence of invisible figures. In the case of Lord's séances, the sound emanating from the musical instruments was described as music, not chaotic, random noise. As such, the music became indicative of intelligent though invisible agency. The appearance of Black Hawk himself also became characteristic of Lord's séances. Throughout the 1850s and 1860s, the time when appearances of Black Hawks's spirit were most frequently published, all records of his spectral appearance were described in association with Lord. Only after Jennie Lord dropped out of Spiritualist print in the 1880s did another medium conjure him.

The methods by which Black Hawk appeared and was authenticated in 1857 were consistent with Lord's later manifestations of him and were formative to the Spiritualist experience of apparitions. They also represented the uncanny, haunting nature of Spiritualist manifestations. Black Hawk's spirit achieved prominence by association with Jennie Lord. She was continually referred to as one of the most remarkable, esteemed, and influential spirit mediums in the early years of the movement. Additionally, printed records of Black Hawk's manifestation occurred with more frequency than that of other spirits; in the nineteenth-century monographs and periodicals under analysis in this project, Black Hawk's spirit appeared more than a dozen times, while the number of visits from the next most popular apparition, that of Little Crow, only amounted to half that. Mediums and séance attendants saw Lord's mediumship as a primary model, wrought with many identifying elements that would become expected, even typical components of the nineteenth-century séance, and of Indian manifestations in particular. The previously mentioned 1857 séance was conducted in the dark, evidenced by the fact that the supernatural phenomena recorded here were recounted as being heard, not seen. Dark séances, conducted in the almost complete absence of light, were usually described afterward by witnesses as being of the most extraordinary character, and relied almost exclusively on sound as the means of both confirming the presence of spirits and identifying those spirits specifically. In this instance, Black Hawk's spirit consisted of aural and tactile dimensions. He stomped on the table, and members of the circle felt his *moccasined* foot.[48] The feel of leather here indicated typical Indian costume, and by extension the Indian. Both the sound and touch of cultural costume stimulated the senses in dark séances, especially for the presence of a culturally other spirit.

A greater number of physical details was recorded in the second appearance of Black Hawk's spirit, published in 1861. Black Hawk's presence was recounted by a man named Benjamin Coleman, who in the 1860s was considered "a great pillar of Spiritualism."[49] Coleman was originally from London, traveling to New York and Boston to observe Spiritualist activity, confirming his beliefs and publishing his experiences in the *Spiritualist Magazine*,[50] which later republished his articles as a monograph entitled *Spiritualism in America*. In it, he details a séance in Boston performed by the medium Miss Jennie Lord. He stated that in Boston he "met Miss Lord, of Portland, Maine."[51] He noted that Black Hawk was "the presiding spirit of the band that visit this circle."[52] This particular séance bore many striking characteristics that distinguished it from a Spiritualist experience in which only white spirits were present.

Among the more clearly defined elements of this second recorded séance of Miss Lord's was a strong musical character; Coleman recounts that on a table,

> about two or three feet distant from the back of the chair on which the medium sat, there had been placed various musical instruments—a guitar, a dulcimer, tambourine, harmonium, a horn, and four bells of various sizes, and in the corner of the room there stood a large bass-viol and bow.[53]

He was careful to point out the distance between these instruments and the medium, as proof that Jennie Lord was not, in fact, responsible for the music that played as the séance began. Although Annie Lord was not mentioned by name, Coleman said that the séance circle consisted of nine people—the medium, himself, "three gentlemen holding prominent commercial positions in the city [and] the ladies of the house." It is possible that Annie Lord was counted among the latter.

The conducting of Lord's séances in the dark was crucial, as it required authentication of spiritual presence through sound and touch, rather than sight. The "subdued lights" at the manifestation's beginnings were ordered to be put out by Black Hawk's ghost, leaving the circle "in total darkness." Black Hawk was here described as the leader of the spirit circle. Similarly, Black Hawk's name was the first mentioned in the 1857 article. Miss Lord was then "entranced" by Black Hawk, and "[h]is orders [were] spoken through the medium." Coleman was more careful later in his account to distinguish between Lord and Black Hawk as separate entities, by emphasizing "the full shape and size of Black Hawk's hands as they pass over [his] head." The hands of spirits in particular were commonly used as a reference point to make distinctions between the mediums and their guiding spirits. Toward the end of his account, Coleman remarked that

> the whole exhibition was a most marvelous and convincing proof of the presence of intelligent invisible agencies and, apart from all other considerations, the *precision* with which heavy instruments were hurled at times about our heads in the dark, touching us lightly and playfully, was in itself proof positive, that spirit eyes guided, and that no human being of this world handled them. Every sense but that of sight being satisfied, the *séance* was quite as satisfactory to me as if the manifestations had been made in broad daylight.[54]

Both Jennie and Annie Lord were consistently described in print as being small in stature and of a weak constitution. In relation to her manifestational powers, Jennie Lord's weak physical state served as a significant point of comparison between her and her spirit controls. As McCabe pointed out, witnesses to her séances were convinced that the feats accomplished therein, such as the sudden appearance of her chair atop the séance table, with her in it, was beyond her capabilities.[55] Performances of this nature served several purposes. The phenomena described above contributed to Spiritualists' distinction between Lord and the ghosts she claimed to conjure. The phenomena seemingly emanated from outside the medium's person. Signifying the spirit control as a strong Indian, and a male at that, was therefore integral to the establishment of authenticity of the spectral phenomena recorded in this instance. Additionally, ascribing both Indianness and masculinity to the manifesting entity undermined the feminization of Indian males in a political sense, opening the door to discussions of Indians as males, deserving of political autonomy.

The auditory aspect of the séance, including music and song on the part of the séance participants, was an ongoing element in Lord's performances here and elsewhere, but one of the most important aural characteristics of Black Hawk's appearance, which Coleman was clear to point out, was Black Hawk's "broken English."[56] Coleman carefully reproduced Miss Lord's speech in the stereotypical style of the cultural "Other." Black Hawk greeted Coleman with "How you do, Mr. Coleman,"[57] and preceded his deeds with "Me do something else for you."[58] This style of speech occurred in Indian as well as other nonwhite spirits, but its significance lies in the fact that it did not *always* occur. Bennett argued that Spiritualists saw patterns of speech as an indicator of the voice's origin, and thus a reliable method of identification.[59] There were other Indian manifestations, and other manifestations of Black Hawk in fact, in which this broken English was wholly absent. In its place were instances of Indian eloquence and "noble" speech, even to the point of poetry, which adhered more closely both to how Black Hawk's powers of speech during his lifetime were perceived by the American public and to how, as Steven Conn argued, nineteenth-century students of native languages commonly described Indian speech—as "rich, poetic and [of] metaphorical quality."[60] Though the novelist James Fenimore Cooper was inconsistent in his application of figurative speech among his Indian characters, he is credited as establishing the trope of Indian speech as highly stylized, wrought with metaphor. His 1826 best-seller *The Last of the Mohicans* was the shining example of Indian speech.[61] The value of Indian oratory was exhibited in the form of recitation, required of young students of elocution. According to Conn, the speeches of chiefs such as Red Jacket served as exemplars of eloquence.[62] Yet that description of Indian oratory was politically charged. The utilization of both eloquent and crude speech in séance rooms reflected the nineteenth-century conflict between noble and savage imagery, and the role patterns of speech played in that struggle.

The broken English in the 1861 séance, as well as the eloquence found in Black Hawk's later manifestations, suggest that speech patterns were crucial in determining the authenticity of an Indian spirit. There were instances of French, German, and even African American spirits speaking through their mediums in heavy accents. The acquisition of new languages not known in life was expected by Spiritualists as a common part of a spirit's progressive education, and one way that spirits could assist mortals around the world, uniting the human family. And yet, some spirits seemed incapable of transcending their cultural and linguistic identities—they could speak English, but only in thick accents that continued to function as racial markers among spirits, especially in dark séances, where aural manifestations and the distinction of sound were integral to the spirit's identity and its authentication. Patterns and styles of speech, including accents and eloquence, thus became central to the process of spirit authentication. In this context, Black Hawk's celebrity and famed oratory became central points of reference. That both elevated skills of speech and their absence indicated Indianness reflects the conflicted nature of the imagined Indian; the former conjured Romantic Indians as the "noble savage," the latter denoted barbarity. Both were deemed "authentic." Further analysis of Indian spirit speech patterns will reveal connections between the abilities of spirits and the sentiments toward Indians that Spiritualists projected.

The content of spirit messages, as well as the style, determined the personality of the apparition. A call to social action was one of the primary purposes of recorded spiritual activity. As such, one of the functions of spectral appearances was to incite and support would-be activists and reformers. In Black Hawk's case, his manifestations through Lord were somewhat of a departure from how he was perceived in life. In the 1830s, he was the forerunner of Indian resistance, and regarded by many Americans as one of the most stubborn, obnoxious, and intellectually backward Indians. His activities and demeanor in Lord's séances, sometimes depicted as "wild," coincided, to a certain extent, with the published portrayal of him as resistant and troublesome. On the other hand, his appearances through her, and more notably through Shelhamer, indicated a spiritual transition, to a place of prominence among peaceful Indian spirits who were sympathetic to Spiritualist causes and lent strength to their efforts. The benevolence of Black Hawk's spirit developed over time, drawing perhaps on the increased sympathy he garnered from the American public at the end of his life, and transforming the image of Black

Hawk into one of sympathy and spiritual strength, and a successful example of the work being conducted by Indian spirits to elevate American white society.

The image of Black Hawk particularly in terms of speech was conflicted, spanning eloquence and the prattling seen in Lord's 1861 manifestation. *The Hesperian* took a middling position on the living Black Hawk's powers of speech. One journalist claimed that Black Hawk "was without the intellect and eloquence of RED-JACKET [another Indian chief], yet he [possessed] powers of speech which could at any time arouse the souls of his warriors to repel the aggressions of his enemies."[63] This passage referenced the moment in Black Hawk's autobiography where he incites his warriors to battle: "BRAVES AND WARRIORS! These are the medicine bags of our forefather, Mukataquet, who was the father of the Sac nation. They were handed down to the great war chief of our nation, Nanamakee, who has been at war with all the nations of the plains and has never yet been disgraced! I expect you all to protect them!"[64]

Black Hawk spoke in public on many occasions, each time drawing a great deal of interest. Each time a lengthy passage from his autobiography was reprinted, Americans eagerly read in translation. This language barrier bred questions about who should lay claim to Black Hawk's eloquence, and many Americans doubted the autobiography's authenticity. The debate over Black Hawk's alleged eloquence demonstrates the significance of such a portrayal; reviewers of Black Hawk's book attributed its elevated aspects elsewhere, maintaining a view of Black Hawk as an ignorant savage. Spiritualists and Indian sympathizers, on the other hand, admired an intelligent, friendly, and sympathetic character, originating, they thought, directly from Black Hawk himself.

The particular speech revisited above rouses morale through the parallels it makes to the initial story of the medicine bundle, further augmenting its centrality. *The Hesperian*, however, did not view this incitement to war as an example of Indian eloquence, which was directly connected to the intellectual capacity of the speaker. It must also be remembered that his speech was made to Indian warriors, and was not delivered in English at all. This fact undermined Black Hawk's powers of speech even further, to the point where the only English Black Hawk was recognized as capable of articulating was through his translator Antoine LeClaire. Any perceived eloquence on the part of Black Hawk was consequently attributed to his biographer.

Reviewers took umbrage with this, scolding LeClaire for his inappropriately stylized translation of Black Hawk's speech on several occasions as inappropriate. Snelling's review of *The Life of Black Hawk* claimed that LeClaire acted badly by intermixing "courtly phrases, and the figures of speech, which our novelists are so fond of putting in the mouths of Indians."⁶⁵ Black Hawk's eloquence was attributed here to the American imagination and the artistic rendering of Indians as noble. Indian oratory was constructed and had no place in public discourse about Indians, lest popular sympathies lean toward a fiction. The argument of a harsher Indian reality robbed them of any redeeming virtue. Reviewers such as the one quoted above asked that authors "cease to make Indians talk sentiment,"⁶⁶ because to *make* them eloquent, to paint them as noble projected misplaced compassion onto undeserving figures. They regarded Black Hawk's "autobiography" as an egregious example of what Jared Farmer called "speaking for Indians."⁶⁷ Steven Conn, in *History's Shadow*, additionally pointed to the danger that acknowledging Indian eloquence presented to justifications for removal and Indian vanishing."⁶⁸ Yet those interested in Black Hawk and sympathetic to the book's peaceful message were eager to make it understood as the kind of work that Farmer labeled a "hybrid text"—delivered to an English-speaking audience by a mediator, to be sure, but believed to be a genuine representation of Black Hawk's own state of mind.⁶⁹ Laura Mielke saw criticism of this type, and explicit differentiation between subject, editor, and narrator, as a reactionary effort on the part of whites to regain control over public discourse and representations of Indians and Indian policies. The expressed concern over issues of authorship regarding Black Hawk's autobiography indicate that language was linked directly to the politicized construction of the Indian image. In this context, Black Hawk's eloquence was deemed politically subversive.⁷⁰ Spiritualist representations of Indian spirits such as Black Hawk undermined the prevailing public view of native peoples, which Conn referred to as generic, silent Indians.⁷¹ The ghosts of Black Hawk and of other Indians were anything but silent. Spirit chiefs utilized sound as a primary method of demonstrating their presence to Spiritualists. Additionally, their speech, especially in the 1870s and 1880s, advocated a distinct position on Indian politics.

The representation of Indians as able to speak was politically motivated in the nineteenth century. This point was driven home by the description of Keokuk, Black Hawk's rival and eventual successor to Sac leadership, as eloquent. In Catlin's descriptions of the Sac Indians, he said that "there is no Indian chief on the frontier better known at this time, or more highly appreciated for his eloquence, as a public speaker, than Kee-o-kuk."⁷² Keokuk became Black Hawk's rival because he was more willing to cooperate with American objectives in terms of land sale. For this reason, Keokuk was publicly praised as being much wiser than Black Hawk, becoming superior to him in terms of both speech and intelligence. In this case the depiction of Keokuk as eloquent was politically appropriate, because such a description praised Indian behavior amenable to American motivations, while simultaneously condemning Black Hawk and other resistant chiefs as dumb barbarians, unworthy of American sympathy.

The political underpinnings linked to Indian oratory are what make Black Hawk's broken English in Jennie Lord's séances worth noting. As Conn argued, nineteenth-century Americans valued language as a marker of Indians' "degree of social advancement."[73] By positing that Indians, living and dead, could speak, and could do so eloquently, was a primary method by which Spiritualists asserted the merit of their answer to the Indian question. Native eloquence demonstrated the capacity for intellectual improvement; on moral terms, the education of Indian peoples, rather than their extinction, was preferable. Spiritualists rejected the soothing rationale that American Indians were destined to disappear. As Brian Dippie pointed out, the morality of America is historically linked to the welfare of Indians. "Sensitivity about the United States's moral stature among the nations of the world," he wrote, "made it difficult for Americans to admit to a deep complicity in the Indians' destruction."[74] Convincing themselves that the natives of North America were incapable of living in a modern, progressive world, many Americans erased any sense of personal or national responsibility. A major objective of white reformers, Berkhofer pointed out, was to educate Indian children in the English language. The power of English speech was seen as a primary indicator of civilization, and thus crucial to the social assimilation of the Indian population.[75] Demonstrations of Indian powers of speech proved sufficiently to Spiritualists that not only was education of American Indians possible, denying the inevitability of vanishing rhetoric, but that it was imperative. Spiritualists repeatedly cited the strides of the "Five Civilized Tribes" to disavow an America deep in moral slumber. Beginning in the early 1800s, the Cherokees, Creeks, Choctaws, Chickasaws, and Seminoles built governments modeled after American republicanism, established educational infrastructures, and succeeded in areas of Christian practice, agriculture, and, perhaps most notably, literacy.[76] As Conn said, complex languages and powers of rhetoric could bestow a new political status on Indians as they "bestowed a measure of humanity, perhaps even equality, on the speakers."[77] The possibility that Indians deserved political equality presented a clear obstacle to ongoing policies of disenfranchisement and removal. Indeed, the ability of acknowledged Indian eloquence to possibly erode such policies and their rationalizations was suggested, Conn observed, early in the nineteenth century.[78] Debates about the validity of Indian eloquence and efforts to authenticate Indian spirit voices were major arenas in which the struggle to clearly define Indians and their relationship to whites was fought. Black Hawk's manifestational broken English, rather than the noble eloquence for which he was known in life, mitigated the sympathetic nature of Lord's apparition, despite the generally benign content of his spiritual speech. Black Hawk's presiding over Lord's séance circles symbolized a cosmic level of peaceful relationships between Indians and whites. On the other hand, the depiction of Black Hawk as somewhat intellectually lacking, through consistent patterns of baser speech, perpetuated the racial hierarchy of the living.

Intelligible spirit speech was also an element unique to Spiritualism; Bennett observed that in Indian manifestations produced by Shakers, no attempt was made to transcribe or corroborate the utterances of Indian spirits as authentic languages.[79] She argued that "forced with the question of how to mimic Indian language or speech patterns, Shakers often spoke nonsense or gibberish (possibly combined with genuine words) or in other cases spoke very crude, stereotyped, heavily accented English … drawing from a range of sources including popular theatrical performance, Indian oratory (and bastardized forms of it), and fiction."[80] Spiritualism continued to draw on these popular, highly available images of Indians, yet utilized them in a different and politically significant way by acknowledging the ability of Indian spirits, and by extension Indians, to speak.

Although the extended use of broken English on the part of Black Hawk's spirit suggests Black Hawk's demarcation as indicative of a lower spiritual status, the perception of Black Hawk in the 1860s had changed significantly from thirty or forty years prior. The speeches he made in his final years, proposing peace and friendship, were emphasized, remembered in continuity with his spectral outreach. When Black Hawk was manifested in the early 1880s, by a medium other than Jennie Lord (which will be returned to later), the broken English of Lord's séances was absent, and Black Hawk's powers of speech were again returned to a noble eloquence. The only remaining trait of "characteristically Indian" speech was Black Hawk's tendency to refer to himself in the third person—his messages typically began with phrases such as, "Black Hawk comes today," or Black Hawk speaks to his friends."[81]

A combination of tactile, as well as aural, manifestations coalesced into spirit performances in dark séances. Speech was not the only culturally specific trait of the Indian spirit; movement was also an important element of American images of the Indian that was manifested in séances. After a series of musical performances, Coleman reported in 1862 that Black Hawk proceeded to give the circle "an Indian dance, and the dull and heavy bumping and thumping sounds as of feet in moccasins, or Indian slippers, kept excellent time."[82] What is especially significant here is the description of the *dance itself* as "Indian." Here again aural, rather than visual cues were the mode of racial authentication, right down to the sound that leather moccasins, the most widely acknowledged form of Indian footwear, would make. This was the second time Black Hawk's presence was observed through the presence of moccasins, but the senses utilized have shifted. By touch and by sound, leather moccasins were central to the recognition of the Indian in both séances. This demonstrates cultural costume as a definitive factor recognizing Black Hawk's spirit as Indian. During a dark séance, the feel and sound of costume, moreso than the look of it, became authoritative. Coleman also recorded a similar manifestation where the sounds heard accurately indicated to him the female ghost in attendance. He recalled "footsteps as of persons walking in their stocking-feet, accompanied by the restling [sic] sound of a silk dress."[83] This sound cue, as did the moccasins, indicated that the spirit was wearing the expected cultural or gender-specific garb. It confirmed her sexual identity and the use of costume and sound as authentic performative modes.

The semi-physical forms of spirits were oftentimes felt by séance observers as a further indication of their presence. In 1861, Black Hawk's hand, rather than his foot, was felt during the séance. "The tambourine," Coleman said, "was then placed on my head, and [Black Hawk] passed his hand over it, by which I could feel its full shape and size."[84] The manifestation of spirit hands was common in séances; by describing the size, shape, strength, and sometimes color of these limbs, séance participants oftentimes drew conclusions about the manifestation's character. In the case of Indian spirits, manifestations of their limbs, recognized primarily through touch, were frequently described as extraordinarily large and strong. Indian spirits were typically remembered by Spiritualists as prominent figures within the séance. As Bennett observed, Indian spirits "were usually believed to be highly perceptive, capable of significant insight, and possessed with powerful oratorical gifts."[85] Black Hawk's spirit in particular was consistently described as being notably powerful. The strength demonstrated in the manifestation was perceived as directly linked to the apparition's spiritual powers, and its ability to act as a medium's guide. In Coleman's account of a Black Hawk manifestation, Black Hawk "concluded this part of his performance by saying, 'Me do something else for you,' and in an instant the medium seated in her arm chair was lifted with a startling bound on to the centre of the table, chair and all."[86]

In a broader context, Black Hawk's demeanor in this séance is indicative of the perceived personality of Black Hawk himself. He spent the majority of the evening moving musical instruments around, hitting people, including Coleman, on the head, and shouting in their ears.[87] His prankish mood suggests that he is an obnoxious figure. This tone was observed in other, but not all, Indian manifestations. Perhaps his puckish behavior was meant to reflect his lack of civilization. Depictions of Indians as being childish was a debated issue in nineteenth-century discourse. Contemporary racial theory was infused with Darwinian vocabulary and a teleological impulse, imported from Herbert Spencer's midcentury writings on evolution as "subject to the laws of progression."[88] Indians stood at odds with civilization, being usually described as savages, or at best barbarians in the upward scale of social improvement, as defined by Lewis Henry Morgan in his 1877 work *Ancient Society, or Researches in the Lines of Human Progress from Savagery through Barbarism to Civilization*, which advocated a teleological understanding of human evolution as "one in experience, one in progress."[89] Since the fifteenth-century discovery of the New World, Christians had struggled to make sense of Adam and Eve as the sole progenitors of the human race. Samuel George Morton's theory of polygenesis, rather than the biblical interpretation of monogenesis, accommodated the obvious human variety. It elegantly termed physical differentiation as ordained by Providence, not by environment or condition. Racial difference was thus made immutable.[90] The relationship between the savage and the civilized man was likened to that of child and parent. The issue was whether or not educating Indian savages would enable them to catch up to contemporary civilization. Scientific findings that indicated smaller skull measurements among American Indians suggested that such intellectual development was not possible. Interpretations of this kind built upon the idea that Indians were governmental children of the United States.[91] The ghosts of female Indians exhibited childishness more frequently, but not while accomplishing feats of strength. In female manifestations, their childlike nature helped to demonstrate their innocence, a point I will return to in chapter 4. Despite what may have been perceived by Spiritualists as an enduring childishness on the part of Black Hawk's spirit, he was most cooperative. His increased helpfulness to living whites indicated for Spiritualists an improvement in his character, and in the tense relationship between himself and Americans.

The dancing done by Black Hawk's spirit in Miss Lord's séance was a rare circumstance in Spiritualist circles, and was connected to the "authentic Indian" in the terms in which it was described—as coming from Indian feet in Indian shoes making loud Indian sounds.[92] In another instance, dances performed by Indian spirits are labeled as "wild" and dangerous to the mediums that came under Indian "possession."[93] Dancing became another example of how images of Indians were constructed.

What is important about Miss Lord's mediumship was the effort and detail recorded in the authentication of the Indian spirit. Epes Sargent, a participant and recorder of Spiritualism who introduced Benjamin Coleman to Miss Lord,[94] recounted in one of his books another séance conducted by her:

> Under test conditions, and while the medium's hand and feet were held, a large bass-viol was taken from the corner of the room and played on vigorously and well. Several familiar psalm tunes ... were given. That it was a preterhuman performance I absolutely *know*. The spirit operator first touched us all on the head with the viol-bow. The spirit-hand, twice as large as that of the medium, proved its intangibility by being placed repeatedly on our heads; it took down the hair of two ladies present, and carefully put it up again, and indicated in various ways the intelligence guiding it—and all this while the medium was held.[95]

There were certain elements of this séance that indicated Miss Lord's mediumship operated under some level of standard procedure. Most important was the presence of music. The large bass-viol described by Benjamin Coleman was again utilized, seemingly without human agency, and several familiar songs of a religious nature were played. In the case of Black Hawk, members of the circle were encouraged to chime in—thus, familiarity with the tunes can be assumed.

The spirit being manifested here did not have a name and was not described as Indian. The performance was not dependent on authenticating a racial identity, but was instead dedicated to the unequivocal demonstration of an otherworldly presence. The emphasis was on insisting the manifestation was *not* of the medium's making, as evidenced by the repeated mention of her bound state and the reference to the size of the spirit's hand in relation to her own. The absence of certain features in this séance present in Black Hawk's performance serve to demonstrate how racially specific those elements were.

Despite the fact that this spirit did not speak, we are told that the "intelligence guiding it" was satisfactorily demonstrated. Although powers of speech were usually connected with intelligence, this spirit might be considered Black Hawk's intellectual superior. Any form of violent movement was absent from this séance, and the behavior of this spirit connoted a very polite tone, quite opposite to that of Black Hawk. This spirit *touches* participants on the head and *places* its hands on them; none of the thrashing describing Black Hawk's movements was present. Also, the spirit was said to *carefully* redo the females' hair, a delicate procedure in itself, which suggests the spirit's familiarity with contemporary white modes of coiffure. This spiritual performance was devoid of any of the specifically Indian elements utilized in Black Hawk's séance, and instead, if anything, asserted the spirit's whiteness. This opposition highlights Black Hawk as an *Indian* spirit, revealing the modes in which Indians, as ghostly manifestations or otherwise, were perceived by Spiritualists as authentic.

Another manifestation of Black Hawk through Miss Lord that had taken place two decades prior was recorded in 1882 by Emma Hardinge Britten, an eminent Spiritualist and medium. It was performed at a house in Massachusetts, and demonstrated a different method of Indian spirit authenticatication. Britten recalled:

> At the house of Mr. Bullens of Chicopee, Massachusetts, the materialized form of "Black Hawk," an Indian spirit, stood in the garden on a bright summer's day, about the year 1862, in the paved pathway, and became visible to myself, my mother, Miss Jenny Lord (the medium), and both Mr. and Mrs. Bullens. He remained there for about the time we might count thirty, then slowly melted out; he was some twenty paces from us, and when we went to the spot where he had disappeared, we found a rough likeness of his well-known face chipped in the paving-stones where he seemed to have stood.[96]

This manifestation was distinctive from the appearance recounted by Coleman a year earlier because of the change in conditions. Under the full daylight of summer, Black Hawk was authenticated in the open air, quite different from the dark, enclosed space of Miss Lord's abode. There was no speech, movement, or behavior whatsoever. Only visual cues were called upon to identify him. His *well-known face*—this was not a coincidental naming of an Indian spirit, but was *the* Black Hawk so widely recognized by the

American public. Thanks to the sketch work done by George Catlin, his portrait was as widely known as his exploits.[97] In the *Religio-Philosophical Journal*, the Indian "chief" Seneca was similarly manifested. He was described almost entirely by the sight of his dress. The anonymous witness recalled, "He had on a red blanket trimmed with beads, wore leggings and moccasins, his head was decorated with feathers, and his whole appearance was extremely majestic."[98] Seneca's costume was authenticated through color, rather than the particular sounds of Indian-made materials.

In the *Religio-Philosophical Journal*, J. R. Randall emphasized visual elements of an Indian manifestation more strongly, describing the Indian's costume as well as physical features. He wrote:

> There came into our view a large, portly INDIAN SPIRIT, WASTINAH, we were told, was his name. He was dressed gorgeously in dark and light colored furs, black feathers, nicely arranged on his head, the double skirt over his tight leggings being trimmed with ermine fur. It was a noble form to look upon ... I could see the features, snapping black eyes, and coarse black hair, very plainly ... on this evening there were four materializations of white persons that were recognized, but they were the same that appeared on the evening before, only they were plainer—each one remaining longer and in a greater amount of light.[99]

The color, arrangement, and layers of costume seen by Randall were what he recorded in this instance, rather than the more common appearance of Indian spirits through sound and touch. Randall also emphasized the dramatic nature of the Indian appearances, in contrast to the four "plain" white manifestations, which seemingly failed to capture his interest in the same way as the four Indian appearances.

Although there is no record of a spirit photo of Black Hawk, the above description of his visual manifestation paralleled spirit photos of other Indians, in that the images of Indians themselves were easily authenticated— as Bennett observed, "Indian spirit guides who appear in spirit photographs are easily recognizable by their feathered headdresses and authentic clothing."[100] Photography was a medium increasingly being used by white observers. Photographs of Indians, as well as hand-drawn portraits like Catlin's, were widely circulated, making certain images and certain figures such as Black Hawk well known. Here again, Indian modes of dress became important to authentication. In the 1862 manifestation, Black Hawk's face was clearly seen, whereas in Coleman's account his dress was verified through aural cues of stomping leather moccasins, and their texture as felt in the 1857 séance.

Black Hawk's last recorded manifestation through Jennie Lord took place in Stockport, New York, in 1865, and was described very similarly to his other appearances. A *Banner of Light* article described the central purpose of Black Hawk's presence, which was, yet again, to prove the existence of spirits and authenticate his own appearance. The anonymous witness of Lord's séance ended his brief story by saying:

> The spirit of the noted Indian Chief Black Hawk was present, and did many things which were wholly unaccountable, and made a deep impression on all present. We are not prepared as yet to say that we are converted, but that we were greatly astonished cannot be denied, and I shall avail myself of further opportunities to witness the workings of the spirit through the noted medium, Miss Lord.[101]

In 1870, Emma Hardinge Britten reported meeting the spirit of Black Hawk near Rock Island, the place of the Black Hawk memorial, and claimed to also have met Annie Lord Chamberlain during the same visit. She claimed that at the place called "Black Hawk's tower," he offered to become Britten's guardian spirit; she went on to "contemplate the degrading conditions into which the enlightenment of *Christian* civilization has reduced the once noble savage."[102]

The racial tropes used by Miss Lord to authenticate Black Hawk's spirit were fairly consistent in their reflections upon Black Hawk's person. However, Black Hawk's spirit was portrayed differently by other mediums, and the changes signify sentiments of a different kind. Emma Hardinge Britten, the medium present at the visual manifestation of Black Hawk in 1862, mentioned another spiritual manifestation of the chief in *Modern American Spiritualism* in 1870 that took place at a conference in New York.[103] The son of a Mr. Conklin had taken ill, and instead of sending the report to Conklin through magnetic telegraph, the messenger went to "the office of the *Christian Spiritualist* … where a public circle was then in session. 'Black Hawk,' an Indian chief announced himself, and volunteered [to relay the message via spiritual telegraph]."[104] Black Hawk was acknowledged as the Indian chief, not a homonymous figure, and here he was offering assistance, instead of being mischievous. The speech in which Black Hawk volunteered was not recorded, but in this instance he was capable of *writing* through Conklin the following message: "Go right home—your little boy, Sammy, is very sick. Black Hawk."[105] Not only did Black Hawk identify himself again to the father away in Washington, but he was able to communicate in written English without error.

Jennie Lord and her sister disappeared from the public séance circuit by 1880, presumably because of failing health or financial difficulty. Jennie Lord was consistently described in print as being of a delicate constitution. In September 1865, she published a letter in the *Banner of Light*, writing from her father's house in Maine that "my health is slowly improving, and I am in hopes to fulfill my engagements in the West in October."[106] Earlier in June of that year, she had announced travel plans to Cleveland, Chicago, and Quincy, Illinois, in the autumn.[107] A letter by their father Dr. Cyrus Lord to the *Religio-Philosophical Journal* in 1875 alluded to Annie Lord Chamberlain's refusal to give public séances at her residence, "as her health will not permit."[108]

Financial difficulty seemed to accompany the Lord Sisters as well. While living in New York City in March 1876, Jennie Lord posted this advertisement in the *Banner of Light*: "Mrs. Jennie Lord Webb, Medium for Independent writing, can be addressed at 18 W. 21st Street, New York. Persons at a distance wishing messages from spirit friends, or business letters answered, can obtain them by sending lock of hair, one dollar and three 3-cent stamps."[109] In June of the same year, another article issued the following statement: "It is to be hoped that [Lord] may receive that generous support she so richly deserves. Media entering the field when the spiritual movement was in its infancy, and when it required much more stamina that it does now, should not be forgotten or neglected."[110] An 1878 article called on Spiritualists to lend Mrs. Lord Webb financial aid: "At present a suffering and needy invalid, her physical powers having succumbed to the strain brought to bear on her nervous system, so that she has obliged to discontinue her sittings entirely, and is therefore greatly in want of such assistance."[111] In the mid to late 1870s, both Jennie and Annie Lord advertised permanent private residences where they could be reached via correspondence or visited to undergo spiritual tests and proofs. The spirit of Black Hawk, however, did not cease to manifest once the Lord family became absent from Spiritualist print.

Black Hawk's Spiritual Progress

During the 1880s, Black Hawk's spirit manifested through a medium named Miss M. T. Shelhamer, working in Boston as the resident sitting medium for the *Banner of Light*. Mary Theresa Shelhamer was "a message medium for a Boston spiritualist semimonthly called the *Voice of Angels*" from 1878 before transitioning to the *Banner of Light*.[112] Black Hawk was one of the many spirits who spoke in the *Banner of Light* via Shelhamer. His spirit through her took on a very different tone from Lord's manifestations. "Black Hawk comes today," he said in 1880,

> not with the hunting-knife or the tomahawk, not glowing like the hues of the setting sun with the war-paint, but he comes to bring peace to the great lodge; he comes from the happy hunting-ground to bring strength to the white maiden, that the voices of the spirit may go forth, sending out their words of love like the snowflakes that fall swiftly from on high, bringing down a new message of whiteness and peace to the pale faces.[113]

This spirit message is perfectly clear and poetic. There is a renewed emphasis on his peaceful, spiritual nature, pleading for whites to be conscious of a coming spiritual judgment, and to prepare by actively working toward racial unity. In Shelhamer's manifestations of Black Hawk, his ghostliness was less focused on the senses through which he was perceived. His specter more strongly represented a literal haunting in its ominous message. Cox observed that "a dead Black Hawk pardoned even the most recent sins for all to hear."[114] This kind of message was new for Black Hawk's ghost, and more clearly defined his position as a spirit that educated, guided, and empowered whites.

During the 1880s, Black Hawk's spirit messages as produced by Shelhamer continued to support Spiritualist efforts for peace. He was also seemingly aware of contemporary political developments. In 1882, he sent encouragement to the "white chief in the far west, in Michigan":

> Black Hawk would say to the white chief, work on strongly, faint not by the way; fail not in your purpose; but press on earnestly and nobly. The work is not altogether of the material, for spiritual labor is entwined within it, the spiritual and the material go hand in hand. Black Hawk, as one of the spiritual band, brings strength and power to the pale-face in body.[115]

Although the overall intention of these later spirit messages was relatively consistent, his message in 1885 was strangely inconsistent in linguistic ability. The underlying eloquence remained, but the syntax became a bit muddy:

> Like to meet the council of spirits that gather here to do big work. Black Hawk see Big Eagle chief; see White Feather; see Half Moon; see heap braves and squaws here, who bring magnetism to those who need, and who carry it out over the plains, across the big waters to the pale-faces and red-faces who want strength and must find it somewhere. Good moon.[116]

The reason for this stylistic change is unclear, for the very next year in 1886, Black Hawk's final recorded appearance in Spiritualist literature returned to the poetic eloquence of Shelhamer's previous manifestations. The messages that spirits such as Black Hawk's conveyed challenged the dominant view of Indians as "silent," to use Conn's words.[117] Conn argued that silent Indians could cut a sympathetic figure without disrupting white assumptions about Indians. By contrast, the primary activity of Indian spirits was to speak. Spiritualists heard these voices as originating from Indians and representing a stance of Indian resistance (albeit on a constructed level) against their marginalization through silence.

Miss Lord's manifestations of Black Hawk accumulated to just that—a demonstration that the ghost himself was present. His recognition on both a racial and spiritual level was paramount. There was no overarching agenda communicated to the séance circle by Black Hawk's spirit. A clear social, political, or moral message in Black Hawk's spectral appearance was almost wholly absent. His manifestation's central act was defining Indianness itself on a sensory level, which was characteristic of manifestations of the 1850s and 1860s, giving way to ghostly warnings more prominently in the 1870s and 1880s. This trend in Indian manifestations will be returned to in future chapters.

The lack of a stronger political message may have resulted in part from Jennie Lord's position as a medium. She was considered one of the most prominent mediums in the early stages of the Spiritualist movement, and was consistently referred to as a lady by those within the movement. In 1864, an article claimed that "all who engage her services will be pleased with her powers as a medium and her accomplishments as a lady."[118] A year later, the *Banner of Light* described her as "intelligent and refined; affectionate, sensitive, and gentle, and will be well received wherever she goes."[119] She was not ridiculed by name in existing anti-Spiritualist literature and was distinguished by those within the movement as not holding what one Spiritualist called "promiscuous gatherings, [but rather] makes engagements for private parties."[120] Although beginning her career as a public medium, holding séances in such places as the Scientific and Progressive Lyceum in Brooklyn, New York, Lord increasingly restricted herself to conducting séances in private settings, at the homes of others or at her own dwelling.[121] She was not described as a political activist for any cause, and Black Hawk's performances through her were not deemed particularly subversive. Perhaps as a result of that, Lord was able to retain the label of "lady," despite the many attacks of skeptics on the propriety and mental health of public female mediums and activists in particular. Those who wished to delegitimize Spiritualist gains, such as the New York medical professor Alexander Hammond, drew parallels between "the absolute identity of the symptoms, in all characteristics, with those in our day asserted to be due to spiritual possession, and with those met within the various forms of hysteria."[122]

Despite the lack of an overtly political message, the complexity of these manifestations doesn't lend itself easily to labels of cultural play or performance, because the figure of Black Hawk changed as a result of his spectral appearances. Jennie Lord's séances made the spirit of Black Hawk a staple of Spiritualist experiences. "All who know anything of spirit-influence," an anonymous *Banner of Light* contributor states, "have heard of the chief Black Hawk."[123] Black Hawk was arguably the most prominent ghost within the movement. Spiritualists saw an increasingly strong, helpful manifestation, increasingly intelligible and progressing through the spheres. He demonstrated a burgeoning spiritual connection between living whites and Indian ghosts that Spiritualists connected in their minds to America's relations with living Indians. As Cox claimed, "even the hardest-hearted of living Indians, a veritable Black Hawk, was softened in the spirit world. Where once 'pale-faced spirits found little welcome at his council fire,' this repentant warrior now welcomed all with open arms and spiritual gifts."[124]

Emma Britten explained Black Hawk's demeanor as the progression of his character after his transition to the spirit world. At first glance, her words seem to paint a more sympathetic portrait of Black Hawk:

> No sooner does he become a spirit, than he practically adopts the neglected duties of Christianity, and by deeds of love and mercy

shows the white man how to prove the truth of his creed ... Many of the once powerful and renowned chiefs among the redmen delight to work out a new and beautiful mission for themselves.[125]

This statement is critical of white religious hypocrisy, but beneath the surface a benign racism resides. In one way, Britten was chastising the Christian nation, arguing that Indians (both living and dead) were better at treating mankind with the love, integrity, and civility. Seen another way, the presence of Indians only benefited Americans in their spirit state. They were not helpful while living, when allegedly devoid of Christian virtue. Their spiritual uplift, then, was perhaps a justification for their deaths. Indian spirits were content to reside in the "happy hunting ground." Furthermore, the Indians most involved in assisting whites were "powerful and renowned"—put bluntly, notorious—chiefs, and Black Hawk's name is the first on her list.[126] In the public mind, he had a long, challenging spiritual journey ahead of him. Yet, his publicized journey was perhaps the most successful of the popularly known Indian ghosts. Black Hawk's spirit moved away from war and vengeance, just as Black Hawk himself claimed he intended to at the end of his life: "I won't go to war again. I will live in peace. I shall hold you by the hand."[127] Speaking of living Indian orators, Cox claimed that some nineteenth-century Americans saw language as having the "power to transform individual Indians ... into something more approaching a masculine ideal [and] had the force to make individual Indian speakers into real men."[128] Eloquence was additionally related to civic virtue, defined in nineteenth-century America as an especially masculine trait. "Admiring Indian eloquence," Conn argued, along with "acknowledging their oratorical skill, came provocatively close to investing individual Indians with power and giving Indian groups the ability to imagine themselves as nations ... it may well have been possible for some to figure Indians into the equation that linked eloquence, power, and nationhood."[129] It is my claim that Spiritualists did just that in depicting the speech of spirit chiefs as eloquent. The actions of spirit chiefs such as Black Hawk confirmed for Spiritualists Indian manhood and the fight to claim them as Americans, rather than recognize their sovereignty. This point of discussion will be more prominent in chapter 3.

The voice attributed to Black Hawk's ghost and other Indian spirits was used by Spiritualists, as might be expected, to critique their own culture. The underlying criticism of American moral hypocrisy present in Black Hawk's autobiography was continued in his spiritual demeanor; Mielke wrote that through his autobiography Black Hawk claimed a kind of moral authority, and a code of conduct to be imitated.[130] This same authority to define morality and ideal manhood—and by extension, ideal American citizenship—was claimed by Spiritualists through spirit chiefs. They also sought to define ideal womanhood, which will be the focus of chapter 4. Conn claimed that the pervasive idea of Indians as eloquent had receded by the later years of the nineteenth century, but that was not the case within Spiritualist circles. If perceived Indian powers of speech had declined in American public consciousness, then Spiritualists gave the power of Indian oratory new life. Mielke posited that Black Hawk's autobiography "insists on white responsibility for Indian tragedy ... and then instructs the audience members to change their behavior accordingly."[131] The work's underlying argument was embraced by Spiritualists, who sought to foster this strain of sentiment after Black Hawk's death by representing his spirit as the admirable figure Black Hawk himself described, and by using portrayals of him as noble and eloquent to demonstrate the capability of civilization. Spiritualists used their allegations of the ongoing presence of Indian spirits and their ability to improve as tools to resist the dominant rhetoric of Indians as inevitably vanishing, and justifiably so. This argument was furthered by Spiritualists who provided records of séance activity as evidence of spiritual progression and intellectual capacity. Throughout the last half of the nineteenth century, Spiritualists resisted hostile discourses on Indians and Indian policies by continuing to assert Indian eloquence, and all it implied. The eloquence that Conn claimed was "a thing of the past" in the years following the Civil War was maintained throughout the remainder of the nineteenth century by the haunted appearance of Indians.[132]

His spiritual journey also lasted longer than other spirits. In the twentieth century, the spirit of Black Hawk "dominate[d] the black Spiritual churches."[133] His appearance in this context is originally connected to Leafy Anderson, whom "most Spiritual people in Louisiana assert [founded] the religion."[134] Although the exact time of her movements remains unclear, according to Albanese, "Mother Leafy Anderson had organized the Eternal Life Spiritualist Church in Chicago ... as early as 1913," migrating to New Orleans around the year 1920.[135] Anderson claimed a connection to Black Hawk through her assertion that "she herself was half Mohawk."[136]

Anderson's portrayal of Black Hawk's spirit differed from those within American Spiritualism in the nineteenth century, yet Jason Berry claims that Anderson was in fact influenced by this earlier movement. "Leafy

Anderson was a Spiritualist—one who believed in the power of human mediums to communicate with the spirits of the dead. Nineteenth-century Spiritualism flourished in the Northeast and Midwest. New Orleans had a concentration of Spiritualists, especially among the creoles of color."[137] Anthropologists Claude Jacobs asserts in *The Spiritual Churches of New Orleans* that "if [Anderson] was from the upper Midwest, she would have known [that] Spiritualism was tied up with Indian spirits ... heard those stories."[138] It is possible that Anderson was exposed to a lingering influence of Jennie Lord's manifestations of Black Hawk, from Lord's presence in the Chicago area as late as 1875.[139]

The use and significance of Black Hawk's spirit in the Spiritual church has been studied to some extent. Jacobs and Kaslow claim that his "preeminent place ... suggest[ed] he was 'more than an Indian spirit or powerful guide,' but instead a 'master symbol.' "[140]

Revered Jules Anderson of the New Orleans Spiritual community explained the significance of Black Hawk's spirit to Berry. Anderson claims that

> as a teenager, I didn't know anything about Black Hawk at the time. So I prayed, and I went through this sensational experience I never had before ... I heard a voice. It spoke to me. "These are my saints and I will teach you how to use every one." But the one that stuck with me out of all those was Black Hawk. Not long after that ... I was walking down the street in the French Quarter, and this big Indian guy just came up to me, in the spirit. It wasn't a real man. He was an Indian, but he was dressed in ordinary American clothes, and he walked to me and folded his hands, like we see the statue of Black Hawk in Illinois. And he just walked right into me, and it was like a possession type thing I went into. And it was from that day on that I began to have this personal relationship with the spirit of Black Hawk.[141]

In this instance, the spirit of Black Hawk was not recognized by traditional Indian costume, but rather by the particular posture the portrayal of him the Rock Island memorial in Illinois adopts. Anderson continued his discussion of Black Hawk's spirit, saying, "Black Hawk is a spirit of justice."[142]

In a 1979 Spiritual service conducted by Anderson, Berry retells how Anderson "chant[ed] the words 'Black Hawk is a watchman' with people in the pews calling back the refrain—'He's on the wall!' "[143] In 1981, Hans Baer wrote that "Black Hawk is regarded as a warrior who can cause justice to be done, and his intercession is frequently sought in court cases, or in seeking the release of loved ones from prison."[144] This particular function of Black Hawk's spirit is an interesting parallel to both the story of the Indian prisoner whose murder, in Black Hawk's eyes, instigated his aggression toward the United States, and the fact that Black Hawk himself was a temporary prisoner of the United States in the later years of his life.

Leafy Anderson proclaimed the spirit of Black Hawk was "the patron saint of the South," whose position in the Spiritual church persists to this day.[145] Black Hawk's spirit, and his role as protector, are celebrated at a special feast on December 17th, which is "usually performed at a night service [featuring] incense rituals [and] a sumptuous dinner."[146]

For the men and women of the Spiritual community, Jacobs and Kaslow claim, "Black Hawk will probably remain their master symbol for some time to come, given the significance of the Native American in Southwestern Louisiana black culture [and] the continuing struggle of blacks against racism."[147] Although Black Hawk's spiritual appearance functions differently than those in nineteenth-century Spiritualist circles, his spirit continues to be a powerful symbol of changing relations among Indians, whites, and blacks in America.[148]

Irrespective of shifting attitudes toward living Indians, the manifestation of Indian spirits such as Black Hawk had an enormous impact on how middle and professional-class Americans defined, interpreted, and understood the specter of the Indian.

THREE

Spirit Council

The Mission of Dead Chiefs

Introduction

During Spiritualism's heyday in the late nineteenth century, more than eighty spirits were identified as deceased Indian chiefs. Spiritualist historian Robert Cox noted the high frequency of Indian manifestations, which in many cases overwhelmed the number of white apparitions. He cites Spiritualist investigator H. H. Farness, who in 1887 sarcastically claimed that "there is no Cabinet, howe'er so ill attended, but has some Indian there."[1] Molly McGarry also acknowledges the centrality of Indian manifestations to Spiritualism, which she claims was "at once in keeping with a larger nineteenth-century cultural imaginary and also specific to a Spiritualist cosmology and reform ethos."[2]

The pervasiveness of appearances by Indian chiefs in séances served several important functions, which form the basis of this chapter. They contributed to contemporary debates about race and gender as related to civilization and power. Spirit chiefs appeared to Spiritualists and were recognized by them in pointedly racial and gendered terms. Such specters were consistently and distinctly identified as Indian, and as men. As chiefs, they were also men of power, who asserted authority in séances by exhibiting a specific model of manhood to be admired and mimicked by their white male spectators. The self-professed purposes of spirit chief manifestations and the content of their messages were integral to this assertion of authority. They undermined the concept of civilized, honorable conquest; in its stead, they prescribed spiritual progress for Indians and whites, both dead and living, by advocating forgiveness among Indians and encouraging action among whites. This was done by offering spiritual support for white reform efforts and threatening divine retribution if interracial peace was not achieved.

The ghosts of Indian chiefs were recognized as such through several types of especially sensory experiences. Through sound, "Indian" ghosts were identified by means of culturally specific modes of speech and costume. They were also noted for their stature and physical strength. By the middle of the century, Amy Greenberg argues in *Manifest Manhood*, several definitions of manhood competed for supremacy. Among these were what she calls "primitive manhood," which focused on virility and power through violence, and "restrained manhood," centered more strongly on the concepts of a virtuous citizen and family protector.[3] During ghostly manifestations, Indian spirits claimed a bit of both for themselves, advocating a manhood and womanhood less stark in their definitions, if not in their distinctions from each other. The form that Indian specters took, along with the content of their messages, reflected Spiritualist positions on changing notions of gender, as well as their attempts to define masculinity in a way congruent to their sociopolitical goals. The contest to define gender in the nineteenth century, Greenberg states, was intimately connected to the defining of America itself and the connected issue of national expansion.[4] It also deeply affected domestic concerns over race and issues of national morality in relation to America's racial policies. This chapter details how Spiritualist experiences of manifestations and their reactions to them were involved in such discourses.

Spiritualists understood the waves of chief manifestations at séance tables as part of the grand mission of all Indian ghosts: spiritual progression. Nineteenth-century "progress" was intimately connected to the state of racial relations in the United States and, as Braude also claims, lay at the core of Spiritualist thought.[5] By claiming manhood and positioning themselves as spiritually and morally superior, an oft-feminized trait, spirit chiefs legitimized the messages of racial reform they transmitted. Through their communications, Indian spirits sought progress for themselves and their living counterparts. They furthered their own progress by shedding thoughts of vengeance against cruel and unjust whites, turning their thoughts toward an afterlife of racial equality in the eyes of the Great Spirit. They reached out to living Indians, sending messages of peace to resistant chiefs, urging them off the warpath.

Spiritualists also acknowledged the service that Indian ghosts provided directly to them; by emphasizing the racial equality of the spiritual realm, dead chiefs underscored the moral wrongs of white society that were impeding its progress—namely, the unjust treatment of Native Americans and near-constant warfare. Spirit chiefs opposed Indian wars, warning of an impending judgment. Several spirits alluded to a coming retribution for white misdeeds to Indians. This warning was given so that change could be effected by whites in the world of the living, so they might avoid divine wrath. Spirit chiefs additionally encouraged and supported white activism on the behalf of living Indians by empowering their white mediums, decrying the wrongs of the United States government and by suggesting alternatives to warfare, the details of which will be covered in chapter 5.

Identifying Spirit Chiefs

The majority of Indian manifestations came not through records of séances conducted in private houses, but through the published messages purported to originate from spirits at public séances. These messages were communicated on a regular basis by the sitting mediums for the *Banner of Light*. The published messages of spirits took up a full page, one-sixth of the weekly periodical, sometimes exceeding that. The position of sitting medium was most notably occupied by Mrs. J. H. Conant in the 1860s and 1870s, and Mary Theresa Shelhamer in the 1880s.

Born in New Hampshire as Frances Ann Crowell in 1831, the medium popularly known as Mrs. J. H. Conant was recognized by fellow Spiritualists as being "remarkably subject to the influences of spirits purporting to have been while in earth-life, members of the aboriginal tribes of North America."[6] One stated reason for this was that she claimed partial Indian ancestry. In her biography, Conant explained that her connection to the spirits, whom she described as "the invisible ones," began during childhood. The spirits told her as a child that

> her great grandfather, known to the whites as "Swift-Foot," was an Indian chief of renown in the early history of the new World, his name, Quinsigamond … that he was married to a French Canadian woman, the grandmother of Peter Crowell being the result of that union; that his daughter's Indian name was Meona, her English, Betsey.[7]

This same connection to Indians also explained why the Indian spirits who spoke through Conant were "replete with natural eloquence and power."[8] Her personal relationship with Indian spirits was authenticated by Colonel Samuel Tappan, a U.S. Indian agent, member of the Indian Peace Commission, and third husband of famed Spiritualist medium Cora Hatch.[9] He confirmed the dialects Conant often spoke as genuine Indian languages, "afford[ing] the strongest proof to Mrs. Conant concerning the reliability of her guides."[10] While working for the *Banner of Light*, Conant did not give any private meetings.[11] The séances conducted for the *Banner of Light*, held on Washington Street in Boston, were open to the public and conducted on Monday, Tuesday, Wednesday, and Thursday evenings, accommodating approximately 100 to 125 people at each sitting.[12] According to Ann Braude, the Boston newspaper "sponsored a public free circle at its offices and published the communications received there in its pages each week. Mrs. J.H. Conant exercised her mediumship at the Banner Free Circle from its inception in 1857 until her death in 1875."[13]

Native American spirits, though described by séance observers as unique from other manifesting entities, were, compared to one another, described in very similar terms. As Cox observes, Indianness among spirits was largely generic as a result of the repetition of basic descriptive tropes.[14] The speech patterns of Indian spirits, for example, exhibited the same inconsistent oscillation between savage ramblings and noble speech found in Black Hawk's manifestations. A rare instance was recorded in 1852 in a monograph by Adin Ballou, in which the spirit of Red Jacket appears:

> Red Jacket, he delivers Indian speeches, sings Indian songs, and performs the Indian dances. Having heard him speak and sing in the Indian language, I was very much charmed with his delivery, which was eloquent and appropriate, so far as we could judge of his speech in a foreign language … Two of the company present, who were acquainted with Indian languages, spoke of his speech with approbation as a genuine Indian harangue, and a fine specimen of oratory.[15]

Red Jacket, who lived from approximately 1750–1830 and was a Seneca chief known in life for his oratory skills, spoke to a séance circle in his native tongue through a medium called Mr. F. Speech was used in this instance as the method of spirit authentication in an unusual way—the language of the speech was confirmed by witnesses to be authentically Indian, and the circle was convinced of the medium's ignorance of this language.[16]

Forms of elevated as well as broken English were continually recorded as issuing from the lips of Indian ghosts. Spiritualists saw the broken English as a remnant of the spirit's earthly personality; eloquence, on the contrary, was a sign that spiritual progression had taken place. A particularly poor display of English published in 1869 rendered an Indian spirit's message almost incomprehensible, condemning the soul to a state of perpetual backwardness:

> Me Indian, me see the depths of your soul, me see deep sorrow, me see much care, much to perplex, and me no leave you but care for you, all me can … Me see among the thorns many beautiful gems, soul gems that sparkle brighter than the sun. Me see they spirit covered with dark shadows, but me is not hindered from seeing they pure spirit, it is much beautiful and me can see what your noble soul would do if unshackled … Me sees much me no tell for want of your words.[17]

This Indian seems to have accepted his fate at the hands of "beautiful pale spirits" and the will of the Great Spirit, but clumsily attempts to offer his aid by creating a connection between dead Indians and living whites.

The damper that pidgin English put on spirit messages was sometimes acknowledged by the Indian spirits themselves. In 1872, the spirit of Powhatan spoke through the medium Dr. Dunn, claiming, "Me Indian, me no speak like white man."[18] The same year, the ghost of White Wing sent this message, published in The *Banner of Light*:

> Me White Wing. Me come here to learn, so I can speak through my medi, like I speak here. [Then you have a medium? *Sic*] Yes; she the squaw of one of the great fathers—my medi, Nellie. You have great chief—big father—and you have another chief, next to him. [You mean the Vice President?] That be he. She be his squaw—the Vice President's squaw. Me want to learn how to speak, so me come here. White Wing will do good. White Wing will carry messages, and never tell no lies. Good moon.[19]

Learning to communicate intelligibly in English, according to White Wing's message, was a process. It was part of the spiritual education all souls received on their journey to enlightenment, and was an integral component of the Indian spirit's mission. The spirit of White Wing acknowledged this, as did the white spirit named Martha in 1884. In a supplemental message to an eloquent communication by Red Wing, Martha's spirit states, "The Indian speaks the language of the whites much clearer than he does his own native tongue, for he has been a glorious spirit-light to guide many souls home for half a century of time, and he has acquired culture and refinement through a part of the work he accomplished for humanity."[20] To convey their message of peace to whites properly, spirits assumed their message needed to be properly understood and clearly conveyed. Thus, the more eloquent the Indian spirit appeared, the more Spiritualists recognized that ghost's helpfulness.

Poor English on the part of Indian spirits became something of an expected element of their manifestations. In 1875, in Havana, New York, the ghost of the Indian chief Seneca was manifested through the medium Mrs. Compton. Dr. H. B. Storer, the author of the reporting article, described Seneca as possessing a voice that was "clear and distinct, speaking not 'baby talk,' but broken English, with ejaculations entirely characteristic of the Indian manner of expression."[21] In a monograph on Spiritualism entitled *Startling Facts in Modern Spiritualism*, Napoleon Bonaparte Wolfe spoke of the famed medium Mrs. Hollis-Billings and her controlling spirit Skiwaukee, purportedly a former Cherokee chief who went by the name of "Old Ski." Dr. Wolfe said of Old Ski, "He has not yet mastered English grammar, and occasionally makes some very funny remarks in his quaint mixture of Cherokee and Lindley Murray. Addressing me, he said: 'Em old chief, want em test?' "[22] The spirit of Old Ski proceeded to tell the story of how Dr. Wolfe got his famous name, stumbling over the anecdote through a profuse number of "ems."

This style of delivery among Indian manifestations continued into the 1880s. In 1884, the following message was recorded in the *Banner of Light* under the name White Eagle: "How chief—how? [How do you do? *Sic*] Good, Me White Eagle. Me come to chief … the big white chief here say: 'Step in, brave, and do the work.' So White Eagle here … and then White Eagle, he speaks the word for the spirits who no can speak for themselves; and that is the work going on and on."[23] Although by this period the work of spirits had been ongoing for three decades, some Indian spirits continued to lack the power of elevated speech recognized in other ghosts.

The eloquence of Indian spirit communications was recognized by Spiritualists simultaneously with broken English as a cultural identifier. Of the two acknowledged forms of Indian speech, eloquence was more commonplace, becoming a pronounced element of spiritual appearances in the 1880s. In 1881, the spirit of Big Beaver conveyed the following message in the *Banner of Light*, demonstrating his progress and his increased ability to communicate clearly:

> Many, many snows fell upon my head; many, many summers beat upon the red man ere he passed to the hunting-grounds beyond. In darkness and in weakness he returned to this hunting ground in search of light and strength ... Now he comes from the great hunting-ground, where amid the green fields and the mighty forests he listens to the voice of the Great Spirit, and finds himself possessed of words which he may give forth unfalteringly; he gains strength and enlightenment in returning to this mortal hunting-ground; he speaks to the pale-faces in words of love.[24]

This message is clear, poetic and explicitly acknowledges the upward change the spirit has undergone, thus allowing him to provide a heightened level of spiritual support for mortal whites. Another 1881 spirit message from Flying Arrow also pointed to the importance of words and clear communication within the séance:

> And to the others who know of Flying Arrow, he comes, speaking the pale-face words, that they may be felt. He is known in one place as the Indian spirit who returns as a messenger to bear the words of life from the hunting grounds beyond. He is entrusted, as he comes to speak to his friends, with a message from the councils in the highest hunting grounds, with a message of cheer for the white chieftain. He speaks as the messenger of the numberless maidens who gather in the hunting grounds beyond; but he speaks also for himself to his friends who know him and his work, bidding them to be of good cheer.[25]

The message explains that in order for Indians to accomplish their goals in the spirit world, they must gain the attention of white mortals. This was to be done through not only coherent but also eloquent speech, so that, as Flying Arrow put it, "the words may be felt." These messages were intended to have an emotional impact on their white audience, rousing their sentiments in order to instill love of the Indian. Flying Arrow also implied that his ability came from the "higher" hunting grounds, and that his powers of communication were used not only to help whites, but to give a voice to other Indian spirits who had not progressed to his state of enlightenment. Not all Indian spirits were equal, and the lower spirits must thus be represented by an eloquent spirit of higher status.

The sounds produced by Indian spirits during séances, in a general sense, were especially significant in authenticating the presence of "Indian" ghosts. Noises emanating from the spirits were often described as being Indian both in their nature and in their volume. At an 1874 séance in Watkins, New York, the spirit of Seneca was manifested through the medium Mrs. Compton. Mr. G. C. Hibbard, a local merchant who witnessed the séance and sent his letters to the *Banner of Light* for publication, remarked that Seneca "delivered a 'war-whoop' that could have been heard a distance of two squares," marking his appearance as noteworthy.[26] In the *Religio-Philosophical Journal*, another professed Indian chief appeared through Mrs. Compton. Upon his retiring from the séance, observers recounted that he gave "a WHOOP LOUD AND THRILLING."[27] This sort of noise seems to have become an anticipated part of Mrs. Compton's séances. In 1875, the spirit of Seneca again "gave the war-whoop, an ear-piercing and blood quickening yell that might have been heard a long distance in the open air."[28] A few days later, Seneca appeared again and "gave first what he calls the peace-whoop and then, at [the witness Dr. Storer's] earnest request, the ringing war-whoop" before disappearing from the séance.[29] The spirit of Seneca appeared in 1876 in Carpenter, Pennsylvania, giving both the peace-whoop and "war whoop with startling effect."[30]

Manifestations of this type were remembered by witnesses as both awful and awesome. The *Religio-Philosophical Journal* related that in one particular 1875 séance the Indians "signified their presence by a DREADFUL CLATTER AND NOISES of various kinds, mingled with sundry war whoops. Thus ended a very remarkable demonstration of spirit power."[31]

The loud noises, and the description of them as "clatter" or as "war whoops," evoked images of wild red men to Spiritualists, but without the attendant fear. But for some observers, the sound of Indian spirits was as distasteful as the sound of living Indians. John Trusdell described a witnessed Indian manifestation in his 1892 monograph as

> a dance of a pack of howling, leaping, sky-larking Indians, who beat on the drums, rattle the tambourines, blow the horns, ring the heavier bells, and make a din so hideous that one easily fancies himself caught in the melee of a dance of live redskins, about starting on the war path. If Horatio [Eddy] were unbound and using all four of his locomotive and prehensile members, he could not imitate this dance. The

creatures yell and one can hear their stamping on the floor in cadence with their rude music.³²

The violence of these manifestations was described in terms that were culturally unique, and replicated the established image of Indian males in particular as fearsome warriors. They continued to claim distinctly male identities through this motif, recognized by whites as a crucial element of their primitivism. But in this changed context, Indians, who did not appear to be dramatically changed in character, and who were still terrifying to an extent, were nonthreatening. Their warlike traits remained apparent, but now Indian males possessed spiritual power exhibited through their strong spiritual bodies. That power and close contact with the material realm became significant in identifying the traits of Indian spirits. In 1874, Dr. Wolfe recorded a conversation in *Startling Facts in Modern Spiritualism* that he had with the medium Mrs. Hollis-Billings about spirit sound and the strength of Old Ski's manifestations:

> [Mrs. Hollis-Billings claimed that] the spirits say the horn [used during the séance] enables them to concentrate their power, to focalize the waves of sound. You know how that is.
>
> *Do they ever try to speak without using the trumpet?*
>
> Yes: and some spirits succeed: but the sound is always very feeble, in comparison to what is spoken through the trumpet. There is an Indian spirit that can be heard, when he speaks, in any part of the house, without using the horn.
>
> *How does it happen that he can speak so loud and not use the horn?*
>
> He is an Indian, and they are found, as a general rule, to have more power to manifest than other spirits. Then again, he has been in the spirit-world so long that he has completely outlived most of the infirmities of his natural life; besides, he is almost a giant in stature, and possesses more strength than we find ordinarily among men.³³

The volume, clarity and strength of these manifestations were understood by Spiritualists as a reflection of the spiritual strength of Indian specters.

This perceived strength manifested on multiple levels during séances, including the nature and volume of noises produced, the physical abilities of the manifestation, and the spiritual encouragement and empowerment that the Spiritualist community received as a result of their communications.

The physical bodies projected by Indian specters exceeded early-nineteenth-century white definitions of male strength, linked, as Greenberg states, "to a well-muscled body."[34] In the 1864 *Banner of Light* article "Physical Manifestations," the anonymous Indian spirit acting as a control was described as a "gigantic genius."[35] In the 1874 article "Strange Phenomena" by J. R. Randall, "a very tall Indian" named Santo appeared. Randall recalled that "the closet door [was] six feet and a half high, and Santo had to stoop in coming out of it. When he straightened up, his head reached above the door casing. He seemed very anxious to have us understand that he was a 'Big Injun.' "[36] The spirit of Seneca, described in 1875 as "a tall and muscular Indian chief seven feet high!" emerged during one of Mrs. Compton's New York séances.[37] A séance recorded by the *Religio-Philosophical Journal* in the same year recounted the manifestation of another male Indian in these terms:

> Minwaw, Minnie's husband, now appeared, rushing into business as if he were a common monarch of all he surveyed, pushing every chair and person (medium excepted) back to the wall with herculean force, to give himself plenty of room to perform his feats in. Adjusting the instruments by placing them on the laps of the circle, he opened the ball by a few keen, loud yells, very Indian like in exultation over prospective success; and had there been a dozen persons in form, all in action at one and the same time, I think they would have fallen far short of representing Minwaw in his GYMNASTIC EXERCISE. His voice was as loud as any man's could be.[38]

A cover article for an 1875 issue of the *Religio-Philosophical Journal* described the spirit of the Indian Santum as being 6'4", and "followed by 'Big Oak,' also very tall."[39] A manifestation of the chief Seneca, "apparently over six feet in height," appeared through Mrs. E. J. Markee in 1876 in Carpenter, Pennsylvania.[40] In 1877, the "stalwart Osceola" appeared through a medium by the name of Mr. Taylor in Chicago. The author of the reporting article, William Wiggin, wrote that Osceola was a "full three inches taller than the medium, and looking like a man that would weigh twice as much ... This Indian had to stoop when passing through the cabinet door."[41]

Such appearances coincide with Bridget Bennett's notion that "Indian spirit guides were frequently credited with significant power by white mediums."[42] On the one hand, depictions of Indians as tall and strong coincided with images and portrayals of Indian warriors as noble, majestic figures, and secured their identities as distinctly male. On the other hand, the strength of their manifestations was an indicator of their spiritual force—their powers to communicate. Further, their stature and power differentiated them from their "frail," and predominantly female, mediums.[43] They were authenticated through the strength that observers found impossible to attribute to the mediums, noted as petite and fragile in comparison. In April 1864, for example, witnesses of Jennie Lord's séances in Peoria, Illinois, observed that

> she has a very gentle and delicate appearance, and hardly appears to be able to undergo so much fatigue as her manifestations require. She gave some three or four sittings a week, at private houses … those who have studied magic as a trade, are generally of the male sex and not innocent and gentle women, whose fragile forms would barely admit any voluntary attempts at feats of strength.[44]

In this case, Lord's frailty, in contrast to the strength of spirit manifestations, contributed to the integrity of her séances.

The dominating personalities of Indian chiefs were often central forces of spirit manifestations, appearing most strongly at both the beginning and end of séances, and appearing, at intervals, to be managing the series of less remarkable manifestations in between. Séances during which an Indian was manifested were consistently recorded as those of the most extraordinary and remarkable character. They were also touted as the spiritual phenomenon most likely to confirm widespread belief in spirit communication, due to their potent materializations, dispelling the doubts of even the staunchest skeptics. The spiritual power exhibited by Indian ghosts was seen by their mediums as essential to their social causes—it was this strength and power that Indians lent to their mediums, to develop their clairvoyant powers and improve the material world. Spiritualists' recognition of Indian chiefs as spiritually strong was significant in both a racial and gendered context. According to Amy Greenberg, late-nineteenth-century definitions of manhood, heavily influenced by Darwinian theory, centered around strong bodies.[45] In *Manliness and Civilization*, Gail Bederman describes how the African American athlete Jack Johnson "positioned himself as a real man by laying ostentatious claim to a male body, male identity, and male power [and that], an ideal male body [of the 1890s] required physical bulk and well-defined muscles."[46] It was this physical form of manhood to which Indian spirits laid claim, by dint of their height and spiritual strength. This masculine authority was recognized by Spiritualists and utilized by their spirit friends to legitimate the content of their messages. Hence, the manner by which spirit chiefs were made known to their audiences legitimized their mission. As Amy Greenberg points out in her discussion of Darwinism, men of inferior races were often not considered men at all, but were, rather, described as being effeminate.[47] In *Notes on the State of Virginia*, Thomas Jefferson promoted the scientific notion that the smaller skulls of African Americans prevented them from becoming the intellectual equal of whites even with proper education. He also spoke of the North American climate as "producing savages."[48] Indian men were not recognized as men; historically speaking, white denial of Indian manhood was used to help rationalize the conquest of North America by dismissing any claims Indian males made of ownership as illegitimate. Their savagery was perceived as "an innate flaw in their racial character."[49] It rationalized the disappearance of Indians in the face of American progress, a force with which degenerate Indian minds could not hope to coexist.[50] A spiritual claim to manliness, in counterpoint to such beliefs, justified the persistence of the Indian warrior motif, as seen in their manifestational forms, spirit costume, and the consistent use of the title of "chief." The appearance of strong Indian bodies during séances established Indian masculinity. The path that Indian spirits trod in the afterlife did not completely jibe with America's emasculating view of Indian men. Their position on the morality-tinged spiritual spectrum was more fluid and malleable, uniting different interpretations of manhood to a more perfect form—essentially, imbuing spirit chiefs with both the will and ability to serve and protect. Mediums described their cosmic ranking on an individual scale. They did not uniformly declare that Indians progressed through the celestial spheres as a racial whole. It was a strong reflection of the American value of individual over tribal identity.

Despite the low visibility in the majority of séances, participants frequently identified Indian spirits through their culturally specific costumes. Philip Deloria argues that costume was "always a crucial element in Indian play,"[51] and it can be used in part here to understand Spiritualists' recognition of Indian apparitions. In *Transatlantic Spiritualism*, Bridget Bennett observes that Shakers were disinclined to use costume as a way to denote the "Indianness" of spirits for practical concerns to the Shaker performance.[52] The frequent use of costume to distinguish Indian spirits was a common element of Spiritualist manifestations, if not Shaker ones. Washtinah, a spirit manifested through Horatio Eddy and reported in the *Religio-Philosophical Journal* in 1874, was "dressed gorgeously in dark and light-colored furs, black feathers, nicely arranged on his head, the double skirt over his tight leggings being trimmed with ermine fur. It was a noble form to look upon."[53] The title of the article retelling Seneca's 1875 manifestation refers to him as "AN INDIAN WITH A RED BLANKET ... HIS HEAD IS DECORATED WITH FEATHERS, AND HIS BLANKET TRIMMED WITH BEADS. His whole appearance," witness A. E. Tilden wrote, "was extremely majestic."[54] In 1875, in Pennsylvania, Seneca "had a red blanket over his shoulders and two feathers on his head ... He allowed the man sitting next the wall to handle his blanket. The man said it felt like a heavy woolen blanket ... He came out a second time and had a white blanket on, and gave what he called the peace-whoop."[55] This white blanket, in contrast to the red one, is interesting to consider alongside the "peace-whoop." The white blanket may in this context represent peace, in opposition to red, seen as the "color" of Indians and perhaps connected to their perceived tendency to war. The spirit of Osceola purportedly wore "the full dress of a brave on the war path, paint, feathers, &c." when he appeared in Chicago in 1877.[56] Emma Harding Britten wrote of a séance in her autobiography during which she saw "a tall Indian dressed in war paint and feathers, carrying his war hatchet upright in his hand, bow and arrows at his back."[57]

The images of these spirits, however dim they appeared in dark séances, were what might be expected. Indianness, it seems, meant to have a very limited wardrobe regarding color and choice of material. To be Indian meant to be a giant, clad in leather, feathers, beads, and paint. This visual concept, observed in the nineteenth century in a variety of popular forms, including novels, plays, poems, and even early ethnographic works, did not originate within Spiritualist circles. Barnett wrote that "the excellent physical condition and appearance of Indians had been remarked by whites from the earliest contact [and] enhanced the fearful quality of the captors."[58] This tendency, as seen in captivity narratives, was continued by authors of fiction, who characterized Indian men as "fine physical specimens, proficient in wilderness skills, stoical, and given to figurative speech."[59] As Daphne Brooks observed, the "Indian chief" was a central "national character" in nineteenth-century performance.[60] In the context of the séance, spirit chiefs represented the climax of the performance as the center of the "physical demonstration" of the evening. The physical attributes of Indianness have been quite persistent, continuing to reach modern popular audiences through television and cinema.[61] Cox argues that such generic representations of Indianness were perpetuated by Spiritualists in the absence of a more genuine appreciation of Indian cultures.[62] Yet Indian costume had a meaning beyond stereotype in the Spiritualist context, as one of the only methods through which Indian spirits could be identified and authenticated. Not all spirits were living celebrities like Black Hawk; shy of that kind of publicity and a personal knowledge of individual Indians, generalities such as cultural costume and the occasional war-whoop became the norm.

Chiefs Make Spiritual Progress

The character of Indian manifestations was one of the ways in which "Indian" as a distinct identity was defined in the nineteenth century. This identity was allegedly maintained in the afterlife. Eminent Spiritualist writer Hudson Tuttle claimed that "death effects no alteration in the form, or organization of the mind, but leaves the spirit the same individual, with exactly similar thoughts and ideas."[63] This included racial difference. While the stereotype of Indians as "noble" was relatively positive, and although Indian spirits who traveled through the spirit world became educated, enlightened, and peaceful, they still belonged to a separate racial category. Such characteristic consistencies are also present in Cox's research, leading him to write that, even in death, "Red Jacket remained the orator, Samoset the leader, and Pocahontas the altruist and intermediary."[64]

Perhaps this is true for how Indian spirits appeared in séances, and the means by which Spiritualists recognized scores of ghosts as Indians. Yet the "prejudices" of spirit chiefs were not everlasting, and they *did* undergo, to a large extent, spiritual change. Partly as a result of those changes, Cox claims, Spiritualists came to believe in an afterlife devoid of distinctions and categorizations based on differing religious or political affiliations.[65] Adding the element of race to this statement can perhaps lend some insight to the contradictory nature of Spiritualists' expressed attitudes about Indians. The racial stereotypes established in popular culture that were articulated in séances were necessary for Spiritualists' initial recognition of Indian spirits. Yet the ultimate message conveyed by such apparitions, and acted upon by Spiritualists, suggested an erasure of those distinctions based on the rhetoric of "civilization" and scientific racism. They instead move toward a definition of Indianness that did not require the presence of superficial and performative signs of Indian identity. According to Cox, "Spiritualist Eugene Crowell claimed that both 'Indians and Negroes, as they progress, constantly assimilate in appearance and character to the white race,' becoming 'blended with the whites' in the highest spheres."[66] Such a belief would explain Spiritualists' advocacy of educational programs that were, in reality, culturally devastating to Indian peoples, despite their insistence on the most conciliatory and peaceful-minded solution to the Indian Question. Such ambiguous racial attitudes on the part of Spiritualists will be returned to in chapter 5.

The primary undertaking of Indian manifestations was to aid in the spiritual progress of themselves as well as mortals. One of the major methods of development for the spirits themselves was to transcend hatred against white men for the injustices these ghosts endured during their lifetimes. Cox also acknowledges the impulse for reconciliation among Indian spirits.[67] During the late 1860s and early 1870s, several ghosts spoke of shedding this earthly, primitive emotion in favor of the higher aspiration of love. The expression of such ghostly sentiments runs contrary to McGarry's conclusion that Indian specters shifted from vanished figures in the 1850s to militant ones in the 1860s and beyond.[68]

Spirit chiefs defied categorization as "vanished" through their constant and uncanny returns, all while advocating peace, not war. As Cox claims, "Indian leaders like Black Hawk, Powhatan, Thunder, Logan, and Little Crow were erased as figures of resistance, only to reappear as the ultimates of forgiveness."[69] In 1863, for example, the spirit of Powhatan spoke through Dr. E. C. Dunn in Rockland, Illinois, claiming that "the tomahawk is ever buried with the warrior."[70] The following message from White Eagle was communicated in 1867 through Dr. John Field and published in the *Banner of Light*. It described the shift of sentiment toward whites that occurred as part of his spiritual transition:

> Wise and good man, the Great Spirit hath said it—that the Indian must be the white man's friend, for the white man is in many things a squaw. The white man has smoked his pipe with his friend, and poisoned the smoke with a lie. Then the red man sharpened his arrows for war, but the Great Spirit spoke, and said that the Indian must love; but the Indian saw no love in his heart toward the white man until his new hunting-grounds were found in the spirit-land. Thus the Great Spirit called the warriors and chieftains together, and taught them how to love.[71]

Although in many instances white women were praised by ghosts for their spiritual work, in this passage being a "squaw" was used as a derogatory term to indicate that white men's actions toward Indians to this point had been less than manly, less than honorable. Such spirits affirmed their own manliness while simultaneously questioning that of whites. The message also provided the reason for Indian hatred of whites—their untrustworthiness and inconsistency in dealing with Indians. But the main thrust of this message was that peace was the will of the Great Spirit, and only in death did Indians heed the will of the Great Spirit in earnest.

The death of Indians, in this context, was described as a positive transition, and one that was necessary for the improvement of the Indian character. An 1869 spirit message from Moke-to-va-tah explicitly acknowledged that Indians were better off dead, because of their improved spiritual state: "Moke-to-va-tah brings back no hate. The white chief of many warriors came upon him, kill his women and his children, yet he brings back no hate. The Great Spirit hath prepared for him a better hunting-ground than here. It is well he went."[72] This message forgave whites not for their deceitfulness, but for the murder of Indian women and children, who were categorically perceived by all involved as the helpless victims of warfare against Indian tribes. Another spirit message in 1873 claimed that Indians were contented to be dead rather than alive. The message read:

> Me be Ounondita, son of Barbanseta, chief of the Navahoes ... Ounondita lives in the land of the spirits, where the Great Father's blessing is broader than here, where his sunshine is clearer, where the red man has more hunting-ground than here. The white man did well for Ounondita when he sent him there; Ounondita did well for him when he sent him there, too.[73]

Indian spirits may have decried the many injustices inflicted upon them, but spiritual progression required a transcendence of that anger. White guilt was not alleviated by such a message; rather, the purpose of the haunting was to force recognition of the ghost. The dead, and the injustice their return represented, had to be heeded by whites in order for mortals to move forward. Spiritual enlightenment thus required the haunting to be dissipated, by bringing the forgotten Indians back into the foreground.

The hatred of these Indian spirits was not entirely forgotten, but was acknowledged and regretted. Only through the transition of death, these spirits explained, could this character flaw be rectified. An 1874 article discussed the intention of Indian spirits in relation to current affairs; the spirit of Little Crow was described as "awaking to consciousness after his physical decease, his spirit at once became cognizant of the bitter fruits which his kindred were eating from the trees which his deeds had planted on earth, and he felt an earnest desire to undo, to some degree at least, the wrong he had accomplished."[74] The desire for vengeance did not disappear completely among Indian spirits. Spiritual elevation came only through the willful act of forgiveness and the offering of peace. In 1870 a message from White Antelope claimed:

> There be strong chiefs in the hunting-grounds, in what me call the dark hunting-grounds; they be powerful, they no be glad because of what the spirits say here, so they be trying to send out a force to this place, to put a damper on. And Red Jacket say to the Indian band, "Gather round and rout 'em"; and we have, and they be fled, they be in a bad way. They no want light to get to the squaws and braves, they want 'em to be in darkness, so we come, to-day, a great band of Indian spirits, to bring force and strength from the spirit-world. Red Jacket sends us; he says no bad spirits will come.[75]

White Antelope made a distinction between Indian spirits living in an enlightened versus a "dark" hunting-ground, claiming those from the dark hunting-ground were "bad spirits" who continued to wish whites harm. White Antelope, Red Jacket, and other enlightened chiefs were, however, able to drive the dark spirits away from the "talking sheet" (presumably the *Banner of Light*) because of their superior spiritual status—they were members of a "great band" dedicated to spreading goodwill among the mortals who would listen to them.

The forgiveness of Indian spirits was not absolute, but was targeted specifically to those whites who heeded messages from the spirits. Their forgiveness was earned through white recognition of the reason for their appearance. In their enlightened state, spirits gained the ability to distinguish between helpful whites, deserving of Indian assistance, and those whose actions were set in opposition to the Great Spirit's will. "White Antelope comes," he said in a message published in July of 1867 in the *Banner of Light*:

> And his heart, like the heart of Little Crow, is hot. There is vengeance in his soul, planted there by the Great Spirit … white man, you put

in your talking sheet, and White Antelope will be your *friend*, not your *enemy*. He has learned in the hunting-ground of the Great Spirit who are his friends; and he follows his friends with kind deeds, and his enemies with vengeance.[76]

White Antelope named "the warrior Chivington," the American colonel responsible for the 1864 slaughter near Sand Creek of about one hundred Cheyenne and Arapaho by the Colorado militia, about seven hundred strong, as his enemy.[77] His friends were those who would publish and disseminate his message. In 1873, a message from Moketavata responded to the white man's desire "to know if Moketavata has any hatred in his heart, in the upper hunting-ground, against the white man. No, no; Moketavata has no hatred for him, but he scorns him and despises him because he is a coward."[78]

Although publications local to Sand Creek initially praised the American military for its bravery and martial superiority, information about the horrors of the Sand Creek Massacre later came to the foreground of Northeastern periodicals on Indian affairs. According to Coward, many soldiers testified that women and children comprised half of the casualties at Sand Creek.[79] Coward states that the Sand Creek Massacre did not gain much national attention in print, instead being overshadowed by stories of Indian violence against Western settlers.[80] However, news coverage of the investigations into the Sand Creek Massacre were featured prominently in the *Banner of Light*. This and related stories remained a primary focus of the news section of the periodical for the majority of its run. According to Coward, "the Sand Creek Massacre inspired little editorial outrage," even among eastern papers.[81] The *Banner of Light* did, however, repeatedly refer to the incidents at Sand Creek to incite moral indignation among its readers. The massacre was used as a prime example of the government's and army's complete lack of manly restraint in dealing with Indian peoples. Coward writes that in 1864, "news reports—unofficial and outside the established news-gathering process in the West—soon surfaced, contradicting the original press accounts … 'now reported was an atrocious massacre of unarmed men, women and children.' "[82] The investigating commission was led by Samuel F. Tappan, connected to Spiritualism via his marriage to Cora Hatch. The violence against Indian families was consistently portrayed by Spiritualists in print as the antithesis of the nation's claim to sexual, racial, and moral superiority. According to Prucha, the Sand Creek Massacre became a prominent example of American mistreatment of Indians that Indian reformers would not allow the public to forget.[83] The continual discussion of these events by Indian spirits amplified the event's infamy even further.

Through their forgiveness of such offenses, spirit chiefs progressed through the celestial spheres. Death allowed Indian spirits to right the wrongs of their lives by lending aid to whites, telling them of the Great Spirit's will and trying to achieve peace on earth. In the context of relations between the races, the spirits of Indian chiefs thus achieved an elevated status—that of educators and guides. Cox asserts that "in the highest circles, according to Horatio Wood, 'almost perfect harmony exists ... There is a mingling of thought and sympathy ... a sort of mutual affinity and desire to assist each other in progressive advancement.' "[84] In Wood's estimation, sentiments of peace that flowed from spirit chiefs originated in the higher spheres. Indian ghosts then, were advanced beyond the character of the lower spheres, wherein the residue of revenge remained. From this position, chiefs claimed a moral and spiritual superiority; they had overcome their hatred of whites, but the opposite had yet to happen. Bridget Bennett claims that "crediting Indians with having particular access to spiritual truths ... had long been part of the way in which they were culturally constructed."[85] Cox discusses Spiritualists' acknowledgment of the spiritual superiority of Indian ghosts, quoting Spiritualists Eugene Crowell and Charles Hammond:

> [T]he cultural inferiority of Indians, Crowell cautioned, did not signify spiritual inferiority ... One of the first mediums to invoke spirit Indians, Charles Hammond, proclaimed that the "untutored inhabitant of the forest" occupied "a higher position, and a purer circle" than the "murderers, liars, thieves, robbers, misers, winebibbers, gluttons, and many others" who proliferated on earth ... for all their rude, uncultivated habits, Indians were thus held up as spiritually superior to whites.[86]

Racial reconciliation was required in the higher spheres, and spirit chiefs made it their mission to spread this new peace toward white mortals still residing in the lowest, mortal sphere.

On the other hand, praise of Indians in their spirit state could indicate that these messages justified the concept of Indian "vanishing" and helped to assuage white guilt over the vast numbers of Indian dead due to American maltreatment. Whites also benefited from chiefs in their spirit state, as they learned about the spiritual realm and how to bring about their own illumination. At the same time, that spiritual growth was only achievable through a peaceful demeanor on the part of whites and Indians. Cox, like McGarry, argues that Spiritualist beliefs confirmed and celebrated the figure of the vanishing Indian by acknowledging the benefits of Indian death for all parties.[87] Though Indian ghosts admitted to being better off as spirits, they were nevertheless determined to rectify the wrongs of their own lives by bringing Indians and Americans together. Spiritualists likewise became actively involved in carrying out a spiritual mission of peace. Indian ghosts were not relegated solely to the past. Their persistent and frequent apparitions rendered them simultaneously past and present, refusing to be repressed through superficial acknowledgment. An active encounter with Indian specters was necessary to resolve their supernatural disturbance of the present, through Spiritualists' political advocacy on behalf of living Indians. In the same way that Indian specters claimed to forgive white misdeeds as central to their spiritual progress, whites also needed to correct the racial injustices of the past and present. As a consequence of this creed, Spiritualists actively sought to enforce established treaties that the United States currently violated, and to reform ongoing federal policies affecting Indian peoples. This point will be returned to in the final chapter.

In conjunction with this effort, many spirit messages were directed toward living Indians, encouraging them to seek peaceful resolutions to political tensions with America. Indian ghosts discouraged violent resistance to white encroachment. The process of peacemaking and imitating the racial equality of the spiritual spheres required the participation of both whites and Indians. Two Indians in particular were the targets of these messages: Red Cloud and Big Eagle. Both were Sioux chieftains, and both forcefully resisted Indian removal, engaging in warfare with the United States in the 1860s and 1870s. Especially for Red Cloud, whom Coward describes as the "most famous and feared chief of the early 1870s,"[88] the presence of these chiefs in American print was ongoing. According to Jeffrey Ostler, nineteenth-century Americans saw Red Cloud as a preeminent leader of Indian resistance.[89] His movements and encounters with American armies and government officials were reported in newspapers across the country, as well as in Spiritualist publications such as the *Banner of Light*. Such periodicals reprinted stories of Sioux leaders protesting the invasion of the Black Hills and fraudulent practices of federal agents. Spiritualist journalists used such news as a springboard for their political views. For example, an article in an 1875 issue of the *Banner of Light* echoed the sentiment of the *New York Times* to demonstrate the breadth of changing sympathies toward Indians:

> In reference to the whole of this Indian business the *New York Times*, in the course of an article, remarks that "there can be no doubt that the Indians have been the objects of quite as much ill-treatment as the negroes ever were, and, if such sins are inevitably followed by retribution, as many events in the history of the world seem to prove, why should we escape more than others"[90]

The article, and the *Banner of Light's* reprinting of it, questioned the conviction in what has been termed American exceptionalism, claiming instead that "justice is eternal and holds her scales evenly always."[91]

With a single exception, spirit messages to living chieftains were delivered by the spirit of Little Crow, through the medium Mrs. J. H. Conant in the *Banner of Light*. One message to Red Cloud came purportedly from Pogonakasheek in 1873. He also spoke through Mrs. Conant, but the eloquence of this Indian, relative to Little Crow, was lacking. "Me Indian," he said, "Me come to send talk to Red Cloud. Me want Red Cloud, when he goes to the Great Father at Washington [presumably, President Ulysses Grant] to keep his thoughts cool, so his words will come right."[92]

Little Crow, who had died in 1863, was the former chief of the same band of Dakota Sioux later led by Big Eagle. It was toward him specifically that Little Crow's messages were directed. The earliest of these messages appeared in 1864. Little Crow's spirit requested that his correspondence be delivered to Big Eagle personally; at the time, he was being held as a U.S. prisoner in Davenport, Iowa. Little Crow said to Big Eagle:

> The Great Father (the President [sic]) will send white men to talk to you, to ask you if you will speak peace to my people. Tell the Great Father you will talk peace to my people. Big Eagle, put up your knife, wet your powder, that he need have no fear of you … When the winds whisper to you, Little Crow will whisper too, and tell you how to live in peace with the white men. Little Crow comes talking to you from across the River of Death. Hear him, for the Great Spirit will smile on you if you do, and will frown on you if you do not.[93]

The spirit of Little Crow was aware, it seems, of the current political atmosphere, and warned Big Eagle against displeasing the Great Spirit through warfare. His own position on such affairs when alive was reversed. Here, both Indians and whites are subject to spiritual judgment and retribution.

A decade later, the spirit of Little Crow again reached out to Big Eagle, to convince him that peace was the only acceptable solution to current pressures. Red Cloud was the topic of discussion. Little Crow's advice to Big Eagle was the following: "When Red Cloud come [sic] to your lodge, counsel him to peace. He is a great chief; his people cannot afford to lose him; they will, if he goes to war … As you believe in the Great Spirit and his red children in the upper-hunting ground, counsel him to peace."[94] Little Crow's spirit, only recently deceased, and his conversation with Big Eagle, a living chief, was not consigned to the distant past, as McGarry suggests, but was deeply invested in the present. Using an 1853 appearance of Powhatan's spirit, recorded in the *Spiritual Telegraph*,[95] as her primary example, McGarry claims that the figure of the noble Indian and his passing was "distanced from the antebellum present,"[96] and that a central component of Indian manifestations was "Spiritualists' calling of bygone tribes to the séance tables of the present."[97] Ghosts such as Little Crow, however, functioned as simultaneously near-past and present among Anglo-American Spiritualists.

The peace that Little Crow's spirit advocated, in the context of nineteenth-century expansionist policies, would have meant peace on white terms. Since 1819, Congress had financed education programs established with the express purpose of "civilizing" Indians.[98] The curriculum of such programs included learning the English language, the Christian Bible, and Euro-American customs and culture. Most importantly, Indian pupils were taught individualism, rather than identification as members of a tribe. In essence, such schools attempted to form a new identity for Indians in the absence of traits traditionally accepted as Indian. As Robert Berkhofer claims, Americans saw tribal Indians as lacking industry, independence, and a drive for material success—all necessary traits for proper American citizens.[99] Speaking in terms of identity, the ultimate goal of schools like the Pratt and Hampton Institutes was to erase Indianness completely. Berkhofer writes that " 'civilized' Indians disappear as Indians."[100] Such a process may have been sought by Spiritualists as a resolution to the haunting of Indian ghosts. Living Indians would virtually disappear as distinctively Indian, and the strides made by them would eliminate the need for the Indian dead to return to earth.

Although many Spiritualists professed their adherence to the vision of cultural assimilation, they may not have perceived Christianity as a necessary component of Indian progress. This is evidenced by their praise of native religions. Perhaps as a result of their own ambiguous relationship with institutional religion, and their newfound respect for (a largely imagined) Indian spirituality through ghostly encounters, Spiritualists were more willing to tolerate native religions than other whites. These views on religion and spirituality may have constituted the difference between Spiritualist activists and other benevolent-minded reformers. Despite what native scholar and activist Ward Churchill rightly calls their genocidal impact, the Indian residential schools were the best attempt made by whites to improve living conditions for Indian peoples. These issues will be returned to in chapter 5.[101]

Although spirits such as Little Crow also argued for peace on the part of whites and better treatment of Indian peoples, his spirit advocated education. It was also one of the primary policies promoted by Spiritualists as a peaceful answer to the "Indian Question." Little Crow's spirit said that if Red Cloud went to war against the United States, he would die, predicting, in a broad sense, the failure of Red Cloud's attempts to resist white expansion through force. He further suggested that this would be an unacceptable state of affairs, especially for those Indians whose interests and general welfare Red Cloud was attempting to protect. The message did not express an excited anticipation of the arrival of Red Cloud to the upper hunting-ground. It instead set up a different approach to the discourse of vanishing Indians and its relation to the proliferation of Indian spirits. While Indian death had been portrayed as beneficial for both races, the complete removal of Indians from the Earth was not desirable, and was not justifiable even in light of spiritual progression. Spiritualists happily reported Red Cloud's willingness to negotiate peace with the United States. A *Banner of Light* article in 1870 recorded that "even Red Cloud, whose war-record we published recently, now that Sheridan has been withdrawn, sends a messenger to General F.F. Flint, commanding at Fort Laramie, with information that they would all be at the fort by the middle of September, after first meeting the principal chiefs, to make arrangements to go on the reservations. So far so good."[102] The hope of this peace was twofold: that Indians would cease to fight, and that Americans would cease to provoke them. Spiritualists did not, then, consistently "project these spirits into an afterworld that both rationalized and validated Indians' passing from this world,"[103] as McGarry claims. Not all Spiritualists accepted Indian vanishing as inevitable or as fate.

Spiritualists' newfound knowledge of the Great Spirit's will allowed them to project onto Indian spirits a sense of moral superiority, thus creating a position for themselves from which to criticize the hypocrisy of America's claims of being a Christian and civilized nation. Spiritualists who perceived parallels between Native American religious practices and their own did not always actively distance themselves from such connections by reinforcing ideas of Indian primitivism.[104] In many instances, the praising of Indian spirituality was utilized as an effective critique of Anglo-American and Christian hypocrisy. For example, in 1863, the spirit of Tecumseh appeared in Ohio through the medium William Bilmie. Tecumseh's message was primarily a call for equal rights for Indians. His argument rested on the position of Indians in the spirit world:

> On the earth I fought for what I called my home and my rights. In this better land I do not have to fight. The Great Spirit here gives us equal rights with pale faces. Here we live in harmony; here we are not driven about by a race calling themselves *civilized*. When I look at your churches and think of your conduct, and your notions about religion, I say, what *barbarism*! … In presence of the Great Spirit, the Indian stands on equal footing with the white man."[105]

Tecumseh argued that though on earth the red man's religion seemed primitive to white Christians, he now found "there was more truth in the little I believed, than they will find in a great deal that pale faces say they believe."[106]

A similar praise of Indian religions was echoed by the spirit of Onalaski, whose 1864 message claimed that Indians knew of the Great Spirit in life by his presence in nature—in the water, the forests, the winds.[107] Messages such as these claimed a closer connection to divinity through Indians' proximity to nature. White association of Indians with nature has been well studied by many scholars. The general consensus among historians of this topic is that the figure of the natural Indian, distanced from corrupt institutions and organized religion, was used as a powerful critique of Western culture and religion.[108] Spiritualists fell largely into this category, convinced that the new status of Indians was a demonstration of their moral superiority in the cosmic hierarchy. By asserting intimate knowledge of the Great Spirit in life and death, Indian spirits undermined the religious and racial superiority imposed by white Christians. From this position, they criticized the application of so-called Christian principles to the treatment of living Indians. Indian spirits did not claim to be racially superior, but instead worked to correct white men's thinking so they might acknowledge Indians' equal worth. The ultimate goal of Indian spirits was to make whites realize, as the spirit of White Eagle said in 1867, that whites and Indians were "brothers in *truth*."[109] Spiritualists' own aversion to organized religion made Indian religions seem all the more attractive and closer to the truth for their perceived similarities to Spiritualism. Spiritualist attitudes toward native religions as a result of their experiences will be discussed further in chapter 5.

In 1868, the spirit of Red Jacket explained that the mission of Indian spirits was to forge new and friendly relations with whites. He appeared through the medium Dr. Henry T. Child, and his message was published in the *Religio-Philosophical Journal*. In this message, Red Jacket's ghost continually addressed himself to his "Brother," the paleface:

> Brother, I come no more with vengeance or hate in my heart. I have buried the tomahawk long ago. My scalping knife is forever laid aside. And I come now to tell you that the Red Man *still* has a mission, even as he roams the hunting ground of the spirit land … I come to you and I call you brother—and the chain of friendship is bright between us … in all manifestations from this life, to the children of the earth, the Red Man labors, and in a most especial manner, in bringing health and strength to the pale face, and to all the children of the Great Spirit, wherever they may be, or of whatever name or nation.[110]

Red Jacket's message explicitly acknowledged that Indian spirits had a sacred obligation to assist whites. They were required to educate in the universal love of the spirit world and forge a new peace.

The state of equality in the higher spheres of the spirit world was placed in sharp contrast with the injustice between races on earth. McGarry argued that the cosmic spheres perpetuated the differentiation of peoples found on earth.[111] While the spirit world definitively operated as a hierarchy, the equality of those spheres and the fluidity with which Indian ghosts traveled through them was a prominent component of spirit communications. How the place of Indian ghosts in this hierarchy was negotiated will be revisited in more detail in chapter 5.

Ghostly Warnings

Native spirits criticized American society by pointing out the contradiction between whites' religious claims and their political actions. The most common indictments against whites were the many instances of deceitfulness and murder. The responsibility for Indian warfare was oftentimes placed squarely on white shoulders. The spirit of Moke-ta-va-ta, for example, claimed in a message in 1874 that "the battle did not come because the Indian had not kept faith with the white man, but because the white man had broken his with the Indian, and had stolen upon him like a wolf in the night, and had assassinated, as my white father says, twenty of my braves and forty of my women and children."[112] The deaths of women and children, counted here as twice as numerous as the death of warriors, were repeatedly emphasized in the outcry against warfare. Bederman writes that in the discourse of "civilization," savages were defined as men who preyed upon women, rather than protected them.[113] Not only did Indian spirits assert that warfare between whites and Indians was initiated by whites, but they claimed it was conducted in a manner dishonorable by both race's standards. Nineteenth-century white claims to manhood, as linked to conquest, were undermined by spirit messages acknowledging Indian women as victims of warfare.[114] In these and similar messages, the guilt of white society was not alleviated by ghosts; they acted as traditional hauntings that instead brought past wrongdoings into the present. Their presence was used as a way of alerting whites that their actions displeased the Great Spirit, and only steps taken to rectify this situation could prevent an unfavorable spiritual judgment.

Warnings of spiritual retribution were a frequent component of Indian spirit messages, appearing prominently in the 1860s and the 1870s, continuing to a lesser degree in the 1880s. The primary message of such warnings was that whites would be punished for their wrongful treatment of Indians, suffering more than those whom they had wronged. In 1860, for example, a spirit message by "The Indian" explained that the Great Spirit "frowns upon" white wars with the red man, and that "the same spirit of evil that came upon the red man shall come forth upon the white man with greater power."[115] An 1862 message from Philip of Narragansett urged people to heed the purpose of his presence. Philip came, he said, "to warn you, white man, of the danger that surrounds you, and to counsel you to fall down before the Great Spirit, asking forgiveness for the sins you have committed."[116] Indian spirits like Philip did not expect whites to undergo the same slow process of illumination that Indian ghosts experienced upon their deaths. Parts of their spiritual progress could be accomplished while alive. It was the responsibility of Indian spirits to guide whites toward this enlightenment during their lifetimes. According to Bederman, ultimate progress was defined as a "millennial vision of perfected racial evolution and gender specialization," an achievement of perfect "manliness and womanliness."[117]

How Spiritualists defined perfected gender and racial evolution was largely determined through Indian spirit communication. Such frequent ghostly messages conveyed distinct ideas about the virtues of ideal manhood and womanhood, emphasizing reform in racial relations as most important. Bederman states that "manly" was officially defined in 1890 as having moral dimensions. Spiritualists argued that morality, outwardly expressed as male honor, was absent from white/Indian relations.[118] As a result of Indian apparitions, the duty to strive for perfection became linked in the minds of Spiritualists to peaceful relations with living Indians. Spiritualists saw heeding spirit messages as all-important. Discussing early-nineteenth-century definitions of manhood and the national character, Bederman writes that early-nineteenth-century definitions of manhood required racial competition and the ability of civilization to triumph over savagery.[119] By the 1840s, Greenberg argues, the American race had achieved a martial superiority, backed by scientific racism.[120] As Haller wrote, "The physical scientist's evidence of morphological evolution and teleological implications of the century's belief in progress merged into the ethnologists's supra-organic schema of development ... a value judgment projected into a scientific process."[121] For men such as John Wesley Powell and Lewis Henry Morgan, who failed to recognize agriculture among Indian societies, Indians were doomed to die at the base of human civilization, with "no hope of elevation."[122] White manhood, in this context, was defined in relation to Indians. Spiritualists continued to see definitions of gender as linked to race. Their image of heaven was completely structured, yet not by race or gender. Men and women of all colors occupied all spheres to some degree.[123]

As a result of their experiences at midcentury séance tables, Spiritualists observed Indian chiefs progressing away from a manhood defined by the body toward one linked to a sympathetic mind over the course of their manifestations. They expected white manhood to evolve along the same path to include higher moral aspirations. As Coward notes, the figure of the Noble Savage has long been celebrated by Americans as an alternative social model.[124]

Berkhofer likewise points out that such a model was liberal in tone; the morality of noble savages was not constrained by decadent and corrupt institutions.[125] The contest between these two conflicting definitions of manhood, both intimately connected to race, raged in the nineteenth century, and bore national consequences. Spirit chiefs' nobility, emphasized through their conversations, rather than their bodies, evinced a tendency toward a manhood dependent upon upholding moral codes and operating as a powerful tool for self-reflection and critique. Thus, earlier séances that detailed manifestations with exactitude were instrumental in cementing Spiritualist practice and theology. But later séances that contained ghostly messages more readily reveal the social philosophy expounded by Spiritualists.

The importance of acknowledging spirit chiefs' depictions of heaven as a racial utopia took on national significance. If the knowledge Indian spirits imparted was not heeded, the nation's spiritual prosperity was put at risk. As Greenberg states, Americans celebrated their lack of imperialism while simultaneously engaging in colonialism.[126] Spiritualists sought to undermine this pride, turning it on its head as a source of national shame, by placing colonialism in opposition to the Great Spirit's will. Philip's spirit said, "Ay, the Constitution of your United States expires before your eyes … for the Great Spirit has written its death seal … Oh white man, send your prayers to the Great Father of Spirit, that your fair land may not be clothed in darkness and desolation."[127] The conquest of Indian nations, as Bederman notes, was central to the national identity; it was for this reason that the evolving Spiritualist attitudes about race and gender were discussed in terms of their cosmic national consequences.[128] In such apocalyptic tones, Indian ghosts such as Philip offered a premonition of destruction through divine wrath, and an opportunity to alter that fate. This message fulfilled the expected role of ghosts; just like Jacob Marley in *A Christmas Carol*, Philip's specter revealed a bleak yet malleable future.

On several occasions, spirit chiefs targeted specific Americans in their warnings. In the late 1860s and early 1870s, the actions of Colonel John Chivington were mentioned in particular by multiple Indian spirits as an example of white wrongdoing. He was a former Methodist minister,[129] and the leading officer of the Sand Creek Massacre. His actions served as a demonstration of white hatred for Indians, and a model to avoid. White Antelope was one of several Cheyenne leaders who perished in the surprise attack at Sand Creek in 1864; Chivington led the assault against a group of unarmed Indian men, women, and children, resulting in the deaths of about 150 Indians.[130]

The spirit of White Antelope decried Chivington in an 1867 message as a "great murderer" and a "liar."[131] White Antelope asked that his Spiritualist friends convey his message to Chivington, that "when his murdered squaws and braves rise before him, White Antelope will come, but with no canoe to bear him to the upper hunting-ground, and with no blanket to shield his most cowardly soul."[132] White Antelope described the role that Indian spirits served in aiding whites to the spheres of spiritual enlightenment; this aid came as a result of the new bonds formed between Indian spirits and living Spiritualists. A man such as Chivington, whose voice White Antelope said "the Great Spirit is deaf to [will] walk the earth in shadows and thorns will spring up and pierce his feet."[133] He was not to be aided by Indian spirits; his ghost was doomed to wander the earth in darkness for disregarding the message of peace that Indian apparitions took great pains to communicate to the living. Chivington's victims, White Antelope stated, would instead achieve a higher spiritual status.[134]

In July 1867, White Antelope conveyed another message against Chivington, this time calling him a "squaw" because "he goes out to murder squaws and papooses; and when the braves meet him in an open fight, he goes like a coward."[135] General William Sherman was also described as a coward who murdered Indian women and children. In 1867, the spirit of Little Crow produced a message through Mrs. Conant that claimed Sherman "can go to war against squaws and papooses, but he has no courage when he's on the warpath."[136] The masculinity and honor of Sherman and Chivington, prominent officers of the United States Army, were called into question by Little Crow's spirit, who claimed that more women and children were victimized by white men than warriors were killed in fair combat. Bederman writes of manly honor as being earned in the late nineteenth century through self-restraint and benevolence toward those deemed unable to protect themselves—namely, women and children.[137] The role of males as protectors was expanded by Indian spirits and their audiences to include Indian men and women. Indian men as well as women required protection because they had been effeminized in American culture. Their perceived inability to successfully protect and provide for their own families portrayed Indian men as less manly than their white counterparts. Nineteenth-century codes of manhood also required industry and self-reliance. These were deemed essential traits of U.S. citizens. Yet Indian men were believed to be lacking these traits since the colonial period.[138] They had not earned the right to justly be called "men" in the eyes of American society. Therefore, Indian men were placed in the same dependent category as women, as wards of the federal government, as even their *humanity* was examined in scientific debates about the origins of Indian peoples. Berkhofer states that the majority of nineteenth-century Americans questioned Indian membership in the human family due to their absence from the Bible and their perceived primitiveness when contrasted with Western culture.[139] The definition of manliness and manly honor as exercised through benevolent protection suggested that its opposite, such as greed and predation upon Indian families, could be defined as unmanly. To fail as a protector was a sign of moral weakness. Such arguments were embedded in spirit communications. They served to undermine American claims that the nation was built on principles of manliness and honor. In comparison to the "unmanly" acts of white traders and agents such as Chivington and Sherman, forgiving spirit chiefs appeared as increasingly moral, and increasingly manly.

The redirection of warfare toward women and children was a primary criticism of war with Indians. The violence demonstrated by a superior white force was misdirected, affecting the sympathetic families of resistant chiefs and warriors. This in turn tainted the manhood and bravery of the individuals involved. Spiritualists expressed outrage and regret over this public display of moral hypocrisy and national dishonor. Bederman states that early in the nineteenth century, Americans had prided themselves on their "violent masculinity—their ability to outsavage the savages," and argues that this imperative superseded concerns of morality.[140] Little Crow's spirit challenged that meaning of manhood, as exemplified by Chivington, declaring a new cosmic imperative of peace and racial equality. The benefits that open communication with Indian spirits provided were in Chivington's case revoked, because "he [had] given the red man great cause to hate him."[141] The rejection of Chivington's approach by American society was urged by the spirits of White Antelope and others, so that the hope for a racially and spiritually enlightened future might be fully extended and brought to fruition.

White Antelope spoke of a prolonged spiritual punishment for Chivington and said that treatment of the Indians would be an integral component of spiritual judgment. In two messages in 1872, he referred to Chivington as "the White Warrior with the Black Heart,"[142] and he told Chivington to "turn to the book of your own life, and see if your heart is all right toward the Indian; see if there is nothing of greed, of craft and wickedness left there. If there is not, then appeal to the Great Spirit for mercy, and He will answer."[143] Only by changing attitudes away from war and toward peace could whites receive the Great Spirit's love and mercy. Reforming the treatment of living

Indians was thus declared as necessary for the spiritual development of whites. Only then might the United States accurately claim to be a morally progressed nation. The reform urged by Indian spirits had to happen on a personal level to achieve individual illumination, but the future of the nation as a whole was also at stake. Warfare with Indians was portrayed by spirits as the ultimate source of national shame, rather than pride. To wash away that shame, the manifestations of Indian spirits had to be confronted, their warnings respected, and their commands put into action. By framing acknowledgment of Indian ghosts as necessary to progress, the guilt inherent in those manifestations refused to remain repressed.

During the 1880s, Indian spirits produced messages that confirmed their spiritual work. Braude argues that by the 1870s public mediumship was often a source of embarrassment rather than empowerment for female mediums. Yet regarding the continuing presence of spirit chiefs throughout this and the following decade, mediums gained renewed strength.[144] The messages during these years acted as encouragement to mediums and their Spiritualist audiences, lending them the strength to carry on the reformatory mission set forth in Indian manifestations. They encouraged and supported white activism on behalf of living Indians by empowering their frail, white, female mediums on the one hand, and suggesting alternatives to warfare on the other. Shelhamer wrote in 1908 of her first meeting with Conant, explaining the essential quality that the presence of Indian spirits provided:

> Mrs. Conant affirmed that our vitality and health had been impaired almost to the verge of chronic invalidism by the well-meaning but unscientific spirits who had so constantly use our organism as to drain us of magnetic life without understanding the strain upon nerves and brain, without reinforcing with life-giving vitality from the other side. She declared that a change at once must be made ... that for a time the larger power would be manifested by Indian spirits, whose magnetic forces were necessary, not only for the building up in the medium a new supply of vitality and of general health, but which would in part be always needed by her in the successful pursuing of her labors in the spiritual cause.[145]

As early as 1863, a spirit council including King Philip, Tecumseh, Billy Bowlegs, and Osceola wrote a message to Indian activist John Beeson, calling for a form of reservation system for Indian peoples. The council claimed that "we in spirit life wish *four* Grand Reserves to be specially set apart, having for their purpose the advancement and protection of our nation."[146] Though these spirit chiefs originated from the Wampanoag, Shawnee, and Seminole, they referred to Indian peoples as united under one nation—the Indian nation. They saw protecting the welfare of all Indian peoples as their responsibility, resulting in a spiritual pan-Indianism uncommon among living Indians. They ended their description of the four reserves with a premonition of a unified Indian nation, if their reservation system was made a reality:

> You will find these Four Grand Reserves to be the means of restoring harmony among the various tribes; and we tell you we expect to see these Four Grand Reserves consolidated into one Grand General Reserve, and our people having but one language, and one religion, living in harmony and union. We wish our race to become a powerful and united nation. For in union there is strength.[147]

In a message from July 1882, the spirit of Red Wing explicitly addressed "the question, What shall we do with the Indian? Which has been propounded by the American nation."[148] The answer to this question was found in the education of Indians. Henry Knox, the first Secretary of War, argued that the act of civilizing Indians through education was "difficult but not impossible." According to Beaver, Knox asserted that the cost of education programs would pale in comparison to any policy based in force.[149] In 1819, the "Civilization Fund" was created. It allotted $10,000 a year to provide basic instruction and agricultural methods to Indians. The fund was repealed in 1873.[150] As David Adams notes in *Education for Extinction*, by 1880 there was a general consensus among Americans that a campaign to exterminate Indian nations was neither a sustainable nor a desirable solution.[151] The educational approach to racial tensions, by which Indians were taught how to live as modern Americans, was advocated by Red Wing's spirit. "Take these children of Nature," he said, "surround them with good influences, place them in schools of learning as you place your white papooses; give them an education."[152] Red Wing's message depicted living Indians as innocent, childlike, and easily taught. Proponents of Indian education described putative students as blank slates, eagerly awaiting the means to their own intellectual elevation.[153] Americans debated the efficacy of a civilization project, questioning the ability of Indians to learn and adopt civilization. Steven Conn, writing on the intellectual history of studying and understanding Indians, describes this as a central debate about the future of individual Indians. The disappearance of Indian ways of life, however, was still accepted by many Americans as fact.[154]

Spiritualists positioned themselves largely in favor of Indian education. Contact with the spirit world had shown them the centrality of education and self-improvement to spiritual life, as pointed out by Cox.[155] They had witnessed the strides made by Indian spirits, and were convinced that living Indians would prove to be the equals of their spiritual counterparts in intellectual ability. Conant's biographer John Day declared, for example, that Conant's interaction with Indian spirits "proved the utter fallacy—to her mind—of the idea that civilization and education are impossible of attainment by the Indian."[156] Spiritualists challenged the destined aspect of Indian "vanishing" that created the safe distance by which many Americans nostalgically mourned Indian cultures. Their experiences at the séance tables bred an acknowledgment of national responsibility. When the call for Indian education was echoed by the celestial voices of their spirit guides, the impetus for reform became divinely sanctioned. Just as Indian spirits demonstrated their ability to improve themselves in the afterlife, so too did Spiritualists believe that living Indians were able to improve their lives, by developing their minds and becoming economically productive. Red Wing said that the Indians were ready and willing to learn how to live in harmony with white society, but it was the responsibility of "white braves of the country who pretend and profess to be teachers and instructors, it [was their] duty to provide means of instruction."[157] Spiritualists, as a result of their experiences at the séance table, became firmly convinced of the fallacies of the argument that Indians were unteachable, and decisively positioned themselves in opposition to such views. They advocated Indian education, which Francis Prucha argues was the most clearly benevolent and powerful aspect of late-nineteenth-century Indian policy.[158]

General spirit messages of encouragement were more common than specific policy suggestions. Spirit chiefs assured mediums and followers that they were not alone in their endeavors. Repeatedly in the 1880s, spirit messages were expressly published to lend the spiritual strength of Indian manifestations to the sacred cause of Indian policy reform. The spirit of Wasso stated in an 1881 message that the spirit council was assembled and ready; "the band in the hunting-grounds [are] all ready to send the strength to white man and squaw."[159] In the fall of the same year, the spirit of Meshkino claimed he was "appointed to come to the squaw, to assist in the unfolding of the power within, to bring it out for the welfare of the spirits and of the pale-faces in the flesh."[160] Red Eagle's spirit claimed in 1883 that the momentum of Spiritualism and its good works was "gathering power and force," even though the change was purportedly coming slowly.[161] The spirit of Red Wing came in 1884 "from the council in the upper hunting-grounds" to "help the medy [medium] who needs the strength which the Indian forces bring to her."[162] He said, "fear not, little squaw … the braves and squaws who have sent their good tidings through the little messenger bring to you peace and comfort, and they will not see you fall nor faint, but they will keep you in a good condition for the noble work."[163] The spirit of White Eagle explained in May 1884 that the primary desire of Indian spirits was to "take weakness away from pale-faces; make 'em strong."[164]

The relationship between spirit chiefs and their mediums was described by Spiritualist philosophers as one of dependency. The medium derived all her physical and spiritual strength from the presence of the chief in her band. Female mediums were often described in failing health. This fact bolstered the arguments of skeptics, especially those who claimed that Spiritualism was a delusion that left women physically and mentally depleted. Such opinions, issued largely by males of the medical community, drew parallels between "the absolute identity of the symptoms, in all characteristics, with those in our day asserted to be due to spiritual possession, and with those met within the various forms of hysteria."[165] Spiritualists described the physical bodies of the mediums as instead absorbing strength from their spiritual controls. Rather than draining their mediums, spirit chiefs claimed to strengthen their earthly friends, enabling them to withstand the trials that accompanied their spiritual work. This included demonstrating the power of Spiritualist communications and conveying those communications to the world. Mrs. Conant's biographer John Day, for example, explained that while many spirits affect their mediums like

> magnetic vampyres … the red man has from the first been a spring of healing power to the exhausted media upon whom the demands of their calling rest like a heavy burden … Especially does Mrs. Conant return thanks in her heart to those of that race who have been her constant attendants and supporters in hours of physical prostration and suffering.[166]

Through this assistance, both whites on earth and Indians in the spiritual realm came closer to achieving the racial harmony perceived as the Great Spirit's will. Although Deloria claims that women did not regularly "play Indian" until the twentieth century, women in this context were empowered by these masculine Indian identities throughout the nineteenth century.[167] Whether these relationships are interpreted as external racial performance (playing Indian) or as spiritual cohabitation (being Indian), the appearance of these spirits contributed to Indian advocacy and legitimized the place of women in public society. Braude argues in her work that "Spiritualism became a major—if not the major—vehicle for the spread of woman's rights ideas in mid-century America."[168] Indian spirits, as central figures of the séance, were an integral part of this. It also extends beyond the 1870s, which Braude saw as a time when empowerment and calls to public reform waned among mediums.[169]

Empowerment of women through the Spiritualist movement did not disappear in the 1870s and 1880s; rather, it took new shape in the form of trance mediumship. By becoming (moreso than playing) Indian, they gained new-found strength by methods previously thought by Deloria to have been exclusive to men in the nineteenth century. The mediums' aims at reform likewise did not dissolve but were instead redirected, away from issues of abolition and toward Indian policy. Their goal toward racial egalitarianism persisted throughout the course of the movement's life. To a large extent, Spiritualists did not perceive a change in the movement's racial mission in the 1870s and 1880s, merely a change in the targeted parties. Links between abolition and Indian reform were openly expressed on several occasions; in the *Banner of Light*, for example, one article claimed that "while thousands are turning their eyes toward the negro, pouring out money and sympathy for them, the Indians are left helpless, to perish, or to remain the savages the papers report them to be."[170] Trance mediumship was the predominant ability claimed by mediums with Indian control spirits, and through these manifestations Spiritualist women became moral authorities, undermining a masculinity defined by violent conquest and challenging the nation's proclaimed virtue. The morally upright manhood advocated by Spiritualists was to be embraced and shared by white and red men alike, as evidenced by the repeated fraternal language used by Indian ghosts who referred to white men at the séance tables as their "brothers."

The physical strength of Indian apparitions reflected their heightened spiritual power, and as such was a central component of their spiritual appearance. Spirit chiefs were tall, strong and continued to function as leaders in the afterlife. Many spirits who appeared had been leaders of Indian resistance in life; in death, they became the guides to spiritual progression for Indians and whites alike. They gained strength and spiritual power by fostering peace with whites, and lent that strength to their delicate mediums on Earth so that they in turn could spread their mission to both races. The overwhelming presence of spirit chiefs in séances and Spiritualist literature signals their centrality to the Spiritualist experience. The purpose of the spirit council, and its widespread dissemination throughout Spiritualist circles, had a profound impact on the racial attitudes and political viewpoints of American Spiritualists. Those attitudes were ultimately expressed through their political activism on behalf of living Indians, to be discussed thoroughly in chapter 5.

FOUR

SPECTRAL ROMANCE

Sympathy for the Indian Maidens

INTRODUCTION

Female Indian spirits visited séance circles as often as spirit chiefs did. They exhibited many of the same physical markers of Indianness as their male counterparts, and professed very similar reasons for their presence. But specific elements of their bodies and interactive style were unique to female manifestations. Likewise, the methods they employed to accomplish their goals were unique to their sex. This chapter focuses on spirit maiden manifestations that were part of the larger mission of Indian ghosts, yet were sexually distinct. Whereas male spirits were largely recognized as powerful chiefs, female spirits were categorized as the innocent, naturalistic, and highly sympathetic victims of Indian warfare and interracial violence. That sexual differentiation, according to Gail Bederman, was a sign of white civilization.[1] Late-nineteenth-century Americans believed, she argues, that sexual specialization—the variation between manhood and womanhood—deepened as white society approached perfection.[2] By defining spirit chiefs and spirit maidens as sexually distinct from each other, Spiritualists encouraged the recognition of Indians as civilized beings, capable of eternal improvement. Additionally, descriptions of Indian apparitions were imbued with qualities that Spiritualists embraced as part of their masculine and feminine ideals—among them education, restraint, and Christian compassion.

The sensory methods by which Spiritualists recognized female Indian apparitions were similar to those used to identify spirit chiefs, yet additional physical traits marked them as females. Long hair, associated in white society with femininity and beauty, was a prominent feature of their appearances.

Female spirits were not noted for their strength, but rather were lithe, lively spectral bodies, often leaping and frolicking during séances. In terms of their speech patterns, broken English was less persistent among spirit maidens than it was among chiefs; poetry instead was a defining feature of spirits such as Ouina and Metoka, who were manifested on multiple occasions. Some female spirits claimed to be princesses, but others did not. Explicit tribal affiliation or political associations were less common among female spirits, and the names of many spirit maidens did not stem from Indian cultures. Names such as Sunbeam and Spring Flower seemed to indicate a closer connection to eighteenth-century Romantic ideas of the noble savage and an innocent association with nature. Such ideals were confirmed by the content of their poetic messages. Spiritualist imagery of the Noble Savage was distinctly feminine in tone, allowing spirit maidens to appear definitively both as Indians and as females.

Spirit maidens' differing nature from spirit chiefs was reflected in their distinct approach to the same spiritual mission advocated by chiefs. Female spirits directed their messages almost exclusively at whites, and represented a more explicit portrayal of Indians as subjects deserving of American sympathy. They depicted their previous lives as natural and innocent, until met with violent and tragic ends. As Bridget Bennett observes, from the late eighteenth century to the 1830s, the "vanishing" quality of Indians made them highly romantic and tragic figures.[3] Spiritualists expressed interest in Indian romances, and often their own depictions of Indian ghosts reflected their exposure to such literature. Though the figures that appeared in séances bore many similarities to their literary counterparts, Spiritualists used romantic imagery to challenge the rhetoric of vanishing—both in its inevitability and in its desirability. Female manifestations in particular were central to this. This chapter will discuss how spirit maidens, by detailing their lives on Earth, built stronger connections between themselves and living Indians in terms of intellectual capacity, deepening the emotional connection Spiritualists had to their stories. Spiritualists extended that sympathy to living Indians, whose plight they recognized as ongoing.

Spirit maidens provided a human dimension to dominant white perceptions of Indians as animalistic. They described their tranquil, domestic, and natural lives, and allowed Spiritualists to empathize with stories of tragedy and violence. The presence of female spirits in séances served an especially important role in this process. Spirit maidens were the ones to relate tales, wrought with Romantic undertones, of the corrupting influence of white society. They condemned white violence and simultaneously defined the imagined simplicity and naturalness of traditional Indian lifestyles as a heavenly ideal. They emphasized the link between Indians (living and dead) and the Great Spirit through their proximity to nature, and espoused a largely naturalist view of heaven. The celestial spheres were at once described as an ideal Indian space and a universal Eden for all nations.

In describing their spirit homes, female ghosts defined the hereafter as a return to Indian lifeways, for both Indians and whites, with an infusion of what were considered productive elements of civilization—namely, education and the development of science and art. Alan Trachtenberg describes the prevailing nineteenth-century view of nature and civilization, wherein nature is civilized through human alienation. Indians, being natural fixtures, must either cease to exist as such, or else cease to exist altogether.[4] Reconciliation between man and nature was desirable for Spiritualists, not just for Indians but for themselves, thus challenging the dominant contemporary view of nature. Sentiments of this kind represented one of the most intimate connections Spiritualists recognized between themselves and their ghostly friends. It was through the presence of female spirits that the sentiments aroused in Spiritualists toward the living Indian were most keenly expressed.

Identifying Spirit Maidens

Some of the ethnic identifiers utilized throughout Spiritualist séances to recognize Indian spirits applied to female as well as male ghosts. In contrast to the majestic image of male spirits, however, female spirits were predominantly described as beautiful maidens with dark, flowing hair. During the 1870s, the renowned medium Horatio Eddy, member of a prominent family of mediums, frequently manifested the spirit of the Indian maiden Honto during his dark séances. In a Boston séance in October 1873, a participant by the name of L. A. Bigelow was given a lock of Honto's hair, which he described in his *Banner of Light* article as "fine and delicate."[5] In 1874, the spirit of Honto appeared as "a small and beautiful Indian maiden ... her long black hair hanging in heavy braids to her waist."[6] Honto's hair was similarly coifed in 1875, where "it [hung] down her back in two lots."[7] Séance participant J. F. Snipes claimed in 1876 that Honto's long hair was a particularly "striking" aspect of her appearance.[8] The spirit of "the Indian girl" Minnie was described in the *Religio-Philosophical Journal* in similar tones in 1877;

Minnie, as manifested by the New York medium Sarah Lane, was "dressed in white with her arms bare. On each wrist she wore a bright band, and on her head a head-dress composed of a bright band and feathers, while her hair hung loosely over her shoulders."[9] Honto's spirit was similarly dressed, wearing what appeared to be a white muslin gown to her ankles.[10] The spirit of Sunbeam outshone her male companions in an 1878 séance held in Chicago, appearing to witness S. C. Gardner in a "beautiful costume." He described the male appearances as "grand," but the subsequent manifestation of Sunbeam was in his estimation "the chief event of the evening."[11] The Rhode Island medium Mrs. H. V. Ross was controlled in 1880 by "an Indian girl, called *Bright Star*" who "appear[ed] before the circle with her long, coarse Indian hair flowing down from her head perfectly natural; and ha[d], in a number of instances, taken scissors from someone present, and cut off locks of it, and distributed to the circle and others present."[12] The anonymous author of this *Banner of Light* article claimed to have examined a specimen in his possession, and found it to "resemble human hair, but entirely unlike that of the medium, in texture and color."[13] The materialization of the spirit Summer Blossom in 1881 in Boston likewise prompted an examination of her costume and "very dark, long straight hair."[14]

Indian costume, and long dark hair for females in particular, continued to be a persistent physical component of Indian manifestations into the 1880s.[15] The notable presence of long dark hair among female Indian spirits became a unique aspect of the process of spiritual authentication, evidenced by the subsequent examination of hair samples. In the 1850s, hair texture was sometimes used as a method of racial classification.[16] To be able to take a physical component of the manifestation outside the confines of the séance room, and identify the hair as *not* belonging to the medium, served as a small physical proof of the existence of physical entities outside the medium's person.

Additionally, the constant description of Indian spirit hair as remarkably long and flowing, whether braided or otherwise, became a cultural marker in itself. Long hair had been recognized in Western cultures as an element of femininity and beauty, but it was also highly uncommon in the 1800s for a middle-class female to be seen outside the confines of her home without her hair pinned up in some fashion. Both the excessive length and lack of complicated coiffure indicated a more natural approach to hair styling, a signal that these spirits continued to lack the modesty and order present in white fashion.

The stature of spirit maidens also set them apart from male spirits. Their behavior during séances further categorized them as innocent, ignorant, and sometimes immodest beings. In contrast to the strength and stature exhibited by spirit chiefs, female apparitions were consistently described by séance observers as being light and spry. The spirit of Honto, for example, whose frequent manifestation was a dominant force among female Indians, appeared several times during the mid-1870s. Her spirit regularly interacted with séance participants, on one occasion calling for the medium Horatio Eddy and a Mr. Cleveland to join her in a circular dance: "The three joined hands and began dancing. They then let go hands and went dancing around, passing each other in and out. This lasted about five minutes. Honto then danced by herself in a sprightly manner, throwing up her legs and extra height by way of finale as she entered the cabinet."[17] In her 1877 book *A Southerner Among the Spirits*, Mary Dana Schindler described her encounter with Eddy's famous spirit:

> [T]he personality of Honto, as she appears night after night, cannot be mistaken. Her form, movements, and gestures are so peculiar and different from that of the other spirits seen here, that none but the blind could not distinguish her instantly from the others … her features and Indian color brighten up and display themselves sufficiently to be recognizable at any time … to prove how agile she is, Honto once ran down like a gazelle the steps of the platform, onto the main floor of the circle room, and leaped clear over the railing on to the elevated platform, four feet and a half exact measurement.[18]

Eddy manifested another Indian girl in 1875 in Vermont, whose "bend of the shoulders, and way of the figure, and the quick, light tread were very Indian like. She danced about and materialized spirits for four minutes, and retired."[19] The 1878 appearance of Sunbeam through Mrs. M. E. Week was similarly described as "sprightly," "playful," "beautiful," and "graceful."[20] In Terre Haute, Indiana, in 1883, the medium Mrs. Steward manifested the spirit of Oskaloosa, who was portrayed as "very lively, and danced around the platform like a veritable living human being. She also allowed the audience to shake hands with her, and feel of her hair."[21] Although not always in name, the physical characteristics of spirit maidens represented a typified form of what Jared Farmer termed the legend of the Indian princess—they were young, beautiful (with fine, rather than coarse hair), and helpful.[22]

Female Indian specters were not described in the same physical terms as spirit chiefs. They were not notably tall; the spirit of Honto was reported to be 5'2".[23] They were strong in comparison to non-Indian ghosts, who could not usually produce loud noises or move physical objects, but they were by no means spiritual giants. Rather, they were light on their feet, livening up a séance by playfully interacting with the sitters. Nowhere were they categorized as loud, violent, or intimidating, terms that often accompanied the manifestations of Indian males. In this regard, female spirits more commonly filled the role of Indians as naive children. The youthful innocence exhibited by spirit maidens echoed the imagined white connection between Indianness and childishness. Deloria writes of such rhetoric, describing that white linguistic associations between Indians and children demarcated Indians as "natural, simple, naïve, preliterate, and devoid of self-consciousness."[24] These associations persisted since the first European recordings of contact. In his journal, Christopher Columbus characterized Indians as generous simpletons. The familial and giving nature of native communities served as the basic subject of John White's sixteenth-century watercolors of the Roanoke Algonkins. The appearance of spirit maidens perpetuated such tropes, resulting in Spiritualist appreciation for their open friendliness. Deloria states that the additional consequence of this rhetoric was to transform Indians into wards of the United States.[25] For Spiritualists, such imagery informed their political positions. They abhorred the violence inflicted on their ghostly friends while living, and sought federal protection for Indian families from the predation of greedy and hateful whites. But the maidens' more extroverted performances in séances created stronger bonds of friendship between female spirits and Spiritualists, through their heightened friendliness and approachability. Female spirits were entirely nonthreatening. They were not portrayed as stoic Indians, nor were they constantly bumping their heads on cabinet ceilings and performing feats of strength to assert their spiritual power. In terms of power and manifestational strength, female spirits were not equal to their male counterparts, but their stronger connections served a higher function of sympathy.

Children of Nature

The traits of the spirit maiden as exhibited during séances combined two different foci of the Romantic movement—what Hoxie Fairchild calls "the cult of scenery" and "the cult of the child."[26] The diminutive stature, playfulness, and overt youth inherent in maidens' appearances distinguished them not only as female, but as distinctively childlike in comparison to the majestic manifestations of spirit chiefs. Additionally, these characteristics were intimately connected to the natural environment. They were likened to other delicate creations, such as flowers and deer, and acted as innocent spirits, free to frolic in a quintessentially Romantic view of heaven.[27]

Though they may have appeared comparatively weak in their physical aspects, the prevalence of elevated speech among female spirits was one element through which Indian females were portrayed as spiritually superior to chiefs. The broken English exhibited by spirit chiefs existed to a lesser degree among the ghosts of Indian women. For example, the spirit of White Fawn sent a message in 1879 to the *Banner of Light* in search of her medium, saying, "Me be the squaw that comes to her sometimes. Me call meself White Fawn. Me say she is in the Providence settlement … She was in the Boston settlement but now me can't find her."[28] Mumblings of this kind appeared as late as 1883, when the *Banner of Light* medium Miss Shelhammer channeled the spirit of Star Flower, who claimed the Indian spirit "band directs Star-Flower [sic] not to speak very plainly, yet she hardly knows how to talk the pale-face language unless she does so."[29] The prose in this message is not overly convoluted, but it makes a notable reference to the spirit's lack of higher powers of speech. The only way Star Flower can communicate in English, if at all, is by way of plain language. She cannot, she claims, speak in the loftier and poetic tones more common among other female spirits.

From the mid-1860s to 1890s, the ghosts of Indian women frequently composed poetry during their manifestations. Communication of this kind was entirely absent from male spirit communication. This sexually unique aspect of Indian spirit speech is intriguing, given the significance designated to elevated forms of speech, within nineteenth-century séances circles as well as outside them. The expression of heightened linguistic abilities on the part of spirit maidens undermined the connection between their characterization as childlike and preliterate, which Deloria claims helped to define white depictions of Indians.[30] Though Spiritualist records of maiden manifestations perpetuated the trope of Indians as children, they simultaneously bestowed qualities on Indian ghosts that elevated the political status of living Indians by demonstrating their intellectual merit. The eloquence and powers of speech attributed to spirits was positively linked to their progression in the spiritual spheres. Elevated speech served as an outward, physical sign of inner illumination and, arguably, the progression of spiritual "civilization." Though many spirit chiefs were capable of delivering moving oratory, none demonstrated straightforward poetic abilities. Poetic qualities, Fairchild writes, were possibly the most pervasive element of the concept of the Noble Savage.[31] Within the Spiritualist movement, this quality was reserved specifically for Indian females—not the chiefs. This difference in the mode of communication is one element of spirit manifestations that points to a sexual hierarchy operating in the spiritual realm. One possible interpretation is that, among Spiritualists observing these phenomena, the spirits of Indian women were regarded as spiritually and intellectually superior to their male counterparts. It was not a far cry from the sexual hierarchy at work in their own culture; the white ideal of womanhood carried with it a claim to moral authority.[32] By depicting the innocent and loving nature of spirit maidens as hewing closely to a Christian moral ideal, Spiritualists asserted that Indian women, as well as white women, could act as moral authorities if properly educated. Thus, ghostly maidens, who had received a spiritual education, became for Spiritualists the models of a universal love that transcended both racial and sexual difference. The absence of Indian women from military activity contributed to this notion; as noncombatants, Indian women could easily be seen as morally superior to native men.

Spirit maidens' superior capabilities of speech were positively linked to their relatively peaceful lives on Earth. Fairchild points out that in Romantic literature, the noble savage was generally depicted as a girl, a "child of nature" who has not been tainted by the vices of civilization. This character's moral superiority comes from her intimate relationship with the natural landscape.[33] In the case of white imagery of Indians, it was fairly common in the nineteenth century to obscure any difference between native peoples and the landscape itself. Jean-Jacques Rousseau's Romantic concept of the Noble Savage, whose virtue was unsullied by civilization, became directly connected with perceptions of the American Indian. The True Native, according to Jean-Jacques Simard, was a reduction of multiple cultures into

> a body of powerful symbols, images, and fictions. [He is] a primeval being, one uniquely and perpetually bound to pristine nature and a remarkably durable, inarguably ancient cultural heritage. So powerful are such mental images that any type of social transformation can be interpreted as a catastrophic threat to the native's natural destiny and authentic soul ... [J]ust as they are physically out of place in modern North American society, so are they ideologically denied the experience of history. Because of the phantom image of *the Indian,* Indians are made into a timeless people.[34]

Such a figure was a fiction of the past about Indians not yet exposed to white civilization.[35] Spiritualism was not the first or the last cultural forum to engage in this reductive fictionalization, but Spiritualists drew on the powerful, pervasive imagery to understand the specters that visited them. The impact and lasting aspects of these phenomena have not yet been analyzed. In an 1869 issue of the *Religio-Philosophical Journal*, an anonymous author spoke of spiritual degeneration among Indians "in consequence of the vices of the white race," despite the fact that their spirituality and powers of mediumship were considered "largely developed."[36] This typical representation of the noble savage is thus considered morally superior to that of the naturally distanced, overcivilized white Spiritualists witnessing such manifestations, who viewed this as an ideal model for defining both the feminine and masculine ideals. If Indian women had fewer sins for which they had to atone, logic suggests that their spiritual progression and education would exceed that of Indian males. With fewer bad deeds to make up for, female ghosts could pass farther and more quickly than men into the upper hunting-grounds. The "goodness" inherent in Indians, as Barnett points out, is thus "expressed chiefly by services to whites and susceptib[ility] to Christian ideals."[37] In one spirit communication published in the *Banner of Light*, an Indian spirit tells the tale of being separated from the woman he loved in life by a river, only to be reunited with her once he ceased to be an angry spirit. He rejoined her after becoming humble and more patient before the Great Spirit.[38] Women were spiritually superior, then, because their spiritual existence was an extension of their spiritual lives on Earth. They, moreso than Indian men, were portrayed as closer to nature and closer to the Great Spirit. They expressed no deep feelings of hatred or revenge for white society. Those lingering, earthly flaws were reserved for fallen warriors, who consequently needed to partake in the great mission of spiritual progression in order to ascend through the spheres. Female spirits did contribute to the spiritual work of the chiefs, but in tones that presented the maidens as friendlier and more approachable, deepening the bonds between Spiritualists and the apparitions they claimed to witness. Nowhere were their actions described as a form of atonement, which was often the case for male descriptions of spirit missions.

Although some female spirits claimed to be princesses, they did not address themselves to living Indians as one chief giving advice to another, the way Little Crow's spirit spoke to Big Eagle.[39] They likewise did not claim to lead the Indian bands of the spirit-world; that position was reserved for spirit chiefs such as Red Jacket. Springflower came, as she said, from "Red Jacket's band

[to] bring messages of love."⁴⁰ Spirit maidens did not come as the leaders of the Indian mission, but rather as the messengers. The spirit of Starlight, for example, spoke through the *Banner of Light* in June 1866, claiming that she came "in behalf of the spirit-band."⁴¹ She did not claim any particular position within that band. Some maiden spirits made explicit reference to their mission as originating from their male counterparts; Morning Star's spirit, for example, claimed in 1877 that she came "with many chiefs, with many braves, with many squaws, to give strength and power."⁴² Star Flower also claimed to come as "a messenger from the band."⁴³ Shining Star's spirit in 1881 said that "the red maiden has come a long distance to speak the words which the Great Chief has given her to speak."⁴⁴ In this instance, the Great Spirit is referred to specifically as a chief, which connotes not only his power over her, but his gender as well.

A relatively small number of maidens claimed the title of "Indian princess." In the medium Fannie Conant's book *Flashes of Light*, published in 1872, a poem by the spirit of Metoka is recited through Conant. Metoka is described as "mother of Winona [another of Conant's Indian spirits], and wife of the sachem Wänandago, whose hunting-grounds, over 200 years ago, included the territory on which the city of Boston is built."⁴⁵ The spirit of Em-mu-ne-es-ka, known among Spiritualists as Minnehaha, or simply Minnie, was the "daughter of Omwah, a Cheyenne underchief," according to *Banner of Light* correspondent and Conant biographer John W. Day.⁶ The spirit of Ouina, previously known as Shenandoah and manifested frequently through the medium Cora Hatch, claimed in *Ouina's Canoe*, a book purportedly authored by her in 1882, that her father was "Chief of the Shenandoah nation … more than three hundred [years] ago."⁴⁷

The title of princess, however, did not translate into elevated spiritual power or leadership within the spirit bands. In each instance, their positions were described as deriving from being their fathers' daughters. If anything, the stories of their lives and journeys through the spirit-world were rendered even more sympathetic. The poem by Metoka's spirit, entitled "The Indian Maiden Winona," told the story of Metoka's daughter and her people's tragic end, when "the strange voice of the white man/Rang through all [their] hunting-grounds;/ … Heeding not the maiden's sighing,/Fearing not the warrior's frown!"⁴⁸ According to Jared Farmer, Winona was also the name ascribed by author William Keating to the Indian maiden who made the legendary leap from Maiden Rock, Wisconsin, to cure her broken heart. The scene of her dramatic jump was also the subject of one of many illustrations included in George Catlin's *Letters and Notes* in 1857.[49] Such connections would not have been lost on Spiritualists, who often by their own admission expressed an intense interest in such stories. The repeated use of such a name simply indicated its usefulness in signifying a certain character type, rather a different act than the scrutiny utilized in naming a spirit such as Black Hawk's. Similar scrutiny in authenticating female spirits was virtually impossible, since with few exceptions, the lives of Indian women were not as highly publicized as those of Indian warriors, and therefore not as visible or available to the American public. The almost complete absence of prominent female figures in John Coward's *The Newspaper Indian* attests to this; coverage of chiefs and warriors dominated Indian-related print. As a result, practically the only resources for authenticating Indian females, with perhaps the exception of the George Catlin, were pieces of fiction. In the context of the Romantic literary tradition, such associations were somewhat expected, considering that the qualities of being legendary and being ghostly fit hand in hand. In John Day's article about the spirit Minnie, he claimed she had previously belonged to the Cheyenne, who recently "went down in the storm of [the Sand Creek] massacre."[50] Ouina claimed in her book that she earned the name "murdered princess" among the braves of her tribe upon her death. She was allegedly slain at her father's command for conveying to the council a message from her own dead mother's spirit. She warned that her father's enemy Karawah with "many mighty warriors come[s] from the west-land to slay his people, [and] the great Shenandoah and his people will perish."[51]

The names of spirit maidens were often generic and virtually anonymous. Their names—Spring Flower, Starlight, Wildflower, Morning Star, Blue Flower, Sunbeam, Sunlight, White Fawn, and Dewdrop, to name a few—connoted a connection to nature, rather than specific tribal affiliations. Very few female spirits claimed a particular Indian identity. In John Day's biography of Fannie Conant, Spring Flower was manifested by her as "a Sioux."[52] In an 1875 issue of the *Banner of Light*, the message of "Ninna, a Kiowa" was published.[53] In February 1878, the spirit of Sunlight claimed in the *Banner of Light* to be Shoshone.[54] In 1885 Shelhammer channeled the spirit of "Anoka, a Sioux."[55] These claims to tribal identities did not affect the appearances of these specters in any appreciable way. The methods of manifestation did not reflect such cultural distinctions. Their recognition by Spiritualists as Indian did not vary based on these claims, nor was there a more targeted attempt at spirit authentication.

Acknowledgment of such ghosts, moreso than spirit chiefs, relied exclusively on Spiritualists' general understanding of an imagined, collective Indianness. Although they had names, female spirits were not recognized as the returned souls of living Indian celebrities. There were no female counterparts to figures such as Black Hawk, Philip, Red Jacket, or Little Crow. Living Indian females were largely absent from popular discourse about contemporary Indian affairs, mainly because of the military focus of such literature. The public invisibility of Indian female figures in white literature persisted in recorded Spiritualist phenomena through the virtual anonymity of Indian maidens.

Perhaps the only exception to this was Minnie, an actual Indian who during the later stages of her life lived with the famed medium Cora Tappan and her husband Colonel Samuel Tappan. Tappan acted as an Indian activist in the 1860s and 1870s, participating in the Indian Peace Commission and serving as U.S. Indian Commissioner. He first met Em-mu-ne-es-ka in 1865 at "an Episcopalian Indian Mission School, where she was baptized with the name Minnehaha."[56] He was charmed by Minnie's "sprightly, natural, and artless ways," and adopted her as his daughter. She continued her education in the company of J. H. Conant and participated in the Children's Progressive Lyceum, a sort of Spiritualist Sunday School started at the suggestion of Andrew Jackson Davis.[57] The adoption of Minnie by the Tappan family is the strongest example that Spiritualists did not only build intimate relationships with long-dead ghosts while keeping live Indians at a distance.[58] After her death in 1873 at the age of sixteen, her spirit was occasionally channeled by Cora Tappan, acting in the manner common to spirit maidens. Although this is perhaps the most direct connection between Spiritualists and living Indians, it did not earn her a particularly esteemed place among Indian spirits. Instead, the tragic stories of Minnie, Ouina, and others were used to bolster sympathy among Spiritualists, drawing on their attraction to literary romances.

American readers avidly consumed Indian romances such as Cooper's Leatherstocking Tales and Indian melodramas, which had the effect of turning Indians into sympathetic figures through the recounting of their tragic deaths.[59] Spiritualism challenged the judgment of the Noble Savage as inferior when confronted by white civilization.[60] Rather, Spiritualist praise of an imaged Indianness turned European condescension on its head, claiming that Indian virtue did not exist only in the absence of white society. But at the same time, Spiritualists adhered ever so closely to the principles of progress through education as the ultimate universal truth. Cultural media that characterized Indians as tragic heroes and Indian women as helpless victims peaked in the first half of the nineteenth century.[61] By the time Spiritualism was at its height in the 1860s and 1870s, such tropes were firmly in place. Stories that spirit maidens told of their own demises tapped into this interest by echoing such narratives and painting themselves as tragic figures to their Spiritualist audiences. In this regard, Indian manifestations were yet another cultural medium by which Americans were entertained by witnessing Indian tragedy. The story of female mediators such as Pocahontas formed the base of the trope of Indian maidens as sympathetic subjects. These earlier cultural media helped inform Spiritualist depictions and interpretations of Indians, as evidenced by their pronounced enthusiasm for such forms. In a *Banner of Light* cover article in 1873, Fannie Conant's biographer John Day reported on the life, death, and burial service of Minnie Tappan, writing that "the incidents which have crowded the experience of this young Indian maiden, make her history as attractive as a romance, and offer additional proof of the verity of that trite saying with regard to the comparative singularity of truth and fiction."[62] The purpose of most female manifestations was to garner white sympathy for the plight of living Indians, hopefully motivating them to act on behalf of Indians' best political interests. Laura Mielke posits that George Catlin's observations, made through direct contact with Indians, of "domestic, familial and communal settings" fostered a sympathetic view of natives that was shared by Catlin's broad reading audience.[63] The depiction of Indian families, and especially the presence of women in these depictions, undermined to a certain extent the simultaneous portrayal of Indians solely as warriors, and was integral to the creation of sympathetic sentiments toward living Indians. The appearances of spirit maidens also contributed to this process of empathizing with Indians. The stories told in poems, spirit messages, and medium biographies followed a general formula. They recounted the peaceful, natural ways of Indians that were destroyed by greed, cruelty, and warfare. Even though these spirits did not live publicly visible lives and did not emerge from a body of literary documentation, their stories were nonetheless provided by the spirits themselves. Told from this perspective, facts and specific details would have been extremely difficult to corroborate; as a result these tales are vague and generic. Additionally, some spirits claimed to have lived in the distant American past. In the spirit Metoka's poem "The Indian Maiden Winona," Winona is described as a "beautiful, dark-browed maid" who died at the tender age of sixteen, almost simultaneously with the arrival of the white man.[64] The poem reads:

> In the sunlight, in the starlight,
> In the moons of long ago—
> Ere the virgin soil of Shawmut
> Quivered 'neath the white man's plow;
>
> Ere the great lakes and the rivers
> Listened to the white man's song;
> Ere the Father of all waters
> Bore them in his strong arms on;
>
> ...
>
> Grew Winona, strong and beauteous,
> Fairer than the flowers of spring,
> And the echo of her sweet voice
> Made the hills and valleys ring[65]

The work is saturated with references to nature as pristine and "virgin," and Winona herself is likened to a spring flower, completely connected to and an inseparable part of her landscape, a common trope of Romantic imagery.[66] Her coinciding disappearance from this scene with the arrival of white society suggests that, as a part of the natural landscape, she too must be relegated to being a relic of the past in the face of American expansion and development. As Cox writes, the absence of familial connection required the bonds between Spiritualists and Indian apparitions to be built on alternative modes of shared experience. The American landscape, Cox argues, bridged the gap of intimate knowledge between whites and Indians.[67] The significance of distinctly female apparitions in this context was the unique connection made between nature and spirit maidens, something not readily apparent in the appearances of male phantasms. Ouina, for example, was described in similarly natural tones. Much like Disney's vision of Pocahontas,

> she seemed to have the power to talk with the birds in the trees and with the animals that roamed the valley. Her people often wondered which was the song of the bird and which was Ouina's, as they listened

to them from a distance. She loved the beautiful in life and was sportive as a fawn, but she never had the heart to kill even an insect. She even wept when the warriors would return with slaughtered game.⁶⁸

In this instance, Ouina was likened to a fawn instead of a flower, but is equally innocent and extremely sensitive to all violence. By portraying the lives of Indian maidens in these edenic tones, their violent deaths became all the more tragic. In Conant's biography, she explained that Spring Flower, another of her Indian spirits, was a member of the Sioux tribe and had committed suicide, frequently reappearing at the place of her death.⁶⁹ Em-mu-ne-es-ka (Minnie) was adopted by Colonel Tappan after surviving the Sand Creek Massacre, "to pass on at last under the effect of consumption, while fitting herself at Washington for missionary work among the tribes in the West."⁷⁰ In *Ouina's Canoe*, Ouina's spirit claimed she was killed by her father, for warning him of an enemy approaching. In a 1918 issue of the *Psychical Research Review*, another spirit, a princess named Wahallahee, claimed that "in a fit of anger and disappointed love she committed suicide by throwing herself from a bluff into a river."⁷¹ The spirit of Ne-os-co-le-ta "perished on the Plains, and was covered beneath the snow; that her people were driven from their lodge by the pale-faces, and having no food, and being unable to continue the flight, this little one faltered and perished."⁷²

Through their violent deaths, Indian maids became the victims of circumstance, encompassing issues of both white encroachment and Indian cruelty. Yet warfare was absent from the hearts and minds of these delicate creatures; thus, when tragedy befell them they became prime subjects of white sympathy. Their deaths were connected to the changing world around them and their increasing inability to exist as part of nature. A poem by Metoka's spirit to a Dr. Pike stated that "the weary, wounded spirit" of the Indian maid "fled from earth like a frightened fawn."⁷³ Spirit maids were sadly disappearing alongside the forests and plains they once happily called home.

Spirit maids told stories of both their deaths and their new lives in the Happy Hunting Ground. In their discourse about the celestial realm in which they resided, female spirits emphasized the Romantic, natural aspects of the upper hunting-grounds. They strengthened the link made between Indian habits and lifestyles and the Great Spirit. The lines of poetry allegedly produced by spirit hands were largely reminiscent of eighteenth-century Romantic poetry in style, rhyme, and content, moreso than contemporary poetry of the age.⁷⁴ Metoka's poem talked of "the happy hunting ground" as a place "where the sky is always bright; / Where our hunting-grounds are greater; / Where the water's always clear."[75] Another poem by her claimed that in the spirit land "the forest trees are greenest."[76] A poem by Ouina's spirit described heaven as "the land of summer sunshine," a place of "peace and plenty."[77] In a spirit message produced in 1873, the spirit of Ninna claimed that

> the Land of Souls is green and fair; the water is clear; the sun shines bright, and no white man's rifle there robs the Indians of his rights or life, because the Great Father teaches him better—tells him that his red children have rights as they have, and they hear his voice, and they love their Great Father, and they obey him; so there is peace there—peace—peace, and not war.[78]

According to these descriptions, peace and abundance were the two essential qualities of the upper hunting-ground. This peace was achieved through acknowledgment of one deity for both whites and Indians, and through universal obedience to a spiritual law of racial equality. There was no greed on the part of whites, but neither was there revenge on the part of Indians. Emphasizing this egalitarian aspect was significant because it provided the model for Spiritualists' attempts to create a heaven on earth. They tried to imitate the Summer Land by arguing for Indian rights; it also served as a way to conform to the professed will of the Great Spirit. Earlier Romantic expressions of nature were echoed in spirit descriptions of the afterlife, defining the Romanticist view of nature as the heavenly ideal. In this context, the womanhood (and manhood) practiced there by Indian ghosts also represented human ideals—ones that Americans had forgotten in their unfaltering quest for progress. Spiritualist political stances on social issues such as women's rights and Indian affairs reflected their desire to achieve such ideals on earth, rather than to simply justify the current state of their lives as being ultimately rectified in the afterlife. Such ideas and actions will be the primary focus of the following chapter. The relationships that Spiritualists fostered with Indian specters served a similar function to the cultural process that Shari Huhndorf describes as "going native." Indian ghosts represented an alternative model for religious, racial, and gendered aspects of American life, which could be mimicked to support a regeneration of whiteness. This reception of spirit Indian manifestations represents an earlier expression of this process, which Huhndorf describes in a predominantly twentieth-century context.[79] Ter Ellingson has argued that the noble aspects of the "noble savage" stereotype derived from white contact. Here, the source of goodness in spirit maidens was their naturalness and lack of contact with whites.[80]

Living in the upper hunting-grounds was a privilege, one enjoyed by many Indian spirits. These apparitions claimed to return from their blissful state to act as guides for white-skinned spirits whose hearts were filled with hate and ignorance. Shelhammer's control spirit Lotela said in a message in 1881 that she

> lives in the great hunting-ground, where the green forest waves and the bright flowers bloom; Ouina lives where the wild roses shed their fragrance on the balmy air. That is the spiritual home, but they who live there come back to this hunting-ground to see the pale-faces, to bring messages of love and cheer, and to try to enlighten all who wish to know of their dear ones across the big waters.[81]

The border between the material and spiritual worlds was often described in the traditional, classical terms of a river, one which spirits such as Lotela and Ouina crossed many times. Although the upper hunting-ground was a veritable Indian paradise—with abundant forests, wild game, and sunshine—their residence therein was not permanent. In the dedication to her book, Ouina's spirit claimed, "My home is in the spirit state. / I live with angels in their home. / And what we have we much create; / so this is why to earth I come. / We build our homes with thoughts above, / We plant our bowers with seeds of love."[82] Lines like this might be interpreted as justifying Indian vanishing by defining the benefits of life in heaven, but the deeper message of such spirit communication is more complicated. It suggested an Indian return from a *higher* spiritual and moral plane for the purpose of white education.

As early as 1859 and as late as 1882, Spiritualists and the manifestations they claimed to witness acknowledged the intimacy Indians forged with the Great Spirit through their proximity to nature. The worship of nature within the Romantic movement, Fairchild states, contained elements of Christian deism and Unitarianism, which also strongly influenced Spiritualist religious concepts.[83] An 1859 *Banner of Light* article, entitled "Thoughts on Man's Religious Nature," explained and supported the medium Cora Hatch's position on Indian religions. "In her discourses on the religious nature of man," Hatch proclaimed that "the savages of America worshipped and adored a Divine Being" and rightly feared "the superior powers of Nature."[84] Although efforts to understand native religions on their own terms were virtually nonexistent, the common assumptions about native religions, which had from the seventeenth century led to the perception of nature-based Indian beliefs as satanic, seemed to gain a modicum of respect in Spiritualists circles.

Though Indian religions were only generally understood and highly simplified, that concept of Indian religion was held in high moral regard when juxtaposed with what many Spiritualists saw as the hypocrisy of Christian love. The historical convention that Indians led largely Christian lives even before their exposure to Christianity was used by Romantics in the eighteenth century and Spiritualists in the nineteenth century to suggest that the savage was in fact a divine model of pre-Fall human innocence, to be copied rather than erased.[85] The Indian, and specifically the Noble Savage as depicted in eighteenth-century Romantic literature, served as a body of imagery that Spiritualists adopted with a new purpose. They did not sentimentalize and celebrate Indian vanishing as Romantics did. Rather, they pointed to the benefits of rekindling those dormant virtues in their own hearts, while actively striving to reverse the political effort to make Indian disappearance a reality.[86] Fairchild writes that the figure of the Noble Savage embodied "a promise of what man might become";[87] Spiritualists perpetuated such Romantic threads of thought by proclaiming the lives of spirits as racial, gendered, and religious ideals. Spiritualists, like Romantics, scorned the complexity of religious institutions and the resulting corruption; the antiauthoritarian sentiments of the majority of Spiritualists mirrored the Romantic aversion to religious infrastructure.[88] Spiritualism also fostered interest in Indian spirituality, deemed simple and therefore authentic in its religious experience. "How many have been burned at the stake," a *Banner of Light* article asked, "and canonized by the church for their sacrifice to the faith?"[89] Though idealized, Spiritualist ideas of Indian religion allowed a stark moral contrast to be made, underscoring the outrages that American society had ostensibly committed in the name of Christianity. A spirit message by Shining Star published in the *Banner of Light* in 1881 acknowledged the dependency of whites on Indian spiritual guidance. She said, "The pale-face has waited long and anxiously for the coming of the red maiden, has waited to hear the light footsteps or to listen to the sound of the spirit-voice which speaks to the soul alone. The white man waits and waits, asking for light, for knowledge concerning the path he is to go."[90] Fannie Conant made a similar comparison to Cora Hatch's in her biography, elevating the spiritual status of Indians:

> The life of the Indian, being on earth conducted in accordance with the principles of, or in a more direct nearness to Mother Nature, a knowledge of the control of the more subtle elements of magnetic strength seems

to be possessed by his arisen spirit in a greater degree than by his white brother, whose civilization leads him further and further into the intricacies of artificial customs, appetites, and fashions, till like the bow continually bent, the verve and spring of his *physique* [sic] succumbs to the constant strain, and he becomes but a walking automaton.[91]

In this passage, whites, not Indians, were depicted as more earthly, and farther removed from the spiritual power rooted in nature. Conant did, however, assert that Indian spiritual superiority stemmed from their lack of civilization. In this context, "civilization" has negative connotations; it is an example of the rejection of overcivilization by Spiritualism and other aspects of nineteenth-century culture highlighted by Jackson Lears.[92] Their victimization by whites was not what elevated them to this morally superior status. Their lifestyles before contact with whites, as described by spirits and understood by Spiritualists, earned them this position. It was not white guilt over Indian violence that placed Indian spirits in a position of spiritual authority. That status was a continuation of their superior lifestyles.

Intermediary Spirits

In the 1880s, many of the Indian maidens who appeared through the medium Mary Shelhammer, especially the spirit of Lotela, claimed higher spiritual positions for themselves by asserting that part of their mission was to help less-developed spirits communicate with the living. The spirit of Lotela first appeared to Shelhammer in March 1878, when Shelhammer has just begun filling the role of the late Fannie Conant as the sitting medium for the *Banner of Light*. Lotela's spirit was initially described as that of a seven-year-old child, who "shivered and chattered, but could not make herself understood."[93] Lotela was portrayed in an article entitled "Interesting History of the Indian Maiden Lotela" as slowly transforming into a helpful spirit control. The anonymous author of the article observed that

> it was interesting to watch the progress of Lotela in her subsequent entrancement of Miss S. At first she did not understand the English language. Then, under the teaching of those present, she began to speak words of one syllable, then to form sentences, and finally to give communications for other spirits.[94]

Part of Lotela's education, then, came not from the spirit-world, but from within the circle itself. In the case of most spirits, their education was administered by spirits even higher than themselves. Ouina's spirit, for example, "eagerly sought instruction from the advanced teachers of the higher spheres ... She rapidly unfolded her own soul's powers, and soon became a teacher in the spirit realms."[95] This was representative of the commonly described structure of spiritual education. Experience and information—higher truths—were acquired from higher spheres, and spirits then returned to the lower spheres to convey what they had learned. Lotela was described as "show[ing] remarkable aptness for the work" of learning the alphabet and writing.[96] Such intellectual capabilities were used to demonstrate successful examples of educating Indians, which was an integral issue in the debate about how to answer "the Indian question." In December 1881, the spirit of Lotela allegedly spoke for several other spirits, explaining that she came "as a messenger from the squaws and braves who want to come ... They want to come back and manifest, but they can't get hold of the medy, so Lotela is going to speak for them."[97] Lotela here is portrayed as a well-developed spiritual entity, with a strong connection to the medium allowing her to communicate clearly through the medium. For those spirits whose connection with the medium was more tenuous, Lotela acted on yet another level as translator between the material and spiritual realms. This explanatory introduction of Lotela's manifestation was repeated several times throughout the 1880s.[98]

In the same way that spirits such as Lotela provided insight into the spiritual world, the same helpful communication operated in the opposite direction. In 1885, Lotela helped to produce a message from the spirit of Anoka, purportedly the spirit of a Sioux, telling of her difficulty in effectively communicating with her medium. "Tell my medium that I have tried and tried to come and speak," she said. "I came, but I could not speak. I did not know how to talk, or how to manifest so she would know I had been there."[99] Spirits with higher faculties such as Lotela, then, functioned as navigators of the séance, showing both the living and the dead the means by which they could recognize and converse with one another. This ability was one that developed gradually—for Lotela, over the course of several years—and was not found naturally in all manifestations. The helpful role that Lotela played in this instance, much like the ability of Old Ski's spirit to speak to the circle without a megaphone, demonstrated a level of development above the basic spiritual existence for departed souls.[100] It served as an indicator of higher rank; the communicative skills of Indian spirits were regarded in this context as a result of development and experience within the séance circle. Such powers did not demonstrate a low spiritual status that kept Indian ghosts bound to earth. The suggestion that "primitive," natural aspects of Indian lifestyles resulted in longer journeys through spiritual progress, as in Black Hawk's case, was absent from this portrayal of Indian ghosts' functions in séances.

Indian spirits were thus described as being of a middling spiritual rank. They lived in the *upper* hunting-grounds, but continually returned to earth. They received education from their celestial superiors, so that they might pass on that knowledge to living whites. Their roles as guides, controls, and teachers gave them an elevated status in a spiritual hierarchy. They asserted the superiority of Indian ghosts over white mortals through their access to higher truths; and yet, through their communications with earth, they were only marginally separated from it. The return of such ghosts to séances would, it was hoped, lead to even further degrees of illumination in the future. The process of pinpointing the position of Indian spirits within a larger supernatural hierarchy highlights the complexities of similar categorizations operating in the land of the living. Questions of racial and sexual identity and intellectual capacity were constantly analyzed, and the answers were always complicated. The complexities of spiritual education, for example—the various sources of knowledge and the differing abilities of Indian spirits—mirrored the simultaneous debate among white Americans as to whether living Indians could or should be assimilated through an Anglo education. Just as this question was not definitively answered in reality, with many differing viewpoints publicly expressed on the issue, there was no clear categorization to explain why a spirit such as Ouina's could produce a book of poetry, while Anoka's spirit could barely pronounce a single English syllable. It is important to keep in mind that Spiritualists as a group were not united in their understanding of the spirit-world; nor were they in agreement as to how their knowledge should affect the material realm, regarding racial and sexual difference, or how to satisfactorily answer the "Indian question." This profusion of ideas, attitudes, and approaches was reflected in the variety of published Spiritualist experiences and interpretations of supernatural phenomena. Complex ideas about race, gender, power, morality, civilization, education, and politics operating within the Summer Land reflected the same complexities as they related to nineteenth-century America.

Much like the spirit chiefs, one of the primary functions of Indian maiden manifestations was to both encourage whites to do good on Earth, and warn them that failure to do so could lead to divine retribution. In 1876, the spirit of Morning Star warned in her message that whites should "be just to the red man, or you will feel the frown of the Great Spirit."[101] A Shoshone maiden by the name of Sunlight said in an 1878 message that

> we [the Indian spirit band] advise [President Hayes] to be mighty much good to the Indian, or else he be nowhere; there be no influence that will save him; there be much fight, much bloodshed, much bad things. Me ask him to be good to the red braves that come to him, else he be very much sorry in time to come.[102]

Sunlight's spirit suggested that there would be no spiritual aid for whites if they ignored the pleas of Indian ghosts. Nor would they be granted access to higher spheres—instead, a kind of oblivion waited for them. Only by heeding such messages, it seems, could whites attain illumination. An 1880 spirit message from Star Flower corroborated this point, telling whites to

> be true and faithful to the spirit-teachings, and you will find yourself surrounded by a holy influence, by a great light, that shall bring to you and to those whom you meet, consolation, peace and blessing.[103]

In order to gain access to heaven, the main example set forth by Indian spirits—that of racial equality and mutual love—had to be put into action. Otherwise, the Great Spirit would deem white souls unfit to live in his racial utopia.

Though some female spirits did come to séances with ominous tidings, the intention was always a positive one. Spirit maidens did not seek revenge; nor was it an emotion they had gradually overcome, as was the case for chief spirits. Rather, spiritual punishment for their mistreatment was something Indian spirits actively attempted to avoid. From the mid-1860s through the 1880s, messages of encouragement were prevalent. In 1866 the spirit of Starlight claimed to "bring the blessing of the angels," giving whites "strength," "encouragement," and "words of good cheer."[104] The spirit of Minnie Tappan said to her friends in an 1874 message, "persevere, and I will do everything I can in my new life to help you."[105] The pages of spirit messages in the *Banner of Light* were particularly saturated with such communications in the early 1880s. The spirits of Silver Star, Star Flower, Sunbeam, Forest Flower, Snowdrop, Shining Star, Forest Lily, White Flower, and Snowball all manifested for similar reasons. Silver Star claimed that "inner vision [would] be opened."[106] Forest Flower said that "the Indians send their love; they bring the blanket of peace to wrap around the medy [the medium]."¹⁰⁷ They claimed that the Spiritualist mission to bring peace to living Indians was blessed, and urged them to be patient and not discouraged by slow or mixed results. "Do not falter by the way," Snowdrop communicated in 1881:

> But still feel that we are all with you, helping and strengthening ... You will not see anything very different from what you now have for some moons to come; then you will find changes working out slowly for you, which will open your way where there is broader work. Your usefulness will be increased, your powers will be strengthened, and your band will be able to do much more for the good of others; you will also receive that which you need yourself.¹⁰⁸

The spirit of Forest Lily said unequivocally in the same year, "we come because we love you: we bring you peace and strength, we guide you in life; and by-and-by we will take you over the river and give you greeting in our beautiful lodges in the hunting-grounds."¹⁰⁹ Such messages were entirely devoid of malice, resentment, or anger. They did not overtly underscore white guilt, but were instead largely focused on establishing a sympathetic and long-lasting relationship between living whites and Indian ghosts, upon which the efforts of white Indian activists could be built.

FIVE

RACE AND REFORM AMONG SPIRITUALISTS

INTRODUCTION

The previous chapters detailed how and why Indian ghosts appeared to nineteenth-century Spiritualists. This final installment will focus on how those manifestations affected Spiritualists' ideas about race, gender, and political reform. The presence of Indian ghosts during séances did not result in a unified Spiritualist position on the categorization of Indians, dead or otherwise, as civilized. Spiritualist literature of the late nineteenth century exhibited several schools of thought: that Indians were civilized on their own terms, possessing superior spirituality and morality; that Indians were capable of adapting to white civilization; that so-called savage Indians had been exposed to the hypocrisies and vices of white civilization and needed to be presented with better examples of white superiority; or that Indians were destined to exist only in the Happy Hunting Ground, with their limited time on earth coming to an end. Such concepts of racial difference reflected the contemporary ideas and debates about evolution, social progress, and scientific racism emergent in other expressions of nineteenth-century thought. As a result of their encounters with Indian ghosts, many Spiritualists became convinced of the hypocrisy of their supposedly superior nation. Spiritualist literature overwhelmingly suggested that, as members of a superior race, it was their duty to bring less civilized, less powerful races to their full human potential through honorable dealings. Their conception of a spiritual hierarchy, borne out of séance communications, favored individual progress rather than racial and sexual difference, and informed their support of Indian individualization as federal policy.

Spiritualists' contribution to the mission of racial peace was to publicly decry the immorality and dishonor of violence against Indians, especially when orchestrated by the federal government. Spiritualist periodicals such as the *Banner of Light*, as well as several monographs, consistently and sarcastically exposed the flaws of U.S. Indian policy in print. They pointed out the major instances of greed, dishonesty, murder, corruption, and victimization not only of Indian warriors, but of Indian women and children. A significant portion of Spiritualist journals were dedicated to this endeavor; more than seventy articles related to Indians, Indian warfare, and Indian policy reform were published by the *Banner of Light* in the 1860s. That number nearly doubled in the 1870s, when the Indian wars were most intense, decreasing again to over sixty articles in the 1880s. The purpose of these works, as expressed by the *Banner of Light*'s editors, was to keep Spiritualist readers abreast of the many confrontations between whites and Indians, as well as the struggles and triumphs of specific native tribes, including the Cherokee, Ponca, and Sioux nations. The words and actions of President Ulysses S. Grant, Congress, federal agents, and military personnel including John Chivington, William Sherman, Philip Sheridan, and George Custer, individual traders and settlers, and even the press of the Western border states were all carefully scrutinized and criticized for their unchristian behavior.

Spiritualists blamed several parties, claiming that the injustices toward American Indians perpetrated by the U.S. government and its citizens were the source of national shame. That shame undermined the masculine superiority and respect to which America laid claim. Assertions of national strength were undercut by Spiritualist depictions of violence against Indians as acts of baseness and cowardice. The egregious and ongoing scope of this problem became a dominant concern for Spiritualists, who expressed the belief that both the nation's permanent reputation and its spiritual future were at risk. The responsibility for the seemingly never-ending conflict was placed on white shoulders; acts of violence perpetrated by Indians on whites were commonly portrayed as either justifiable resistance or self-defense. Spiritualists supported their position through constant journal coverage of Indian wars and massacres, federal investigations of government corruption, and treaty violations.

In arguing the need for Indian policy reform, Spiritualists referenced the national effort to enfranchise African Americans. They asserted that the situation for American Indians was far worse than that of the newly freed blacks, because Indians were not in a position to help themselves or to voice their own wishes effectively to the U.S. government. The slave population had benefited from white advocacy for emancipation, Spiritualists argued; Indians had yet to experience significant white benevolence.

Spiritualists echoed the ghostly warnings of divine retribution with a sense of fear and urgency, deeming the correction of injustices a national priority. Through their many printed works on the subject, Spiritualists articulated their conviction that the spiritual and moral fate of the entire nation was wound up in Indian policy. They feared that a failure to correct wrongs against Indians would stunt the nation's progress, turning its claim of liberty and equality into a mockery, and shaming the so-called Christian nature of its citizens. Individual Americans risked unfavorable judgment in the afterlife, possibly doomed to interminable wandering in spiritual darkness. They did not, as Molly McGarry has suggested, create a safe, temporal distance between themselves and their Indian spirit guides.[1] Rather, the continuing disenfranchisement of native peoples was decried in their publications as a moral outrage that demanded immediate action. Furthermore, Spiritualists did not wash their hands of blame for Indian misfortunes, but instead took up their cause as a means to cleanse their own souls, and the collective soul of the nation.[2] They were not content to simply blame others, but called upon all Americans, even those in the highest echelons of the government, to join them in rectifying what they saw as the great hypocrisy of their country's founding principles.

As a result of their séance experiences, Spiritualist activists called for the end of warfare with Indians and supported policy reforms. Many championed bestowing Indians with the rights of American citizenship through severalty, combined with education programs aimed at assimilation; a very small and liberal contingency went so far as to suggest staying out of Indian lands and affairs entirely. One of the few points to achieve a general consensus was to deal with all Indian nations honestly; this could be ensured through the diligent media coverage of events in Indian country, which kept Americans conscious of the state of Indian affairs. Those writing for Spiritualist periodicals meant to keep living Indians present in American minds. They largely saw their goals achieved in the Dawes Severalty Act of 1887, which dissolved the tribes as legally recognized entities. After the passage of the Dawes Act, the work of Spiritualists was more or less complete.

Defining Spiritual Difference

By listening to the ghostly explanations of the hereafter, Spiritualists understood that the spiritual realm was not a unified celestial space, but rather was divided up into different spheres, each with its own characteristics. The progressive levels of enlightenment recognized in ghosts determined in which sphere they resided, and served as the basis for spiritual differentiation. Writing on this spiritual hierarchy in 1856, the Philadelphia pastor William Ramsey explained that "a spirit that is bad must enter one of these seven circles of the second sphere. Development and progression are the established order of the invisible world. Many of the spirits are so bad that it is a long time before they begin their progressive course upwards. But sooner or later this is the case."[3] Spiritualists acknowledged that not all ghosts were created equal. In asserting, as Ramsey did, that the spirit world operated according to the law of progression, Spiritualists confirmed a spectral order. Such a hierarchy was readily understood by people who lived in a society similarly structured upon difference. Yet the existence of separate spheres was not inherently linked to mortal categorization for all adherents; an 1860 *Banner of Light* article, for example, claimed that "the spiritual kingdom, although abounding in all you have in earth-life, you will find has no distinct localities for certain people to abide in. The spheres are certain degrees of development, certain states of happiness and unhappiness."[4]

Spiritual development was thus judged on an individual level, and did not strictly follow the rules of social categorization common to other areas of American life. Spiritualist experiences colored how Americans interpreted scientific racial concepts; the language and rhetoric of scientific racial discourse served to link the progression of civilization explicitly to race. It helped inform Spiritualists' interpretation of information from séances.[5] Spiritualists' acknowledgment of spirit realms opened up a new space of negotiation where Indians could, or in some cases already had, become superior to whites in certain aspects. These notions in turn affected how Spiritualists understood worldly racial difference and civilized progression. It contributed to their emphasis on education and civilization efforts for Indians as essential to progression. Spiritualists' understanding of a progressive cosmos strongly reflected theories of racial and social hierarchy set forth by Darwinism and eighteenth-century racial science, but their conceptualization of the spiritual order took on an ostensibly nonracial tone.[6] It was individual character, as evidenced by moral behavior, celestial education, and acts of guidance and forgiveness, that established one's position within the spheres. Such ideas about spectral differentiation and progression persisted; for example, in the 1903 monograph *Seers of the Ages*, the eminent Spiritualist Dr. J. M. Peebles described spirit life as "an active life, a social life, a retributive life, a constructive life, a progressive life."[7] In her book *Relations of Rescue*, Peggy Pascoe references the writings of Ruth Etnier, a member of the Women's National Indian Association, a political advocacy group with ties to Spiritualism. The association's publication *Indian's Friend* featured an article in which Etnier wrote, "I would beg that in the outset we eliminate the notion … that Indian girls differ fundamentally from the girls of any other race."[8] This was the core understanding of spiritual life and meaning for all spirits, regardless of their progressive pace. Advancement through celestial spheres was described by communicating entities as having upward momentum. The starting position of newly departed spirits was not universal, but rather depended upon the individual's mortal character. A 1918 monograph recorded a conversation in which the manifestations purportedly claimed that the first or lowest sphere "would seem to be the abode of people whose moral development was somewhat low when they pass from things terrestrial … the riff-raff of humanity."[9] Ghosts falling under this category were the closest to living human beings, and thus had the longest spiritual journey ahead of them. The frequency with which Indian ghosts consistently appeared in séances commonly lent itself to the conclusion that, as a group, Indian spirits generally resided in the lower spheres, and were counted among the lowest ranks of spiritual enlightenment. The explanation given in the 1922 work *Pictorial Spiritualism* for the frequent appearance of lower spirits in séances coincided closely with the purpose of Indian manifestations often expressed by the specters themselves:

> [T]he spirits from the darker spheres are often allowed to visit the Spiritualist circle, in order that they may obtain a knowledge of things which were denied them while on earth. Oftentimes they come honestly seeking for knowledge and for light … for them to develop and to outgrow the unhappy conditions acquired during their life on earth, seek[ing] earnestly to unfold into better conditions. They return frequently to the circle seeking more light, and in time they start on their pathway of eternal progression.[10]

Scores of Indian specters attested to this throughout the latter half of the nineteenth century—their own progression rested on forgiving whites their misdeeds and forging new peaceful relations.

But where exactly Indian ghosts as a distinct group fit into the spiritual hierarchy in concrete terms, and what that meant for the progressive abilities of living Indians by extension, was one of the many doctrines that Spiritualists as a body could not agree on. The clear-cut demarcation of a distinctly Indian heaven, or claims that the "happy hunting-ground," as it was called, was part of the lowest of celestial spheres, as described by Cox, was not supported by a unanimous agreement among Spiritualists.[11] In her book *Life and Labor in the Spirit World*, prominent Indian medium and sitting sensitive for the *Banner of Light* Mary T. Shelhamer argued for a "red man's hunting ground," in which tribal distinctions were erased, but where only Indians resided nonetheless.[12] As McGarry pointed out, Spiritualist discourse, taken as a whole, seemed to oscillate between civilization rhetoric and that of paternalism; on a smaller scale, such inconsistencies serve as an indicator of the lack of consensus among Spiritualists regarding questions of the civilization and political status of Indians.[13]

Throughout Spiritualist literature of the late nineteenth century, several major strains of thought emerged. First, that Indian spirituality, as whites perceived it, was a legitimate, respectable religion, and in practice, if not in theory, Indians possessed a higher moral faculty than their white counterparts. In 1857, the *Banner of Light*'s first year of publication, an article appeared within its pages entitled "Manifestations Among the Indians," which referenced several historical accounts of the supernatural abilities of American Indians, dating back as early as 1764. Relating an eyewitness account, the article detailed how a group of Indians at the Sault of St. Mary

> erected a strongly built wigwam [and] confused preternatural voices were heard, while the wigwam commenced shaking. The priest then claimed to receive revelations from the spirits respecting their English enemies. Many passages might be quoted from Cotton Mather and other writers concerning the customs and beliefs of the North American Indians to prove that they had, as they claimed to have, intercourse with spirits.[14]

Spiritualists would not have failed to recognize the parallels between Indian spirituality as described here and their own beliefs. The Indian ceremony referenced here produced, in broad terms, an outcome identical to that of séances—namely, spirit revelation, and in a manner similar to manifestations—through telekinetic activity. The title of the article itself additionally alludes to the similarities by couching the related events in the shared term *manifestations*. In 1867, the *Banner of Light* reviewed a text published in 1796 by explorer Captain Jonathan Carver, which described Indian lifestyles and religion and was presented to the journal's editors by Colonel Samuel Tappan. The reviewer praised the eighteenth-century work for demonstrating "the Indians' regard for truth a hundred years ago, the purity of their social life, their practical examples and religious principles, [that] towered infinitely above the Christianity of this century."[15] The work was briefly quoted, including references to the Indian belief in "a great *country of spirits*" and a practice "to *bring back* their *departed*" to deliberate in the proceedings held around their council fires."[16] Certain points were emphasized in this article to claim that Indians and Spiritualists shared a truth of the afterlife and its operations. Such descriptions simultaneously legitimized an Indian spirituality as witnessed by whites and the core tenets of the Spiritualist movement. An 1869 article in the *Religio-Philosophical Journal* explicitly praised Indian religion, drawing parallels between it and Spiritualism, believed by observers to be mimetical of the heavenly realms and thus the ultimate form of religion. The article claimed that a "high degree of spirituality has ever existed among the Red Man of the forest" and that "with the Indians, spirituality is largely developed, and in all their emotions they feel the presence of the Great Spirit."[17] The article also asserted that "among the Indians at the present day are many fine clairvoyants and mediums, and were it not for this fact, they would not be able to withstand the scourge of the white man to the extent they do."[18] Indian religion, as perceived by the article's author, was praiseworthy for its immersion in nature, and the absence of separation between man and god. Terms such as *clairvoyants* and *mediums* were used to establish a common bond between Indian spirituality and Spiritualism. Indian theology, in this imagined form, was legitimized as a religion; Spiritualism by extension was legitimized by its shared beliefs and practices. An 1873 article in the *Religio-Philosophical Journal* went so far as to say that "the mental ideas of a large number of people in America and England seemed to agree with those of the Indians as to the nature of the spirit world, for the germ of all modern Spiritualism of the day was entirely related to the notions of the American Indians."[19] An 1874 article that reprinted an address "to the Head Chief at the Indian Council" claimed that "the 'GREAT SPIRIT' whom [Indians] revere is the same as '*our*

Father which is in Heaven,' whom Christians worship."[20] Spiritualists of this position did not actively seek to distinguish themselves as separate from and therefore superior to nonwhite or premodern religions based on spirit communication. There are several notable instances to the contrary, in which Spiritualists describe non-Christian religions in parallel terms to their own theology and practice. For example, in an 1879 article in *Fraser's Magazine*, H. A. Giles, the British professor of Chinese responsible for the Wade-Giles Romanization system, described in detail the similarities he observed between Spiritualism and Chinese beliefs. Repeatedly and deliberately, he described Chinese religious practices using Spiritualist terminology. He argued that the word *planchette* was "a fair translation" of the word *chi,* making reference to a work published in the year 100 as a demonstration of China's long-established spiritualist inclinations.[21] He reports that the practice he refers to as planchette "is carried on in the full light of day," and that dark séances have been purportedly conducted in China as far back as 1679.[22] He describes in detail an instance of what he interprets as automatic writing:

> An attendant priest seized a bundle of gild joss-paper, and, casting a look round to see that all was ready, plunged it into a flame of a lamp burning upon the altar. Simultaneously the men who held the writing implement began to work it so that the vertically placed tip spread rapidly round and round in a circle of about a foot in diameter ... until at length the two men who were driving the pencil became suddenly possessed with the divine influence [and] rapidly traced a single Chinese word ... thus the *séance* progressed, until at length the secretary handed to me a perfect stanza of Chinese verse.[23]

The stanza produced begins with a statement of spiritual universality: "The pulse of human nature throbs from/England to Cathay."[24] This anecdote is punctuated by Giles's use of the term *séance* to describe the scene he witnessed, and his decision to emphasize that word to drive home his argument of parallel practice. He makes further connections between Spiritualism, Mesmerism, and Taoist possession. Under Giles's pen, these three philosophies are bound by their occult nature. He speaks of the Taoist ritual of "divine possession" as a form of mediumship. The priest, referred to as "medium" in his passage, undergoes "certain movements, apparently mesmeric passes, by which a state of unconsciousness is induced; whereupon the god takes possession of the temporarily unoccupied body. From that moment every word uttered by the medium is held to be divinely inspired."[25] He refers to "kang-fu" as also being occultish in nature, "rarely practiced in the present day, and then only in secret."[26] It is known in France, he says, as magnetism.

Louis Ebé Boclé, the author of the 1906 *Future Life; in the Light of Ancient Wisdom and Modern Science*, found it "scarcely necessary to draw attention to the very interesting analogy between these crude conceptions [of savage tribes] and the belief in ghosts and spirits still so common among Christian populations."[27] The religion of the Egyptians, he argues, is also grounded in "the notion of complexity in the immaterial portion of man."[28] Here Boclé connected Spiritualism to other religions. He did not, as Emma Hardinge Britten did in her writings, distance it from spiritual beliefs worldwide. Rather, he writes of Spiritualism as the most sophisticated form of religious concepts that have exhibited themselves all over the globe since the beginning of human civilization. The underlying commonality of the dual nature of the soul is presented here as a universal truth, revealed to Egyptians, Indians, and Spiritualists alike. Dr. Peebles, in *Seers of the Ages*, praised non-Christian religions as being closer to understanding the nature of heaven. "Even the ruder tribes of Earth," he says,

> less favored with the supports of civilization, instinctively entertain this truth [of immortal existence]. The poor Indian of America's wilds, child of fate falling before the *more* savage monopoly of his pale brother, is nature's diorama of immortal lights and shades from the spirit hunting-grounds ... Christians [with their] sighs, groanings, moanings, and mourning apparel—black fitting their condition—a church menagerie of sable show and brooding despair—absolutely shock the seers and sages of India, Greece, Rome, the millions of present Spiritualists, and even the North American Indians.[29]

Peebles's use of the word *even* is interesting. He speaks of Spiritualists collectively with global spiritualisms, including native spiritualism, yet he singles them out as being perhaps less respectable than the other traditions he mentions who are largely of Western, if not Christian, origins. Maybe the point of this linguistic choice is to demonstrate the supreme lack of illumination from which Christianity allegedly suffers. Juxtaposed in such a fashion to the poorly respected beliefs of Indians, Christianity is described in a dismal spiritual state. Spiritualism then, by contrast, is theologically superior by way of its self-professed inclusion in the spiritual tradition of the world, broadly defined.

This strain of religious liberalism was not a sufficient element of the Spiritualist movement to affect change in Indian policy regarding religion; however, along with the federal categorization of Indians as wards came the prohibition of native religious practices. The majority of Spiritualists did not object.[30]

A more common understanding of the place of Indians in the spirit world was one where their position was in flux. In the 1870 book *The Revelator*, the boundaries between the celestial spheres were described as fluid. Pierce claimed that "in each circle they had teachers from higher spheres, who come to instruct them and assist them to progress."[31] This kind of thinking resisted the notion that Indian spirits were largely capable of communicating with Earth because they originated in the lower spheres; it was possible for enlightened spirits to travel to lower spheres for the express purpose of communication and education, which was the professed purpose of the majority of Indian spirits. Talking about Indian spirits specifically, Pierce alleged in 1870 that there were a number of Indians living in the fourth circle of the sixth sphere, a relatively high position. "Here the Indians have a portion on one side of the river bank, where they have pretty lodges. Luna, an Indian girl, and Pocahontas, and others are here happy and joyous, all commingling together by the purity of spirit in the love of God."[32] According to Pierce, William Penn, Roger Williams, and John Milton were also residents of this circle, teaching at colleges "preparing teachers to come to earth to teach."[33] The mention of such figures by name demonstrated the prestige of this circle, making the explicit mention of Indian ghosts such as Pocahontas as their neighbors all the more noticeable.

Spiritualists largely expressed the opinion that Indians were in fact capable of adapting to white civilization, a position that supported federally funded efforts toward that end. As early as 1859, articles appeared in the *Banner of Light* that claimed "that the Indians are capable of advancement, we have the most abundant proof in the highest attainments which many individuals among them have made, and in the fact that some entire tribes are proving themselves equal to their pale-faced neighbors in the various vocations of civilized life."[34] Throughout the late nineteenth century, the achievements of several specific tribes toward civilization would be upheld by Spiritualist publications as shining examples of the capability of all Indian peoples to become civilized. In 1870 the *Banner of Light* described the Utes as

> peaceable, and manifest a desire to cultivate the advantages of civilization, among which is education. They desire their children may

be taught, and already have schoolhouses for that purpose. The Utes are well provided for by the Government, and, as a consequence, are contented, and will make no trouble if let alone.³⁵

This last point was included to persuade readers that the circumstances of the Utes might also be a desirable approach for other native nations. Reprinting a letter from Secretary of the Interior Judge Jones in 1872 about the progressive strides of the Chippewas, including improvements in housing and agriculture, the editors of the *Banner of Light*, listed as William White, Luther Colby, and Isaac Rich of William White & Company, declared that "it is a source of supreme pleasure to us to make public all records of actual improvement among the Indians, wrought through the agency of the Government in the fulfillment of its solemn stipulations."³⁶

The most notable of such examples was that of the Cherokees. During the 1820s and 1830s, the Cherokee nation made one of the strongest noted efforts at accommodation. In the 1867 article "Intelligence of the Indian," inventor of the Cherokee alphabet Sequoia, spelled in the article as "See-quah-yah," was lauded for his linguistic achievements: "The following account of the invention of the Cherokee alphabet proves how false is the assertion that the Indian is fit for nothing but extermination."³⁷ Sequoia's alphabet made almost the entire Cherokee nation literate practically overnight, a quality held as one of the cornerstones of "civilization." Cherokee literacy received continual praise by Spiritualists; in 1870 the *Banner of Light* published another article entitled "The Cherokee Advocate," stating that the Cherokee publication of the same name "appears in both the English and Cherokee languages, and is devoted to the advocacy of Indian rights ... [I]t is also the object of its publishers to 'give to its subscribers living in the States all news of interest ... of the civilized nations of the Territory, and a description of the country which they inhabit and *own*.' "³⁸ The Cherokees professed themselves to be civilized in their own publication. Their work was presented as being of interest to the *Banner of Light* readers, who saw the Cherokees as a successful example of Indian civilization, and a model to be followed. In 1871 the *Banner of Light* again upheld the *Cherokee Advocate* as "itself an evidence of the capability of civilization on the part of the Indian, if time and opportunity be given him."³⁹ In 1872, the Cherokee Colonel Boudinot was recognized by the *Banner of Light* as "a highly intelligent, well-educated Indian, to be heard in an argument favoring the granting of civil rights to the Indians with whom he is associated. He represents that his people are civilized ... they are a prosperous people, generally engaged in agricultural and mechanical pursuits."[40] Literacy and education were held in the highest regard; the presence of those qualities in American Indians served as the ultimate proof of their capabilities; as a result, Spiritualists and other advocates of the civilization project centered their efforts around Indian education. In 1877, the *Banner of Light* article "Indian Civilization" reported that "the Cherokees, Creeks, Choctaws, Chickasaws and Seminoles, without any outside assistance whatever, have 169 schools, 189 teachers, and 4400 scholars. Does this not plainly mean civilization?"[41] In 1878, the intellectual abilities of certain Indian individuals were described as excelling those of whites; the author of "The Indian Territory" claimed that "some of the head men of the Chickasaws, Choctaws, and Creeks are highly educated, graduates of collegiate institutions, and much better equipped for the duties and responsibilities of self-government than the average white man."[42]

Spiritualists looked with interest upon educational endeavors from within Indian country, as well as those where white Americans were more explicitly involved. The two largest educational institutions to gain Spiritualist attention in this regard were the Hampton and Carlisle Institutes. Richard Pratt, head of the Carlisle Institute, was one of many Indian reformers who believed their salvation lay not in their extinction or their removal from white society, but rather by their immersion in it and their ceasing to be outwardly Indian. He, like many Spiritualists, claimed to believe that the erasure of racial distinction, of racial Indianness, would put an end to Indian predation.[43] In 1880, the *Banner of Light* published an article titled "Education for the Indians," which recounted the results of a meeting held in the Central Church of Boston. There, General Armstrong brought twenty-five Indian pupils from the Hampton Institute and "spoke very encouragingly of the efforts to educate the Indians. They make good progress in their studies, and seem bound to disappoint those who prophesy that they will return to their wigwams, and that their education will be thrown away."[44] An 1884 article, "The Indian School at Carlisle," claimed that "no better illustration exists of the capabilities of the Indians, and of what they may become if rightly dealt with and properly educated, than of the School for Indian Pupils at Carlisle, P.A."[45] The article gave a short history of the Carlisle Institute, and went on to enumerate the work accomplished by the students. These included the publication of the journal *The Morning Star*, apprenticeships in carpentry and wagon making, and the construction of a hospital by the male students. Their clothing was produced by the female students, engaged primarily in laundering and housecleaning.[46] The transformation of Indian children into "disciplined workers" was described by Hayes Mauro as one of the primary goals of the Carlisle school's curriculum.[47] Another article in the same year explained that the daily instruction at Carlisle was divided equally between study and work.[48]

A third, yet somewhat quieter sentiment also emerged in Spiritualist print, claiming that Indians were, in fact, doomed to vanish, their rightful and permanent place being the Happy Hunting Grounds of the celestial spheres. For example, an 1863 *Banner of Light* article, "The Death of an Indian Chief," retells the peaceful intentions of the recently late Iowa chief Yellow Wolf. The anonymous author criticized the supposed success of Indian civilization. Allegedly echoing the words of Yellow Wolf's interpreter, he wrote that "this living in houses and remaining so long in one place, is having a deplorable effect upon all the Indians here—and if not soon returned to their native prairies, they will all die. Like an eagle in a cage, or a salmon in a mill pond, they cannot bear the heated air of civilization."[49] Described as part of nature, Indians must naturally recede along with it in the face of civilization, according to this source. In 1868, the *Banner of Light* reprinted an article from the *Religio-Philosophical Journal* prefaced by the editors as "well written" and "all true" that stated:

> The destiny of the Indians is known. Fading away is written on their leafy homes ... the present foreshadows no bright future on earth ... but after they pass over the shining river, to their beautiful spirit homes, all they can desire—and with their pure magnetism, sparkling with health and vitality, they return to earth to benefit those who have been instrumental in causing them so much trouble. Beautiful is their mission in the spirit-world![50]

Acknowledging Indian Ghosts

Spiritualists' ideas about race and their racial politics were most strongly expressed through their declarations that it was the responsibility of all whites to assist in the civilization of "lesser" races and to deal honorably with less powerful nations. The latter part of this was especially true for American Indians, considering that it was from them that Americans had stolen the continent. Indian activists refuted the myth of vanishing. The attention Spiritualist publications gave to the dire circumstances of living Indians was intended to keep Indians present in the minds of their readers, resisting the urge to condemn all thoughts of them to the unchangeable past. In 1859, only two years into the *Banner of Light*'s fifty-year publication record, it published an article titled "An Address to the People of the United States in behalf of the Indians" that claimed:

> It is no satisfaction to the human and Christian mind to say, that these people are destined to PERISH, and that, therefore, we may leave them to their fate. For it is felt that, as a nation, we are responsible to-day for the sympathy and protection which they need to-day, irrespective of what may be their circumstances tomorrow … We are, therefore, bound by respect which we owe to ourselves—to the age— and to posterity, to transmit, not mere relics and records of a race extinct, but a living, thriving community of the people from whom we have derived a continent.[51]

Language like this explicitly denied the inevitability of Indian vanishing. By 1862, the actions of Methodist minister John Beeson on behalf of Indians were well known and supported in Spiritualist circles. A *Banner of Light* article reporting on resolutions made at a public meeting held at the New York Cooper Institute in 1862 claimed that "Father Beeson's movement in behalf of the Indian tribes in the United States is a laudable one, and should meet with the cooperation of every true man in the country."[52]

Gail Bederman argued that in the latter half of the nineteenth century manly power, racial supremacy, and civilization were all interconnected.[53] At this early stage of Spiritualism's lifespan, definitions of manhood as linked to peaceful Indian relations had begun to exhibit itself. Nineteenth-century reformers who understood such connections between these concepts recognized the added importance of demonstrating an Indian capacity for civilization. It legitimated Indian men as men, worthy of political power. At the same time, it impugned the moral virtue and manliness of Americans who favored violence as an answer to the Indian question. Spiritualists saw themselves as occupying a distinct position from which they could make such determinations about the manliness, civilization, and moral honor of Indians and Americans. In October 1862 another *Banner of Light* article, "Spiritualists and the Indians," encapsulated

> the reasons why the Spiritualists should, as a body, make a special effort in behalf of the Indians: 1st. Spiritualism gives a better idea of the

condition and of the capacity of the Indian, and of the proper means for his improvement, than the teachings of any of the churches. 2nd. The Indians being the elder brethren of Spiritualists in a common faith, and having done so much by their magnetism in healing the sick, and developing mediums, have a first claim on the sympathy of all in their ranks. 3rd. The Indians have been the longest sinned against by our people.[54]

This perfectly succinct rationale for acting on the part of Indians drew intimate connections between both living Indians and Indian ghosts, and Indian religions and Spiritualism itself. Encounters with Indian specters were here declared to have given Spiritualists a clearer image of Indians and an appropriate federal policy regarding them. There was no distinction made between noble spirits of the past returning to séance tables and their degenerated living descendants, as McGarry suggested, and no removal of Indians from the conscious mind through their ghostly metamorphosis as Farmer suggested.[55] By definition, ghosts are not vanished—they are remainders that have returned. The author also claimed communion between Spiritualists and Indians on the basis of religion. Spiritualism, according to this article, was not an entirely new or insular religion. It was connected to the spiritualisms of other peoples and other ages, claiming to be modern only by the introduction of scientific approaches to prove religious truths. In an 1886 issue of *The Medium and Daybreak*, for example, Andrew Lang's work on "Myths and Mythologists" is cited for defining "savage religion" as "consisting of a belief in ghosts, and magic exercised through prayer; and accompanying this he is 'probably, in certain moods, conscious of a far higher moral faith' … indicated by the ghost philosophy, which is not a mere 'belief' of the savage, but an actual experience."[56] Here non-Christian religions are legitimized. They are interpreted as being a misreading of Spiritualist principles otherwise labeled as universal revelation. He does not criticize "savage" religion; he points out what he sees as an intellectual fault. He reasons:

> It has been proved that horses, dogs, and other animals can see "ghosts," invisible beings, at the same time that mankind in the highest state of moral development have also seen these supernatural phenomena. But the "aura" or "magnetic sphere" of objects, growing and living things can also be seen; and the savage not understanding the meaning of his experiences, attaches attributes to objects, which being

untenable, discredit the experiences which led to them. Clairvoyance is a widely-diffused faculty of savage life.[57]

In this passage, savage intuits are likened to animals that have an allegedly supernatural sense, but do not possess the means to properly interpret it. And yet, the term *clairvoyance* is used to create commonality between "savage" and Spiritualist abilities. Further, the reference to clairvoyance among the "uncivilized" serves to demonstrate their elevated talent for it. Those who can *see* ghosts, he argues, comes from the "highest state of moral development." That is separate, here, from the cognitive ability to interpret experience. In another article of the same issue, Mr. E. W. Wallis writes of Spiritualist truths in

the divining cup, black and white magic, the fascination of the evil eye of olden time, and what was related in connection with witchcraft ... evidence of a modern form of belief in clairvoyance, but that the idea of it, and the practice of it, yea, and even the evidence of it was ancient; and further than this, there was a philosophy with respect to the matter which was by no means modern, and which dated back to times antedating the Christian era.[58]

Wallace uses the terms *ancient* and *modern* interchangeably to refer to clairvoyance of generations past around the world, rendering such labels meaningless. Spiritualism, which some adherents argued was unique in its modern, scientific approach to questions of the soul, is in this passage unique compared to denominational criticism. No discernible difference is described between contemporary Spiritualism and spiritualist traditions of other ages. By building connections to other systems whose beliefs and practices are more grounded in the material world, this sort of logic instead attempted to pull Spiritualism out of a wholly Christian, faith-based context, and establish its legitimacy through its association to these well-established traditions.

Spiritualists utilized their position on Indian policy to further legitimize their own religion. They assumed a place of moral superiority by exposing and openly criticizing the hypocritical actions of their largely Christian nation against American Indian tribes. Most Spiritualists had Christian backgrounds, and continued to identify as Christians throughout their involvement in the Spiritualist movement. But many of their printed materials reflected a desire to legitimize Spiritualism to skeptical Christians. Their encounters with Indian ghosts, who had in their own ways laid claim to spiritual and moral superiority, bestowed that superiority onto their Spiritualist audiences. Spiritualist activists saw their cause as originating in the higher spheres, providing them with a pedestal of universal illumination from which they could criticize the hypocrisy of their own nation's character and policies.

Throughout the *Banner of Light's* lifetime, more than a dozen articles appeared criticizing the unjust treatment of Indians by a self-proclaimed Christian nation. One 1859 article stated that "when men claiming a Christian civilization, and calling themselves American citizens, can thus glory in their shame, it is time to stop speaking of the Indians as 'the savages.'"[59] The virtues connoted by both the terms *men* as honorable and *Americans* as protectors of freedom were called into question here. The 1867 article "Lo! The Poor Indian" exclaimed that "our Saxon face is mantled with shame and soul-humbled in deepest humiliation at the individual and associate crimes that blot the escutcheon of this great, wicked Christian country called United States of America," and arguing that the messages of peace brought by the ghosts of "Powhatan, Red Jacket, Tecumseh, Logan, Little Crow, Antelope, and all Indian spirits" should be observed as an example of justice.[60] In 1868, an article commented boldly on a piece in the *Jamestown Journal* referring to Indians as big game, to be hunted along with buffaloes and bears. It decried such activities as "a common Christian sport in this Christian nation!" going on to claim that "these Indians, that white men 'hunt,' are God's children. They have inalienable rights and immortal souls."[61] In November 1868, the *Banner of Light* reported on a speech that Wendell Phillips gave regarding the Sand Creek Massacre of 1864. He had called the military personnel involved "men, whose mothers baptized them in the name of Christ, [and who] did this deed of infamy, cowardice, and shame!"[62] Both the manhood and the Christian character of these individuals, and the country they were meant to represent, were again under fire. In October 1869, a brief report on a telegraph about tensions with the Montana Indians reiterated the sentiment common to border territories. It stated that "the Indians must be annihilated, we need their lands, and the quicker we wipe them out the better," ending with the comment "what a sad comment on civilization—*Christian* civilization, too!"[63]

Attacks on Christian hypocrisy in America continued into the 1870s. Speaking of tensions with the Modocs, an article appearing in the *Banner of Light* column dedicated to "the West." It opined that "the wicked always abound where Christianity is the ruling religion—so there is no hope for the 'poor Indian' until rational and spiritual religion succeeds in our Government and its policy."⁶⁴ Such an open and explicit rivalry between Christianity and Spiritualism was rare to find in print. Speaking again of hostilities toward the Modocs in the following month, an article titled "Cause of Indian Wars" claimed that "the weakest [in this case, the Modocs] invariably go to the wall, according to the working of our modern Christian civilization."⁶⁵ In a lengthy article appearing in 1879 titled "the Ponca Indians: Meeting in Boston for the discussion of their wrongs and the best method of righting them," Major General Sheridan was condemned for stating his desire to "annihilate the race," described with passion as *the advice he gives to fifty millions of Christian people, with all the resources of civilization, and religion, and art, and wealth, and the inheritance of so many generations of culture, in dealing with the poor, ignorant, dependent, half-civilized, wandering and fragmentary tribes!*⁶⁶ Granted, this tirade does a great disservice to the merit of Indian peoples and cultures—yet the author's supreme goal in comparing the two lifestyles was to demonstrate that, if the gap between Indians and whites was as wide as believed, then reason and "civilization" should have dictated a more generous and benevolent approach to those appearing so obviously and abysmally inferior.

That superiority, which Spiritualists did not wholeheartedly deny, had been abused, in their eyes, leading to such atrocities as the Sand Creek Massacre. In October 1879, a reporter for the *Daily Tribune* of Denver was personally attacked in the *Banner of Light* for authoring an article that suggested that "*the lesson of Sand Creek must be retaught* [and] *the single and effective way to settle the Indian question is to turn it over to the jurisdiction of a Winchester rifle.*"⁶⁷ The *Banner of Light* author responded that "this frantic appeal that the barbarous massacre of Sand Creek may be repeated is worthy of a fiend, although we presume the writer of it calls himself *a Christian*!"⁶⁸ Such vehement expressions continued into the 1880s, when Indian injustice was described as "diabolical" in a *Banner of Light* article that said, "The one excuse generally offered … is the singular one of advancing civilization basing itself upon Christian principles. *Then Christianity has nothing better to rest itself upon than simple greed, taking the name of necessity*! If that is Christianity, let us hasten to have nothing to do with it."⁶⁹ The strong feelings of disgust with Christian Americans surfaced among the most outspoken factions of Indian activists within the Spiritualist movement; they used the issue of Indian policy as a major platform from which to compete with the religious dominance of Christian institutions and to combat criticism of Spiritualism as a delusional, superstitious, regressive, or otherwise illegitimate religion.

Attacks against Christian hypocrisy in America also took a more specific form, pointing to the most common sins committed by Americans against Indians—namely, greed, dishonesty, murder, corruption, and the victimization of Indian women and children as well as men. As David Adams pointed out in his study of the Indian boarding school system, by the early 1880s the image of the corrupt Indian agent was a permanent fixture in the American consciousness.[70] For Spiritualists, such a character represented the very worst side of Americans. Such misdeeds were traditionally recognized as the cause of a haunting, and were cited by Spiritualists specifically as instigating the return of Indians to the séance table. Spiritualists revisited and publicized the racial violence that Amy Greenberg wrote was obscured by the unifying concept of Manifest Destiny in the first half of the nineteenth century.[71] In other words, Spiritualists actively acknowledged the haunted return of Indians by making Indian peoples, both alive and dead, more highly visible to the American press. The manifestations of Indian apparitions did not simply act as an abstract form of removal, as Farmer suggested of the large presence of Indian ghosts in early American literature.[72] The purpose of ghosts, in both a literary and a Spiritualist sense, was to force recognition of wrongs committed through their return, rather than encourage the act of vanishing through forgetting. They were not completely gone; some essential element of their existence, which constitutes the "ghost," remained.

Likewise, Indians did not disappear from the American consciousness upon the arrival of Indian spirits at séances; Indians and the political issues attendant upon them lingered. Spiritualists attempted to fulfill the wishes of their ghostly friends by making pointed claims of Indian injustice, facilitated by the close eye that Spiritualists kept on Indian-related events. The greed of white traders and agents was offered up by Spiritualists as one of the major causes of war with Indian tribes. In the 1860s, the *Banner of Light* published several articles detailing white avarice. In 1867, the U.S. government's Indian policy was criticized for affording "dishonest white men opportunities to enrich themselves *at the expense of the red men*; and when any of the latter, in turn, have ventured to take the matter of redress into their own hands, the result has been a wholesale slaughter."[73] Another article summarizing the reports of the commissioners of Indian affairs for the years 1863–65 touted the reports as proof that these red forest brethren of ours, naturally proud and noble—the original proprietors of this country, have been forcibly, or fraudulently, driven from lands previously granted; deprived of their annuities; demoralized by poison whiskey; deceived by unprincipled traders, and swindled by agents.[74]

Detailing the removal of the Osage Indians and white encroachment in 1869, described as "the usual result" of relying on "the honor of white men" and a legalized robbery, one writer for the *Boston Daily Advertiser* was quoted in the *Banner of Light* as saying that "we do not think of any earthly punishment [as] quite good enough for the greedy squatters."[75] In praising President Grant's peace policy in 1872—which created the Board of Indian Commissioners to oversee Indian affairs, attempted to weed out white corruption, expanded federal funding for Indian education, and called for reservations to be managed by Christian-minded personnel—the *Banner of Light* observed the shift of opinion in other national journals, and declared that "the cheat and plunder, drive and kill policy is evidently going out ... which means that the Indians are beginning to be dealt with in a spirit of justice and humanity."[76] Upon hearing of the discovery of gold and subsequent invasion of the Black Hills of Sioux territory, sacred and protected by the Fort Laramie Treaty of 1868, a *Banner of Light* article lamented that "it is the love of money that precipitates these Indian wars and massacres in any case."[77]

Spiritualists also charged Americans with dishonesty, highlighting the countless violations of the U.S. treaties with Indian nations. In the 1877 article "Indian Policy," the system of entering into treaties with Indians was deemed "absurd," since it seemed that "as white settlements increased treaties were made to be broken."[78] Expeditions into the Black Hills became the target of similar arguments. In 1878, the article "Sheridan's Report," pulling information from his history of aggression in the region, claimed that the war with the Sioux "grew out of nothing but the emigration of whites into the Black Hills region contrary to the distinct terms of the treaty with them."[79] Speaking regrettably about the future, the article continued that "there are still more Indian wars to come, and they are of our own seeking."[80] Another article decrying the invasion of the Black Hills in 1880 asserted that "the history of the world, civilized and barbarian, does not afford more palpable and monstrous instances of bad faith than may be found in the record of dealings of the American nation, which claims to be Christian, with the red men of the country."[81]

Race and Reform Among Spiritualists

These outrages were exacerbated by the many investigations into Indian territories that uncovered rampant corruption among U.S. government agents. In 1867, the *Banner of Light* lauded the work of John Beeson in this field. Spiritualist editorialists proclaimed that his work "brings to light a mass of corrupt dealing, fraud, treachery, lying and deceit, practiced upon the Indians by the overpaid agents of the Government, that ought to put a civilized nation to shame and confusion."[82] Such reporting in the *Banner of Light* continued for several decades, making liberal use of previously published letters and reports to detail the injustices forced upon Indians. For example, an 1868 article described

> a published letter written by the Right Reverend Bishop Whipple, whose residence is near the scene of disaster in Minnesota, that [claimed that] four years ago the Sioux sold the Government one hundred thousand acres of land, and of $96,000 due to the Lower Sioux, they have never received a cent … Hundreds of them waited two months past the time for their annual payment, until famished and maddened by hunger, and while in this extremity … then came the horrors for which Senator Wilkinson affirms "that there was no cause."[83]

In the same year, Spiritualists protested the proposal to transfer the management of Indian affairs from the Department of the Interior to the War Department, objecting that it would mean "slaughter and rapine; fire and murder; war and famine; fat army contracts; frauds and swindles."[84] In 1870, further details of "How the Indians are Swindled" were published by the *Banner of Light*, taken from a report to Secretary of Interior Columbus Delano, compiled by William Welsh, a Philadelphia man and member of the Indian Peace Commission. The excerpt chronicled the inflation of prices for items such as flour, wheat, and cattle, calculating that "a few adroit manipulators of contracts and purchases have made at least $250,000 this year from supplies to the Indians of the Missouri river alone."[85] Welsh provided examples of sacks of flour sold at Sioux City for $3.50 when the price "ought to have been $2."[86] In 1874, a further proof of government corruption presented itself to *Banner of Light* readers that alleged that the previous winter,

> General Shanks, of the Indian Committee of the House of Representatives, made a very full and detailed report on Indian affairs to the House, which was ordered by that body to be printed … It was

well known to be full of facts of the most damaging character for the tricky agents who have the traffic with the tribes in their control, hence the natural desire to secure its suppression. Of course, the [congressional] recess furnished the very opportunity required to effect that object, and it was done. No trace can be discovered of the Report, or of the agency by which it so mysteriously disappeared.[87]

In 1875, paleontology professor Othniel Marsh of Yale College visited the Red Cloud agency to investigate its management, and subsequently wrote to President Grant of his findings. His letter was reprinted by the *Banner of Light*, telling of the inferior, and in some cases unusable quality of essentials such as beef, pork, sugar, coffee, tobacco, and flour distributed to Red Cloud's people. Marsh was further cited for his lack of confidence in a favorable response from Secretary Delano or Commissioner of Indian Affairs John Smith, since they were both explicitly incriminated in his report.

Corruption continued to run rampant in Indian country, even throughout the initially praised peace policy set in motion by Grant. The continual uncovering of scandalous activity within the Indian bureaucracy discouraged Spiritualists who had hoped Grant's policy would lead to a brighter Indian future. As a result, they were forced to seek alternative methods to achieve a lasting peace between whites and Indians. Spiritualists had become firmly convinced of an existence of an "Indian ring," a large group of powerful individuals who frequently and successfully conspired to enrich themselves by disenfranchising Indian peoples. One of the core goals of Spiritual activism on behalf of Indians was to root out corrupt officials, whose actions threatened constant warfare with American Indians and a mounting spiritual debt.

The most serious charge that Spiritualists leveled against the American government and its people was murder—of Indian men, women, and children. In the context of such critiques, living Indian men did not retain the manhood that their ghostly counterparts had asserted during their manifestations. They were effeminate in their portrayal as simpleminded, unable to protect their own families. They had been forcibly emasculated by their victimization alongside their wives and children. The honor of white men was impugned in these passages, as they not only engaged in disgraceful warfare against the seemingly inferior forces of Indian warriors, but were also painted as butchers of Indian families. In 1863, the *Banner of Light* responded to a letter printed by John Beeson on an earlier page of the same issue, arguing the rights of Indians and the need for white action. The article states that "the Indian is a man, and should, in his present weak condition, be protected in his rights by the strong arm of the General Government."[88] In 1874, the *Banner of Light* article "Call for a Public Meeting in Behalf of Indians" maintained that "when aggressive whites seek to rob the red man of his last refuge, and when the starving Indian is driven by thieving speculators to take the war path for food for himself and his little ones, it is all important that the true state of the case should be explained to the public."[89] Later on in the article, Commissioner of Indian Affairs John Smith was quoted as testifying that the previous August, "*twenty-five men* [of the Kansas militia] *completely armed, attacked eighteen unarmed friendly* [Osage] *Indians, with women and children, and killed four of them.*"[90] In this article, Indian men were depicted not as warriors, but as fathers who had failed in their masculine duties. They were unable to provide for or protect their families.

A similar claim of the victimization of Indian males was made in an 1879 article titled "More White Man Rascality." The story was that nine Indians were killed crossing the U.S. border in pursuit of buffalo. "These Indians," the article expounded,

> were not on the "war path," but simply out to provide food for themselves and families, and were ruthlessly attacked because, forsooth, they had "crossed the line"! If this isn't wanton murder under false pretences, we should like to know what it is? How long will this professedly *Christian* government allow such outrages?[91]

Such expressions suggest that, for Spiritualists, Indian men were unjustly emasculated by the actions of white men. The manhood of white men was also thrown in jeopardy by such reports, especially those that included Indian women and children among the casualties. In 1860, the *Banner of Light* recorded the "wholesale butchery of Indians at Humboldt Bay," saying that "what adds to the enormity of the defense [is that] the victims were nearly, or quite all women and children!"[92] Speaking of the Plains tribes in 1866, the article "The Abused Red Men" employed similar language to describe a group of sixteen Indians "butchered by white men in cold blood, fourteen of the victims being women and children! This is a black disgrace to our national name."[93] An 1867 article asserted that Americans increasingly "do know that many a base massacre, under the orders of United States officers, has been visited upon the defenceless women and children of the Indians; in one instance, certainly when the male Indians were off in the performance of a signal service for our own troops."[94] The 1867 article "Lo! The Poor Indian!" went so far as to accuse white soldiers of raping Indian women.[95] Wendell Phillips argued in 1868 that the Sand Creek Massacre, of which Minnie Tappan was a survivor, was "a most infamous atrocity."[96]

Such accounts continued to appear in the *Banner of Light* throughout the paper's run; in 1884, an article about "Destitute and Starving Indians" depicted women and children of the Poplar Creek and Wolf Point Agencies as "gaunt and hollow-eyed," with the men, "strong and vigorous a few months ago, now so reduced by hunger as to be scarcely able to walk."[97] To sympathetic Spiritualists, such actions deprived the nation and its citizens of the right to call themselves honorable. The definition of true and respectable manhood, historically related to the conquest of Indians in America, was turned on its head in the Spiritualist mind. The manhood Spiritualists valued and advocated for the future required a new, amiable approach to Indian nations that extended the role of white men as protectors.

The relationship between manhood and military victory was muddled by the questions that Spiritualists raised about the nature of military campaigns against Indian nations. They paid close attention to the depiction of campaigns in general presses, and the use of words such as "massacre" and "war." In 1862, the integrity of news about Indian violence against whites was questioned in a *Herald of Progress* article about an outbreak in Minnesota. The author wrote, "It is reported that forty-five families had, all but two persons, been killed at Lake Shitik … but these reports are undoubtedly exaggerated."[98] An 1867 *Banner of Light* article questioned the use of the word *massacre* as related to the events at Fort Phil Kearney in Wyoming during Red Cloud's War. In the same year the *Banner of Light* published two additional articles calling the use of the word *massacre* into question, asserting that "every time there is a rumor of an Indian attack anywhere, it is telegraphed East as a fact; but when, a few hours later, it proves to be entirely untrue, the telegraph does not carry the correction."[99] The preceding article's title and the negative stereotypes of savage Indians that they perpetuated suggested that "Indian Outrages," which for many Americans justified their military position in the West, were manufactured by either hateful individuals or those who stood to profit from Indian warfare. Intentional misreporting, the *Banner of Light* claimed, "has its due effect in fanning the hatred so prevalent against the red man," and was deemed counterproductive to Spiritualists' political aims.[100] A month after General George Custer was killed at the Little Bighorn River in 1876, the *Banner of Light* published a letter from Wendell Phillips to the editor of the *Boston Transcript* that lamented:

> What kind of a war is it, where if we kill the enemy, it is *death*; if he kills us, it is *massacre*? ... The general use of this abusive term betrays the unfairness of the American press ... [T]here really was, in 1868, a "Custer massacre," when General Custer—a disgrace to his uniform and the flag he bore—attacked a peaceful Cheyenne village near Fort Cobb [and shot] down scores of women half asleep, and of unarmed, peaceful men.[101]

These were incredibly strong words, considering the freshness of Custer's death, which became for many of Americans the justification for future hostilities, including those at Wounded Knee in December 1890. This assault on Custer's character was confirmed in the *Banner of Light* in 1877 when the ghost of the general himself appeared at a séance, declaring that he was surrounded by hordes of Indian specters in the spirit-land, and was gravely mistaken in his ideas and actions toward Indians while living.[102] The Spiritualist publication the *Banner of Light* openly and repeatedly touted the importance of the press in the formation of the American consciousness, and thus the importance of its own endeavors to set the record on Indians straight. As John Coward stated about the Eastern press, the Spiritualist press, through major journals such as the *Banner of Light*, played a crucial role in Indian reform by providing a forum in which Indian activists could publicize American abuses of Indians and reach an increasingly sympathetic audience.[103]

The expression of similar sentiments about the origins and depictions of war continued late into the century; in 1879, a report of violence at the Red Cloud Agency was described by the *Banner of Light* as coming "from *white* sources, but the half has not been told."[104] Spiritualists continued to doubt the veracity of reports that painted Indians as bloodthirsty savages—everything they had come to believe about Indians through their communications with ghosts contradicted that narrative. This semantic battle that Spiritualists waged cast further doubt on the justification of warfare.

When Spiritualists did acknowledge instances of Indian violence against whites, it was couched in mitigating language; violent resistance was generally justifiable under the circumstances, according to Spiritualists, and in many cases they claimed Indians were first provoked to combat by white vice. In 1864, an article calling for Indian aid by a F. L. Hildreth likened the

Indians to the American revolutionaries, who "fl[u]ng back the English when they would invade our sacred rights and liberties."¹⁰⁵ Referencing hostilities in the Black Hills region in 1876, in the *Banner of Light* quoted the *Boston Post*. An article therein had acknowledged that "the Indians bear themselves wildly and blindly, but they have as good a right to defend their soil as they could have were they as white as milk."¹⁰⁶ As late as 1890, Spiritualist sources identified Americans as intruders and the Indians as defenders. In the 1862 work *Atomic Consciousness*, author James Bathurst acknowledged the poetic justice of the fact that the Plains tribe responsible for General Custer's death were the same people whose protected rights he violated by entering the Black Hills.¹⁰⁷ To the sympathetic Spiritualist mind, the majority of the "endless wars" with the Indians were provoked—by the greed of settlers and traders, the dishonesty of government agents, and the seeming inability or unwillingness of the federal government to honor its promises to Indian peoples.¹⁰⁸ The pre-contact Indian, "when discovered by the white man, was a peace-loving man."¹⁰⁹ He would, Spiritualists argued, continue to be peaceful if whites could only restrain themselves from incurring their anger and justifiable outrage. In the earlier part of the nineteenth century, Bederman wrote, the prevailing definition of white manhood as later perpetuated by Theodore Roosevelt characterized white men as virile and powerful. Indians were not seen as men at all, but rather as devils who preyed on women and children.¹¹⁰ Spiritualists in the latter half of the nineteenth century rejected this kind of popular rhetoric, charging that whites, and not Indians, acted like devils and victimized Indian peoples. This idea of manhood was an unacceptable model for Spiritualists, who defined compassion and moral justness as a continent at peace.

Just as Spiritualism was broadcast as a scientific, rational religion, their argument against Indian wars likewise took a logical tack. Spiritualists complained that, compared to civilization projects, the cost of military campaigns against native peoples was an unreasonably exorbitant and unnecessary expense. Criticizing General Sherman's position in support of military action, an 1868 *Banner of Light* article commented sarcastically that "it is of secondary importance what another Indian war is going to cost the nation, even at the average expense of a million dollars for the kill of every Indian."¹¹¹ Later in the same year, the *Banner of Light* republished figures from a report by a Mr. A. H. Jackson of New York City that delineated the costs of war with the Seminoles, Cherokees, Cheyennes, Navajos, and others, "beginning with the Black Hawk War of 1831–32, which cost directly $2,000,000 and indirectly, in the destruction of property, employment of militia, volunteers, pensions, etc., $3,000,000 more ... attended with a loss of 4,000 of our people."[112] Comments about the cost of the war continued throughout the journal's run; more details on national expenditures appeared again in the *Banner of Light* in 1877, as part of a lecture given by the Revered Joseph Cook and first recorded by the *Boston Daily Advertiser*. Cook asserted that "official government statistics published lately show that the Indian war in Florida cost $50,000,000; the Sioux War of 1853 and 1854, $40,000,000; the Oregon War of 1854 and 1855 $10,000,000."[113] He listed several other similar statistics, concluding that "the facts stands out beyond all controversy that for the past forty years the military operations of the nation against the Indians have cost on the average $12,000,000 annually."[114] Such numbers were provided to readers in the hopes that, even if not on moral, religious grounds, at least from a practical standpoint the American populace would come to see the continuation of warfare in the West as unfeasible, and the emptying of treasury as a real threat, especially considered the depressed state of the economy in the 1870s.[115]

In terms of racial politics, Spiritualists concluded that, by comparison, the circumstances of Native Americans were far worse than those of African Americans. By the end of the Spiritualist movement, the plight of slave populations had garnered enormous amounts of public attention that culminated in their emancipation. Spiritualists argued that the dire straits of Indian peoples, however, were not sufficiently represented to the American people, and therefore had not yet sparked the outrage necessary to effect substantial change. Even in 1865, at the height of the Civil War, fought ostensibly over the issue of slavery, the *Banner of Light* declared that "if any race of beings on the face of the earth has been *savagely* wronged, it is that of the North American Indian."[116] Indeed prominent abolitionists such as William Lloyd Garrison, the Grimké sisters, and Lucretia Mott contributed to reform activities on behalf of Indians.[117] Isaac and Amy Post also contributed to efforts and Indian reform. According to Cox's research, Isaac Post was one of the first to witness the knocking phenomena at the Fox home in Rochester that catapulted the Spiritualist movement. His and his wife's private collection of Spiritualist publications, held in the University of Rochester's archives, made a significant contribution to this book's resources.

In the years preceding and during the Civil War, journalism arguing for abolition and black enfranchisement similar to those for Indian rights was virtually nonexistent in the *Banner of Light* and other Spiritualist publications under analysis. The appearance of black ghosts in séances was likewise exceedingly rare. An explicit statement comparing the two groups appeared in the *Banner of Light* in 1868. The author posed this contradiction to the reader: "We have liberated the *black* man from physical bondage at the South, at an enormous cost of blood and treasure; and now we are driving from his native soil the free *red* man!—subjecting him to worse than negro slavery—starvation and death! And this, too, by a country that calls itself *Christian*!"[118] Speaking in terms of sheer population, the African American community was perceived by whites as disadvantaged but large; on the other hand, whites constantly observed native populations shrinking. Counting those who remained, the death toll among American Indians was calculated to be higher. The death tolls recorded in the numerous campaigns in the West disgusted Spiritualists, and their reactions demonstrated their desire to keep American Indians alive, despite the ultimate good their journey through the spirit-world offered. An 1873 article posited that "there is, somehow, a feeling of bitterness against our abused, persecuted, and almost exterminated neighbors, that does not exist toward any other race … not even the negro, who has had to suffer much from popular prejudice, arouses such bitterness in the feelings of Americans."[119] The article suggested that the reaction to Indians was more visceral, perhaps because of the deeper connection between Indians and an American identity.

In arguing for change, a *Banner of Light* article published in 1879 compared efforts to help blacks and Indians, attempting to rationalize pro-Indian efforts as worthwhile. It read:

> Millions of dollars were expended and thousands of lives sacrificed to liberate the black man from the thralldom of Southern slavery, while to-day we have the sad spectacle presented to us of the policy of the Government to enslave the free man of the Northwest, or otherwise to annihilate him at the cannon's mouth, for by starvation, because, forsooth, *the white man craves his lands!* No wonder we have Indian wars. No wonder the intelligent Utes have recently gone on the warpath: and having succeeded in a late fight with the United States troops, this Christian nation calls the Indian's successful encounter a "massacre!"[120]

The theft of homelands from men who had always been recognized as free seemed here to be a more egregious violation of the white Christian's moral code; rectifying this injustice was therefore deemed an even worthier cause than that of abolition, though one which had unfortunately failed to arouse the same level of popular support. The *Banner of Light* continually and often explicitly attempted to correct this through its publication.

Spiritualists sought to actively acknowledge and undo the wrongs continually perpetrated by the American nation against Indian tribes. They responded in the way that haunted persons traditionally responded to the appearance of ghosts—they discovered the cause of the disturbance, deciphered what the ghosts wanted, and worked to achieve it. They heeded wholeheartedly the warnings of God's punishment communicated by their ghostly friends, and repeated those premonitions of spiritual retribution if policy change was not achieved. Throughout the *Banner of Light*'s production, Spiritualists expressed their embarrassment at the nation's behavior toward Indians and its hypocritical stance as a bastion of liberty and justice. Those expressions became increasingly religious in tone as the nineteenth century came to a close. In 1866, reform to Indian policy was declared a national imperative by an article that posited, "Before we can call ourselves even a civilized nation, we must change our course to the Indians right about. Justice does not sleep always."[121] Two years later, another *Banner of Light* article declared that

> the blood of these wars will hang to the national skirts long after the last red man has gone the way of his fathers and brethren. We must begin and do right in this matter now; not by-and-by, for it will then be too late; and it is as certain as that God lives, who loves justice, that we shall never be permitted to go on to the end of this bloody business with impunity.[122]

The author suggested that, even if Americans were to succeed at exterminating Indians, the nation would continue to be haunted by the memory and consequences of its wrongdoings. The future of America, guided by Providence's hand, was at present uncertain; change had to occur, and quickly, he argued, if America was to avoid divine destruction. An 1869 article referenced the risk of America's international reputation, saying that the nation "desires to make its garments spotless, but so long as these monstrous stains are upon it, all other nations will be looking toward you with derision and with pity."[123] This article's author referenced the persecution of both the Indian and the slave in this account—for him and other sympathetic listeners, the American principles of liberty and equality demanded improved racial relations in order to be rightly called "just." Spiritualists challenged America's claims of civilization and superiority, because of the abuse of power they perceived toward others. An article published in 1873 pondered not only how other countries would view American hypocrisy, but how future Americans would view it—"In the future history of the Indian wars," the piece read, "if there is a just historian to write them, ours will be the cruel and unjustifiable record ... that will make our descendants ashamed of us and our claims to civilization."[124] Spiritualists lamented that the shameful activity was "traced direct to the Government itself, in whose repute that of all citizens is supposed to be bound up."[125]

The nation's honor, among both global powers and future generations, was being threatened by Indian injustices, according to sympathetic Spiritualists. But Americans had also to fear for the spiritual future of the nation, and the overwhelming reach of its impending punishment if steps were not hastily taken to reconcile America's debt to Indian peoples. An 1879 article warned that if the government did not act to weed out corruption in the management of Indian affairs, "the great spirit-world, which rights the wrongs of the oppressed, *will,* and in a manner, too, that shall blanch the cheeks of the whites. That it has the power to do so we are well aware."[126] The *Banner of Light* repeated the warnings of spirit chiefs such as Philip, who foretold "that a great calamity was soon to overtake the nation, in which thousands of 'pale-faces' would lose their lives."[127] Warnings of this nature were accepted as the inevitable outcome of such disgraceful activity.

The Death of Indianness

The reform goals of Spiritualists regarding Indian policy consisted of several components. They saw little hope in the success of the reservation system, and planned to replace it with policies that would offer the protections of the government, both through federal dependency and citizenship. They realized that the reservation system was counterproductive to the creation of an ideal, nonracial society. Reservations kept Indians in a distinct space—to use Alan Trachtenberg's words—"both inside and outside the American polity: subject to its jurisdiction, but without rights of citizenship."[128] Spiritualists did not wish for Indians to be perpetual federal wards, nor did they believe that would be necessary. Indians would be given the means to survive, which included an education in Anglo-American civilization and submersion in white society. Spiritualists urged direct and significant government intervention. They expected the government to provide the necessary funds and protections and to enforce standing policies and treaties.

Spiritualists were strong supporters of government policies that bestowed upon Indians the rights of citizenship. Consequently, many Spiritualists advocated the dissolution of tribal entities and the "civilizing" missions of educational institutions. More than two dozen articles appeared in the *Banner of Light* that supported such efforts. They had exposed the financial absurdity and spiritual risks of war to their own satisfaction, and argued that the reservation system would not "civilize or permanently benefit the Indian."[129] Wide-scale assimilation became the dominant Spiritualist answer to the Indian Question. Writing in 1866, William J. Young proposed an alternative approach in the *Banner of Light* to constant aggression: "I would break up the Indian tribes or communities, and send them among the older white settlements to learn civilization. I would have them forget their kindred and tribe, and, if possible, their language; would have them cease to be Indians."[130] The resolution to Indian injustice, and by extension the resolution to the haunting of America by dead Indians, was described here as achieved not by the cessation of Indian death, which sent them to their destiny in the Happy Hunting Ground. Rather, it was through the death of Indianness. A policy of racial equality was not to be achieved through tolerance, but by an absence of racial difference. Spiritualists did not cling to categorizations of Indians that defined them as static figures of the past, a sentiment that Deloria rightly claimed dominated American conceptualizations of Indians.[131] By leaning toward policies of education and citizenship, Spiritualists sought to help Indians by erasing the racial difference that marginalized them and glued them to historical representations of Indianness. They believed this would help propel unity between Indians and whites forward, failing for the most part to see the catastrophic consequences of such policies for Indian peoples. Yet on the other hand, the prospect of Indian cultural death was not noticeably of concern to Spiritualists. They did not anticipate a change in what they imagined to be a superior moral quality inherent in Indians, so the welfare of Indians was not seemingly put at risk by the reforms they proposed. In order to protect the lives and rights of Indian peoples, Spiritualists argued, they must be given "the privileges and safeguards of citizenship."[132]

Spiritualists thus called for the dissolution of distinct tribes and the absorption of all Indian peoples by the U.S. government, unifying the inhabitants of the continent under one recognized nation. To that end, the *Banner of Light* reported in 1872 that "Senator Pomeroy introduced [to Congress] a bill [by which] before the benefits of naturalization can accrue to the Indian, he must renounce allegiance to his tribe, and prove by two competent witnesses that he is able to manage his own affairs, that he has for two years adopted the habits of civilized life, and maintained his family."[133] The acquisition of the right to vote depended upon an Indian's ability to prove his manhood, through husbandry and the successful support of a family. The logic behind such reform was described in an 1880 article discussing a congressional bill presented by Secretary of Interior Carl Schurz. It proposed "dealing with the Indian as a citizen … [T]his bill contains every pledge and guarantee of permanent peace with the Indians: that there is no more war with them, because there are no more tribes."[134] Spiritualists undoubtedly supported the vanishing of the Indian, but in racial, cultural terms rather than through physical extermination. Providing citizenship to Indians was to be justified by their own efforts, both to acclimate themselves to white culture and to become self-reliant, one of the many virtues required of American voters. An 1883 article stated that "as soon as the Indian is taught that he must work, and by work increase his ponies and stock, he will take a long step toward an improvement in his condition. The self-supporting tribes fully bear out this statement and opinion."[135] Spiritualist attempts to transcend racial difference fostered a still ongoing process of reexamining American ideas and attitudes regarding race.[136]

For Indians to succeed as citizens, Spiritualists supported the dual necessity of their education. Such an education included learning English, math, science, Western history and arts, and a strong work ethic aimed at individualization through the process of ownership. Working also served the function of crystallizing gender specialization to foster the progress of Indians toward perfection, as completely gendered citizens.[137] In 1885, a *Banner of Light* article reported on a recent conference on the Indian question held by sympathetic Americans which recommended that

> the present system of Indian education be enlarged, and a comprehensive plan be adopted which shall place Indian children in schools under compulsion, if necessary, and shall provide industrial education for a large portion of them. The adult Indians, [the conference] holds, should be brought under preparation for self support and to this end the free ration system should be discontinued as rapidly as possible.[138]

Spiritualists were thus strong supporters of the Dawes Severalty Act. Additionally, the Dawes Act was meant to present Indians with American role models in the form of their neighbors. As Deloria put it, "They were to disappear as discrete social groups and exist only as individuals" and, as Sherry Smith observed, the Dawes Act was the culmination of the argument that Indians could and should be taught the ways of Western civilization.[139] Dawes was a Massachusetts senator, with a strong constituency centered in New England, the stronghold of the Spiritualist movement.[140] Senator Henry Dawes's position on Indian matters was presented in 1886 as largely philanthropic. The sole voice of Dr. T. A. Bland, editor of the pro-Indian journal *The Council Fire* and organizer of the National Indian Defense Association, suggested that "*there is no more legal right to break up the government of an Indian tribe than there is to break up the government of one of the States of the Union.*"[141] Spiritualists claimed to have witnessed a great deal of progress and improvement on the part of Indian apparitions; many Indian ghosts had succeeded in transcending to the higher celestial spheres, serving as spiritual educators. A similar course of improvement was expected to occur among living Indians. Spiritualists believed Indians were capable of successfully receiving instruction, and would gradually evolve into productive, independent, and highly educated members of American society. They anxiously anticipated Indians' contribution to the nation's prosperity and greatness. Through this course of action, Spiritualists believed, America's doom might be avoided, its reputation cleansed, and its future secured.

The previous system of interacting with Indian groups as entities separate from the United States was described as a failure—the government needed to treat Indian peoples as temporary wards of the government, to whom an enormous debt was owed. In 1871, the United States Congress confirmed the status of Indians as federal wards.[142] Spiritualists demanded that the government repay its debt to Indian peoples by enforcing established treaties, providing promised protections and provisions, and beginning to deal with Indians honestly and honorably. In the 1880s, Spiritualists called for an increased federal presence in the management of Indian affairs. A *Banner of Light* article claimed that "it is the business of the government in this matter to retrace its steps, and restore to these harassed and worried people the country and rights of which it has robbed them. The power that did wrong must right it."[143] Spiritualists strongly believed that hostilities would end if the government adopted an open and honest Indian policy. In 1867, an article was published that stated, "We sincerely believe that, with good and honest management, we have seen the last of these Indian troubles, and that a permanent state of peace is before us if we are resolved to keep our word."[144] Spiritualists posited that the federal management of Indian affairs should be relegated to civilian supervision through the creation of the Indian Bureau as a separate federal department, and that only persistently hostile tribes should be subjected to military control by the express order of the president.[145] The government was meant to oversee the actions of all those who had interactions with Indians; in 1875, for example, the *Banner of Light* questioned the methods by which the Atlantic and Pacific Railroad company acquired its land grant though Indian territory, urging that Congress investigate the matter before turning the land over to the developers.[146] Ultimately, the responsibility for establishing and maintaining peace with the Indians was placed on the shoulders of the government, which Spiritualists claimed "either ought to stop making promises to [Indians], or keep its promises."[147] By 1875, however, Spiritualists had become disillusioned with the peace policy, and ceased to put their faith in Grant's promises. Spiritualists averred that the new Indian policy was rife with corruption, despite Grant's protestations to the contrary. A *Banner of Light* article affirmed that "the President continues to protest his constancy to the 'humane and Christian' policy laid down by him, but people who have become at all familiar with the secrets of this Indian business are utterly incredulous of the humanity or the Christianity of any such policy. They openly declare the peace policy to be a fraud."[148] In 1877 they expressed hope that President Hayes would be as honest in dealing with the Indians as he suggested in a December congressional message.[149]

After the Civil War, Indian advocates urged policy reform. Success, albeit short-lived, was witnessed in the creation of the Indian Peace Commission and several other organizations that sought to improve the lot of Indians, generally by eradicating corrupt individuals from positions of power. Colonel Samuel Tappan, stepfather to Minnie of the Sand Creek Massacre and the third of four husbands of leading Spiritualist Cora Hatch, was a prominent member of the Indian Peace Commission and a lifelong Indian activist. In 1868, the U.S. Indian Commission was organized in New York to change public sentiment toward Indians.[150] The American Indian Aid Association was also established in New York, the birthplace of the Spiritualist movement, with the intention of publishing scholarship about native lifestyles for the purpose of demonstrating the fallacy of "assuming that the extinction of the Indian race is owing to manifest destiny."[151] In 1879, the Boston Indian Citizenship Association, led by Senator Henry Dawes and others, was formed. In Pennsylvania, the Women's National Indian Association grew out of a Baptist church. In Massachusetts, the Massachusetts Indian Association was created in 1883 to fight for government protection for the Indians and "to aid in educational work for and among the said Indians."[152] This organization was an all-female subsidiary of the National Indian Association, created in Philadelphia.[153] Both of these organizations sought to inform the public of Indian disenfranchisement and generate financial and congressional support for the Hampton and Carlisle Institutes.[154] The *Banner of Light* also noted in 1886 that the National Indian Association sent "agents to Indian Territories and gained facts which it spreads abroad."[155] The most permanent gains for the Spiritualist cause came from the Carlisle and Hampton Indian schools and the passage of the Dawes Severalty Act in 1887. Reporting on the success of the Carlisle School in 1884, the *Banner of Light* asserted that once the assumption that Indians were incapable of civilization was disproved, the actual process of educating them was a "comparatively easy solution" to the Indian Question. The Dawes Act made a reality all that Spiritualists hoped to accomplish on behalf of Indians.

The successes that Spiritualists celebrated through these policies were, of course, undermined by the devastating impact they had on Indian peoples in reality. In many cases, the problems caused by such policies, including federal nonrecognition and high rates of poverty, drug abuse, alcoholism, and suicide in native populations are ongoing. The success in making severalty policy and funding education campaigns brought with them cultural death, but the act of erasing Indianness as a distinct racial category was not observed by Spiritualists to be destructive in nature.[156] Their experiences with Indian spirits and their ideas about the cosmic realm transcended consideration for racial difference, failing to realize that instead of establishing a raceless society, they had furthered white hegemony. They were antiracists, but not, as Pascoe pointed out of activists in the West, cultural relativists.[157] The promotion of cultural relativism would not come to dominate ethnographic and anthropological thought, Sherry Smith argued, until the twentieth century.[158] Although Spiritualists may have been antiracists, the value they placed on individuality as set forth in their accepted cosmic structure led to the support and celebration of assimilation.

Conclusion

Undoubtedly, on some level Spiritualists recognized the Indian specters that appeared at séances as a symbol of the sins and consequent guilt of the United States in its dealings with Native Americans. Spiritualists were literally haunted by the presence of Indians. But for many that guilt was not assuaged; rather, in order to confront the haunting and rectify it, they were galvanized into action. The political activism of Spiritualists on behalf of Indians was thus the result of combining white guilt and fear of divine judgment with a new sense of purpose and responsibility. Indian ghosts were understood as representing and expressing the desires of all Indian peoples, living and dead, and communicating those desires exclusively to the Spiritualists who were open to such communication. Spiritual progression, then, was not interpreted by all Spiritualists as a justification for Indian death.

Throughout the latter half of the nineteenth century, Spiritualists had opposed the categorization of Indians as a vanishing or vanished race; during the height of the Spiritualist movement they kept Indians present in the national consciousness; the meaning they derived from the spectral appearances of Indians kept living Indians from being defined as relics of the past. Yet the culmination of Spiritualist efforts on behalf of living Indians, as a result of their communications with dead Indians, proved to be the triumph of vanishing rhetoric. Indians did not disappear at the end of the nineteenth century because they ceased to exist; they dissolved from American minds because they ceased to be recognized as distinctly Indian. The physical markers of Indianness established in séances and popular culture ceased to be readily visible, through both the acts of cultural assimilation and isolation in reservations situated on the margins of American society. By the end of the nineteenth century, the period of the "Indian wars" was over, the Indian education system was considered a success, and the severalty policy of the Dawes Act was set in motion. The Indian Question had been successfully answered. Indian policy ceased to be a national priority, and thus Indians ceased to be a pervasive presence in American political thought. After the passage of the Dawes Act, efforts among Spiritualists to better Indian circumstances lost steam, largely because their central aims had come to fruition. Perhaps the resolution of Indian reform, as signaled by the Dawes Act, was a larger contributing factor to the turn away from social reform within Spiritualism than has previously been suggested. The appearances of Indian ghosts had served their purpose and, for a flicker of time, fizzled out. By seemingly enfranchising Indians, their ghosts were temporarily exorcised. Though the imaginary Indian appeared in full force in the twentieth century, exhibiting some of the same haunting qualities in New Age Spiritualism and American cinema, for a brief moment, Indian specters ceased to appear, as their living relatives once again became invisible shades.

Notes

Introduction

1. Mary Theresa Shelhamer, *Life and Labor in the Spirit World: Being a Description of Localities, Employments, Surroundings, and Conditions in the Spheres by Members of the Spirit-Band of Miss M.T. Shelhamer, Medium of the Banner of Light Public Free Circle* (Boston: Colby and Rich, 1885), 85–86.

2. Alan Trachtenberg, *Shades of Hiawatha: Staging Indians, Making Americans 1880–1930* (New York: Hill and Wang, 2004), 19; Jared Farmer, *On Zion's Mount: Mormons, Indians, and the American Landscape* (Cambridge: Harvard University Press, 2008), 312; Molly McGarry, *Ghosts of Futures Past: Spiritualism and the Cultural Politics of Nineteenth-Century America* (Berkeley: University of California Press, 2008), 73.

3. McGarry, 72; Robert Berkhofer, *The White Man's Indian: Images of the American Indian from Columbus to the Present* (New York: Alfred A. Knopf, 1978), 90.

4. Lisa Lenker, "Haunted Culture and Surrogate Space: A New Historicist Account of Nineteenth-Century American Spiritualism" (PhD diss., Stanford University, 1998), 30.

5. Renee L. Bergland, *The National Uncanny: Indian Ghosts and American Subjects* (Hanover: Dartmouth, 2000), 7.

6. Bret Carroll, "Unfree Spirits: Spiritualism and Religious Authority in Antebellum America" (PhD diss., Cornell University, 1991), 25. Howard Kerr, *Mediums, Spirit Rappers, and Roaring Radicals: Spiritualism in American Literature, 1850–1900* (Urbana: University of Illinois Press, 1973).

7. Burton Gates Brown Jr., "Spiritualism in Nineteenth-Century America" (PhD diss., Boston University Graduate School, 1973).

8. John Coward, *The Newspaper Indian: Native American Identity in the Press, 1820–90* (Chicago: Illinois University Press, 1999), 11.

9. The *Banner of Light* is regarded as the most widespread of Spiritualist periodicals. According to Sally Morita, by 1860 the periodical had a circulation of approximately 25,000. Ann Taves, *Fits, Trances, and Visions: Experiencing Religion and Explaining Experience from Wesley to James* (Princeton: Princeton University Press, 1999), 184; Sally Jean Morita, "Modern Spiritualism and Reform in America" (PhD diss., University of Oregon, 1995), 78.

10. Judith Richardson, *Possessions: The History and Uses of Haunting in the Hudson Valley* (Cambridge and London: Harvard University Press 2005), 39.

11. Elizabeth S. Bird, *Dressing in Feathers: The Construction of the Indian in American Popular Culture* (Boulder: Westview, 1996), 3.

12. Trachtenberg, 96.

13. Carroll, 3.

14. Ibid., 17.

15. Morita, 11.

16. Carroll, 15.

17. Berkhofer, 47–60. The division of human groups into physically definable categories enabled Americans to understand their world in hierarchical terms and in many cases justified preexisting sentiments toward the enslavement of African Americans and the conquest of native-inhabited territories. Acknowledging the pervasiveness of this scientific ideology among American citizens will be useful in determining how "Indians" as a cohesive group were defined in relation to the American ideal of the national self.

18. Ramsey, 67.

19. Susan Scheckel, *The Insistence of the Indian: Race and Nationalism in Nineteenth-Century American Culture* (Princeton: Princeton University Press, 1998), 114.

20. Brown, 115, 117.

21. See for example: Daniel Richter, *Facing East from Indian Country: A Native History of Early America*, (Cambridge: Harvard University Press, 2003): Colin G. Calloway, *The American Revolution in Indian Country* (Cambridge: Cambridge University Press, 1995): Richard White, *The Middle Ground: Indians, Empires, and Republics in the Great Lakes Region, 1650–1805* (Cambridge: Cambridge University Press, 1991).

22. Kerr, 118.

23. Bernadino Rose Angelino, "Beckoning the Red Man's Spirit: Exploring the Boundaries of Gender, Race, and Commercial Spaces at the Wigwam Spiritualist Temple Onset, Massachusetts, 1880–1913" (PhD diss., University of Massachusetts, Boston, 2010), 63.

24. McGarry, 67.

25. Braude, 81. Braude is more concerned with the overlap between the women's rights movement and the Spiritualist movement. Her work analyzes the content of the spirit messages—predominantly calls for self-improvement and religious and social reform—and demonstrates how women's role in Spiritualism allowed them to gain a new sense of authority and autonomy that predates the movement that began at the Seneca Falls Convention. Carroll states that the potential for learning from Spiritualist sources is great and the movement should not, therefore, be disregarded as a bizarre cultural aberration. Bret Carroll, *Spiritualism in Antebellum America* (Bloomington: Indiana University Press, 1997), 1.

26. Steven Conn, *History's Shadow: Native Americans and Historical Consciousness in the Nineteenth Century* (Chicago: University of Chicago Press, 2004), 2.

27. Philip Deloria, *Playing Indian* (New Haven: Yale University Press, 1998), 8.

28. Rayna Green, "The Tribe Called Wannabe: Playing Indian in America and Europe," *Folklore* 99, no. 1 (1988): 31, 49.

29. Bergland, 7.

30. Sydney E. Ahlstrom, *A Religious History of the American People* (New Haven: Yale University Press, 1972), 488.

31. T. J. Jackson Lears, *No Place of Grace: Antimodernism and the Transformation of American Culture, 1880–1920* (Chicago: University of Chicago Press, 1981). In this work, Lears suggest that the spiritually enthusiastic and backward-looking tendencies of Spiritualism were reactions to the common perception of late-nineteenth-century American life as an "overcivilized" existence lacking true experience. European Spiritualism has also been connected to shifts toward a personalized spirituality and modern subjectivities. See for example Corinna Treitel, *A Science for the Soul: Occultism and the Genesis of the German Modern* (Baltimore: John Hopkins University Press, 2004) and John Monroe, *Laboratories of Faith: Mesmerism, Spiritism, and Occultism in Modern France* (Ithaca: Cornell University Press, 2008).

32. See for example: "Psychometric Reading of Andrew Johnson." By Mrs. Abby M. Laflin Feree in *The Spiritual Republic* Feb. 16, 1867; *The Spiritual*

Republic 1, no. 7 (Feb. 16, 1867): 101; "The Spiritual Significance of Science," by S. J. Finney, *Herald of Progress* 191, vol. 4 no. 35 (Oct. 17, 1863): 5; "The Soul: Clairvoyance, Psychometry" by Mr. E. W. Wallis at Rochdale, *The Medium and Daybreak* (Jan. 22, 1886), 52; *Princess Wahletka's Book of Knowledge.*

33. Albanese, 181.
34. Moore, 5.
35. Dippie, 21.
36. Louise K. Barnett, *The Ignoble Savage: American Literary Racism, 1790–1890* (Westport: Greenwood Press, 1976), 43, 49.
37. Berkhofer, 95, 97.
38. J. A. Mangan, introduction to *Manliness and Morality: Middle Class Masculinity in Britain and America, 1800–1940,* ed. James Walvin (Manchester: Manchester University Press, 1991), 3.

Chapter 1. Uncanny Indians

1. The Fox Sister rappings refers to a series of instances in which three girls allegedly discovered that the loud knocks or raps on floors and walls of their home were attempts by the dead to communicate with them. These raps were organized systematically so that spirits could provide answers to questions from the Fox sisters and the many visitors who travelled to their home to confirm the spiritual nature of this phenomenon. "Origin of Spiritualism in the United States," *New York Times,* July 24, 1888, 4.
2. McGarry, 41.
3. Brown, 184.
4. Ibid., 109.
5. See also, for example, Robert Cox, *Body and Soul: A Sympathetic History of American Spiritualism* (Charlottesville: University of Virginia Press, 2003), 2; Ann Braude, *Radical Spirits: Spiritualism and Women's Rights in Nineteenth-Century America* (Boston: Beacon Press, 1989), 7, 25; Bridget Bennett, *Transatlantic Spiritualism and Nineteenth-Century American Literature* (New York: Palgrave Macmillan, 2007), 8.
6. Emma Hardinge Britten, *Modern American Spiritualism: A Twenty Years' Record of the Communion between Earth and the World of the Spirits,* 2nd ed. (New York: Self Published, 1870), 60.
7. Ibid., 352.

8. Ibid., 356.

9. Ibid., 19; her italics.

10. James Martin Peebles, *Seers of the Ages: Embracing Spiritualism Past and Present, Doctrines Stated and Moral Tendencies Defined* (Chicago: Progressive Thinker Publishing House, 1903), 207.

11. Cox, 2; Braude, 25.

12. Taves, 181.

13. John Buescher, *The Other Side of Salvation: Spiritualism and the Nineteenth-Century Religious Experience* (Boston: Skinner House Books, 2004).

14. Ibid., 167.

15. Taves, 177.

16. J. S. Loveland, "The Necessity of Scientific Culture," *Present Age* 2, no. 26 (Dec. 11, 1869): 4.

17. Dr. Napoleon Bonaparte Wolfe, *Startling Facts in Modern Spiritualism* (Cincinnati: 1874), 98.

18. Mitch Horowitz, *Occult America: White House Séances, Ouija Circles and Masons, and the Secret History of Our Nation* (New York: Bantam, 2010), 2.

19. R. Laurence Moore, "The Occult Connection? Mormonism, Christian Science, and Spiritualism," in *The Occult in America: New Historical Perspectives*, ed. Howard Kerr and Charles L. Crow (Chicago: Illinois University Press 1983), 150.

20. Catherine Albanese, *A Republic of Mind and Spirit: A Cultural History of American Metaphysical Religion* (New Haven: Yale University Press 1995), 6.

21. Ibid., 195.

22. See for example Ann Fabian, *The Skull Collectors: Race, Science, and America's Unburied Dead* (Chicago: University of Chicago Press 2010), 93, Albanese, 133, 180. C. B. F. "Ancient Glimpses of the Spirit Land," *The Herald of Progress* 178 4 no. 22 (July 18, 1863): 2.

23. Horowitz, 4.

24. Albanese, 12.

25. Cox, 2.

26. Robert Laurence Moore, *In Search of White Crows: Spiritualism, Parapsychology, and American Culture* (Oxford: Oxford University Press, 1977), xiii.

27. Albanese, 189. See also, for example, "Shakerism and Spiritualism," by Julia H. Johnson, Tyringham, MA, July 25, 1880 *Mind and Matter*, Oct. 2, M.S. 33: 3, and "True Grounds of Shakerism: Doctrinal Epistle from

Valentine Nicholson to Frederick W. Evans," by Valentine Nicholson, *Herald of Progress* 67 vol. 2, no. 15 (June 1, 1861): 2.

28. Albanese, 186–87.

29. Ibid., 246.

30. Daphne Brooks, *Bodies in Dissent: Spectacular Performances of Race and Freedom, 1850–1910* (Durham: Duke University Press 2006), 15.

31. Ibid.

32. Albanese, 266.

33. Jon Butler, "The Dark Ages of American Occultism, 1760–1848," *The Occult in America: New Historical Perspectives*, 72.

34. Carroll, 118.

35. Prentice Mulford, "The Invisible in Our Midst: Various Conditions of the Spirit-Life Denied," *Religio-Philosophical Journal* 7, no. 21 (Feb. 12, 1870): 1.

36. Ibid.

37. William Ramsey, DD, *Spiritualism, a Satanic Delusion, and a Sign of the Times* (Rochester: Horace Lorenzo Hastings, 1856), 67. Ramsey was also pastor of Cedar St. Presbyterian Church in Philadelphia.

38. *Banner of Light* 5, no. 26 (Sept. 24, 1859): 7.

39. Peebles, 319.

40. Wolfe, 225.

41. Peebles, 319; my italics.

42. C. A. Burgess, ed., *Pictorial Spiritualism* (Chicago: Illinois State Spiritualist Association, 1922).

43. Carroll, 267.

44. Abraham P. Pierce, *The Revelator: Being an Account of the Twenty-one Days' Entrancement of Abraham P. Pierce, Spirit-medium, at Belfast, Maine together with a Sketch of His Life* (Boston: Adams and Company, 1870), 47.

45. Andrew Jackson Davis, "Naturalness of the Summer Land," lecture at Dodworth's Hall, Feb. 8, 1863, recorded by Robert S. Moore, *Herald of Progress* 163, vol. 4, no.7 (April 4, 1863): 5–6.

46. R. Pierce Beaver, *Church, State, and the American Indians: Two and a Half Centuries of Partnership Between Protestant Churches and Government* (St Louis: Concordia Publishing House, 1966), 10.

47. Ibid., 12.

48. Ibid., 63.

49. Jean-Jacques Simard, "White Ghosts, Red Shadows: The Reduction of North American Natives," in *The Invented Indian: Cultural Fictions and*

Government Policies, ed. James A. Clifton (New Brunswick: Transaction Publishers, 1990), 338.

50. Beaver, 61.
51. Ibid., 63.
52. Simard, 344.
53. Linnaeus, in John S. Haller Jr., *Outcasts from Evolution: Scientific Attitudes of Racial Inferiority, 1859–1900* (Urbana: Illinois University Press, 1971), 4.
54. Beaver, 123.
55. Ibid., 134.
56. Ibid., 186, 194.
57. Albanese, 266.
58. Horowitz, 69.
59. Larry Danielson, "Paranormal Memorates in the American Vernacular," in *The Occult in America: New Historical Perspectives*, ed. Howard Kerr and Charles L. Crow (Urbana: University of Illinois Press, 1983), 196.
60. Richardson, 3.
61. Avery F. Gordon, *Ghostly Matters: Haunting the Sociological Imagination* (Minneapolis: University of Minnesota Press, 1997), xvi.
62. Terry Castle, *The Female Thermometer: Eighteenth-century Culture and the Invention of the Uncanny* (Oxford: Oxford University Press, 1995), 184.
63. Richardson, 97.
64. Ibid.
65. Ibid., 127, 202.
66. Castle, 168.
67. Bennett, 14.
68. Coward, 3.
69. Farmer, 342.
70. Alan Trachtenberg, *The Incorporation of America: Culture and Society in the Gilded Age* (New York: Hill and Wang, 1982), 29.
71. Julian Wolfreys, *Victorian Hauntings: Spectrality, Gothic, the Uncanny, and Literature* (New York: Palgrave, 2002), xi.
72. Ibid., 15.
73. Coward, 35.
74. Danielson, 201.
75. Barnett, 84.
76. Castle, 359.

77. Molly McGarry, *Ghosts of Futures Past: Spiritualism and the Cultural Politics of Nineteenth-Century America* (Berkeley: University of California Press, 2008), 67.

Chapter 2. Chief Spirit

1. Kerry Trask, *Black Hawk: The Battle for the Heart of America* (New York: Macmillan, 2007), 2.

2. A treaty made where a vast majority of Sac land east of the Mississippi River was ceded to the United States, unbeknownst to Black Hawk. Black Hawk, *Autobiography of Ma-ka-tai-me-she-kia-kiak or Black Hawk*, trans. Antoine LeClaire (Minneapolis: Filiquarian, 2006), 16.

3. He referred to the British, French, and Spanish crowns as his fathers—all of which he cooperated with amicably at different times.

4. Initially published by J. B. Patterson in 1833. Patrick Jung, *Black Hawk War of 1832* (Norman: University of Oklahoma Press, 2007), 11.

5. Black Hawk.

6. Robert F. Berkhofer, *The White Man's Indian: Images of the American Indian from Columbus to the Present*, (New York: Alfred A. Knopf, 1978), 3.

7. *Hesperian* was a product of the 1836 merger between *The Western Journal* and the *Western Monthly Magazine*. Focused in both Cincinnati and Columbus, Ohio, the *Hesperian* was predominantly a literary journal. Rev. Charles F. Goss, *Cincinnati: The Queen City 1788–1912* (Columbus, OH: S.J. Clarke, 1912), 505.

8. Life of Black Hawk," *The Hesperian: or, the Western Monthly Magazine* 2 (Dec. 1838–39): 168.

9. "Google NGram Viewer," *Google*, Aug. 27, 2012; http://books.google.com/ngrams/graph?content=Black+Hawk%2CBlack+Hawk+War&year_start=1800&year_end=1900&corpus=0&smoothing=3.

10. *Hesperian*, 428.

11. Laura Mielke, *Moving Encounters: Sympathy and the Indian Question in Antebellum Literature*, (Amherst: University of Massachusetts Press, 2008), 85; Donald Jackson, introduction to *Black Hawk: An Autobiography* (Urbana: University of Illinois Press, 1964), 30.

12. Under the original title of *Harper's Magazine*, this monthly publication addressed a broad range of interests, including politics and literature. Harpers.com; accessed Nov. 29, 2009.

13. Randolph B. Marcy, "Border Reminiscences," *Harper's New Monthly Magazine* 39 no. 232 (Sept. 1869): 483.

14. John Kucich, *Ghostly Communion: Cross-Cultural Spiritualism in Nineteenth Century American Literature* (Hanover: Dartmouth, 2004), 39.

15. William S. Snelling, "Review: The Life of Black Hawk," *North American Review* 40, no. 86 (Jan. 1835): 70. The *North American Review* was a literary magazine.

16. Philip Deloria, *Playing Indian* (New Haven: Yale University Press, 1998), 64.

17. Bennett, 110.

18. Mielke 85; Jackson 11.

19. R.G. Thwaites, "War with Black Hawk," *Magazine of Western History* 5 (1886–87): 33. This journal was dedicated to publishing a serialized history of Ohio, from its pre-territory days to "the history of the State under the Constitution." Ibid.

20. Scheckel, 113.

21. Mielke 72, 87.

22. Bridget Bennett, "Sacred Theatres: Shakers, Spiritualists, Theatricality, and the Indians in the 1830s and 1840s," *The Drama Review* 49, no. 3 (Fall 2005): 127.

23. Ibid.

24. "Life of Black Hawk," *American Quarterly Review* 15 (1834): 426. The *American Quarterly* was also a literary journal.

25. Scheckel, 110.

26. Bennett.

27. Cox, 117.

28. George Catlin, *Letters and Notes on the Manners Customs, and Condition of the Native American Indian*, vol. 2 (1841), 211.

29. Trask, 113.

30. Black Hawk, 6.

31. Snelling, 71.

32. Trask, 3.

33. "The Life of Black Hawk," *The Hesperian* 2 (1838–39): 167. See *New England Magazine* 6 (1834): 420.

34. Black Hawk.

35. Ibid., 66.

36. Elijah Kilbourn, *The Soldier's Cabinet* (Philadelphia, 1855), quoted in Samuel Drake, *Biography and History of the Indians of North America* (Boston: O. L. Perkins, 1834), 376.

37. See for example Perry Armstrong, *The Sauks and the Black Hawk War, with Biological Sketches, etc.* (Springfield, IL: H. W. Rokker,1887), 534; Frank E. Stevens, *The Black Hawk War, Including a Review of Black Hawk's Life* (Chicago: Chamber of Commerce, 1903); Drake, 136; *American Quarterly Review* 15 (March and June 1824): and Norman B. Wood, *Lives of Famous Indian Chiefs* (Chicago: American Indian Historical Publishing, 1906), 376.

38. Stevens, 19.

39. Armstrong, 541.

40. Ibid., 540.

41. Stevens, 376.

42. *Transatlantic Spiritualism*, 99.

43. Trask, 3.

44. "Strong Physical Manifestations of Nashua," *Banner of Light* 1, no. 18 (Aug. 6, 1857): 6.

45. Ibid.

46. *Banner of Light* 15, no. 20 (Aug. 6, 1864): 5.

47. "Strong Physical Manifestations of Nashua," 6.

48. Ibid.

49. R. H. Hutton, "The Unspiritual World of Spiritualism," *Victoria Magazine* 1 (1863): 51. The *Victoria Magazine* was a publication of the 1860s that was dedicated to feminist reform and stood at the center of the feminist campaign in Britain. Sheila Herstein, "The Langham Place Circle and Feminist Periodicals of the 1860s," *Victorian Periodicals Review* 26, No. 1 (Spring, 1993).

50. Founded in 1860, the *Spiritualist Magazine* was the leading periodical on Spiritualism in Great Britain. *Occultism and Parapsychology Encyclopedia*, ed. J. Gordon Melton (Farmington Hills: Gale Group, 1996), Accessed on answers.com Nov. 29, 2009.

51. Benjamin Coleman, *Spiritualism in America*, Reprinted from *The Spiritual Magazine* (London: F. Pitman, 1861), 11.

52. Ibid.

53. Ibid. All quotes up to and including the following block quote are also from Coleman.

54. Ibid., 12.

55. John McCabe, *Spiritualism: A Popular History from 1847* (Berkeley: University of California Libraries, 1920), 72.
56. Ibid.
57. Ibid., 12.
58. Ibid., 11.
59. *Transatlantic Spiritualism*, 111.
60. Conn, 8.
61. Barnett, 78.
62. Conn, 85.
63. *Hesperian*, 167.
64. Black Hawk, 98.
65. Snelling, 69.
66. Ibid., 70.
67. Farmer, 285.
68. Conn, 94.
69. Farmer, 285.
70. Mielke, 72.
71. Conn, 79.
72. Catlin, 210.
73. Conn, 81.
74. Dippie, 12.
75. Robert Berkhofer, *Salvation and the Savage* (New York: Atheneum: 1972), 33.
76. Beaver, 76.
77. Ibid., 84.
78. Ibid., 85.
79. *Transatlantic Spiritualism*, 98.
80. Ibid., 110.
81. *Banner of Light* 47 no. 23 (Aug. 28, 1880): 6.
82. Coleman, 11.
83. Ibid., 24.
84. Ibid., 11.
85. *Transatlantic Spiritualism*, 11.
86. Coleman, 11.
87. Ibid., 12.
88. Dippie, 98.
89. Morgan, quoted in Dippie, 103.
90. Fabian, 30, 83.

91. Haller, 96, 112; Fabian, 2; Dippie, 29, 97–100.

92. Coleman., 11.

93. William B. Carpenter, "Psychological Curiosities of Spiritualism," *Fraser's Magazine* (Nov. 1877): 543. *Fraser's Magazine* was a literary journal with conservative leanings, which manifest themselves in this instance through hostility toward Spiritualism in general. Miriam M. H. Thrall, *Rebellious Fraser's: Nol Yorke's Magazine in the Days of Maginn, Thackeray, and Carlyle* (New York: Columbia University Press, 1934).

94. Epes Sargent, *The Planchette, or the Despair of Science, Being a Full Account of Modern Spiritualism, Its Phenomena, and the Various Theories Regarding It* (Boston: Roberts Brothers, 1869), 123.

95. Epes Sargent, *Scientific Basis of Spiritualism* (Boston: Colby and Rich, 1880), 268.

96. Mrs. Hardinge Britten, "Dark Circles and Cabinets," *The Psychological Review: An Cosmopolitan Organ of Psychology, Mesmerism, Mind Reading, Clairvoyance, Spiritualism, Theosophy, and the Occult Sciences* 5 (Jul.-Dec. 1882): 441.

97. Catlin, 210.

98. *Religio-Philosophical Journal* 17, no. 25 (March 6, 1875): 1.

99. *Religio-Philosophical Journal* 16, no. 20 (Aug. 1, 1874): 1.

100. *Transatlantic Spiritualism*, 130.

101. *Banner of Light* 16, no. 21 (Feb. 11, 1865): 4.

102. *Banner of Light* 27, no. 26 (Sept. 10, 1870): 1.

103. Emma Hardinge Britten, *Modern American Spiritualism: A Twenty Year's Record of the Communion between Earth and the World of Spirits* (New York: The New York Printing Company, 1870), 266.

104. Ibid., 267.

105. Ibid.

106. *Banner of Light* 17, no. 26 (Sept. 16, 1865): 8.

107. *Banner of Light* 17, no. 14 (June 24, 1865): 4.

108. *Religio-Philosophical Journal* 17, no. 24 (Feb. 27, 1875): 1.

109. *Banner of Light* 38, no. 24 (March 11, 1876): 7.

110. *Banner of Light* 39, no. 13 (June 24, 1876): 3.

111. *Banner of Light* 44, no. 7 (Nov. 9, 1878): 4.

112. Albanese, 250.

113. *Banner of Light* 47, no. 23 (Aug. 28, 1880): 6.

114. Cox, 206.

115. *Banner of Light* 51, no. 12 (June 10, 1882): 4.

116. *Banner of Light* 57, no. 7 (May 2, 1885): 6.
117. Conn, 80.
118. *Banner of Light* 15, no. 20 (Aug. 6, 1864), 5.
119. *Banner of Light* 19, no. 24 (Sept. 1, 1866): 5.
120. *Religio-Philosophical Journal* 16, no. 14 (June 20, 1874): 4.
121. *Banner of Light* 16, no. 1 (Sept. 24, 1864): 4.
122. William Alexander Hammond, *Spiritualism and Allied Causes and Conditions of Nervous Derangement*, (New York: G. P. Putnam's Sons, 1876), 225. Dr. Hammond was a Professor of Disease of the Mind and Nervous System in the Medical Department of the University of the City of New York.
123. *Banner of Light* 18, no. 24 (March 3, 1866): 3.
124. Cox, 200.
125. Britten, 482.
126. Ibid.
127. Stevens, 261.
128. Cox, 86.
129. Ibid., 91.
130. Mielke, 87.
131. Ibid., 88.
132. Conn, 93.
133. Albanese, 249.
134. Claude Jacobs and Andrew Kaslow, *The Spiritual Churches of New Orleans: Origins, Beliefs, and Rituals of an African-American Religion* (Knoxville: University Press of Tennessee, 1991), 2.
135. Albanese, 474.
136. Ibid., 475.
137. Jason Berry, *The Spirit of Black Hawk: A Mystery of Africans and Indians* (Jackson: University Press of Mississippi, 1995), 98.
138. Ibid., 97.
139. *Religio-Philosophical Journal* 16, no. 14 (June 20, 1874): 4.
140. Albanese, 476.
141. Berry, 18.
142. Ibid., 21.
143. Ibid., 15.
144. Hans Baer, *The Black Spiritual Movement: A Religious Response to Racism* (Knoxville: University Press of Tennessee, 1984), 187.
145. Ibid., 119.

146. William Fagaly, *Tools of Her Ministry: The Art of Sister Gertrude Morgan* (New York: American Folk Art Museum, 2004), 30.
147. Jacobs and Kaslow, 148.
148. Albanese, 476.

Chapter 3. Spirit Council

1. Seybert Commission, *Preliminary Report*, 1887, 151–52, quoted in Robert Cox, *Body and Soul: A Sympathetic History of American Spiritualism* (Charlottesville: University of Virginia Press, 2003), 190.
2. McGarry, 67.
3. Amy Greenberg, *Manifest Manhood and the Antebellum American Empire* (Cambridge: Cambridge University Press, 2005), 10.
4. Ibid., 15.
5. Braude, 40.
6. John W. Day, *Biography of Mrs. J.H. Conant, the World's Medium of the Nineteenth Century*, 2nd ed. (Boston: William White & Co., Banner of Light Office, 1873), 151.
7. Ibid., 30.
8. Ibid., 155.
9. Cora Hatch was married at least thrice, using the surnames Hatch, Tappan, and Richmond at different times.
10. Ibid., 154.
11. *Banner of Light* 20, no. 13 (Dec. 15, 1866): 6.
12. *Flashes of Light from the Spirit Land, through the Mediumship of Mrs. J.H. Conant*, comp. Allen Putnam (Boston: William White & Co., Banner of Light Office, 1872), 10.
13. Braude, 25.
14. Cox, 190.
15. Adin Ballou, *An Exposition of Views Respecting the Principal Facts, Causes, and Peculiarities Involved in Spirit Manifestations: Together with Interesting Phenomenal Statements and Communications* (Boston: Bela Marsh, 1852), 254.
16. Ibid.
17. "From an Indian Spirit," *Religio-Philosophical Journal* 5, no. 17 (Jan. 16, 1869): 6.
18. J. O. Barrett, *The Spiritual Pilgrim: A Biography of James Peebles* (Boston: William White & Co., 1872), 172.

19. *Banner of Light* 32, no. 11 (Dec. 14, 1872): 6.
20. *Banner of Light* 56, no. 7 (Nov. 1, 1884): 6.
21. *Banner of Light* 36, no. 15 (Jan. 9, 1875): 8.
22. Napoleon Bonaparte Wolfe, *Startling Facts in Modern Spiritualism* (Cincinnati: 1874), 156.
23. *Banner of Light* 55, no. 17 (July 12, 1884): 6.
24. *Banner of Light* 48, no. 22 (Feb. 19, 1881): 6.
25. *Banner of Light* 49, no. 23 (Aug. 27, 1881): 6.
26. *Banner of Light* 36, no. 2 (Oct. 10, 1874): 2.
27. *Religio-Philosophical Journal* 17, no. 15 (Dec. 26, 1874): 1.
28. *Banner of Light* 36, no. 15 (Jan. 9, 1875): 8.
29. Ibid.
30. *Banner of Light* 38, no. 18 (Feb. 5, 1876): 1.
31. *Religio-Philosophical Journal* 18, no. 7 (May 1, 1875): 1.
32. John W. Trusdell, *The Bottom Facts Concerning the Science of Spiritualism: Delivered from Careful Investigations Covering a Period of 25 Years* (New York: G. W. Dillingham, 1892), 231.
33. Wolfe, 129.
34. Greenberg, 15.
35. "Physical Manifestations," *Banner of Light* 15, no. 18 (July 23, 1864): 3.
36. *Religio-Philosophical Journal* 16, no. 20 (Aug. 1, 1874): 1.
37. *Religio-Philosophical Journal* 17, no. 25 (March 6, 1875): 1.
38. *Religio-Philosophical Journal* 18, no. 3 (April 3, 1875): 1.
39. *Religio-Philosophical Journal* 18, no. 7 (May 1, 1875): 1.
40. *Banner of Light* 38, no. 19 (Feb. 5, 1876): 1.
41. *Banner of Light* 42, no. 8 (Nov. 17, 1877): 3.
42. Bennett, 11.
43. Coleman.
44. *Banner of Light* 15, no. 4 (April 16, 1864): 3.
45. Greenberg, 9.
46. Bederman, 10, 15.
47. Greenberg, 93.
48. Haller, 74; Fabian, 16.
49. Dippie, 106.
50. Ibid., 30.
51. Deloria, 175.
52. Bennett, 111.
53. *Religio-Philosophical Journal* 16, no. 20 (Aug. 1, 1874): 1.

54. *Religio-Philosophical Journal* 17, no. 25 (March 6, 1875): 1.

55. *Banner of Light* 38, no. 19 (Feb. 5, 1876): 1.

56. *Banner of Light* 42, no. 8 (Nov. 17, 1877): 3.

57. Emma Hardinge Britten, *Autobiography*, ed. Mrs. Margaret Wilkinson. (London: Deansgate and Ridgefield, 1900), 131.

58. Barnett, 75.

59. Ibid.

60. Brooks, 14.

61. See Alan Trachtenberg, *Shades of Hiawatha*, for a detailed discussion of "Indians" in popular media.

62. Cox, 190.

63. Ibid., 103.

64. Ibid., 190.

65. Ibid., 199.

66. Eugene Crowell, *Spirit World: Its Inhabitants, Nature and Philosophy*, (New York: Trow's Printing and Bookbinding, 1879), 55, quoted in Cox, 196.

67. Cox, 198.

68. McGarry, 70.

69. Cox, 207.

70. J. M. Peebles, "The Individuality of the Spirits," *Herald of Progress* 189 Vol. 4, no. 33:1.

71. *Banner of Light* 21, no. 3 (April 6, 1867): 6.

72. *Banner of Light* 25, no. 11 (May 29, 1869): 6.

73. *Banner of Light* 34, no. 5 (Nov. 1, 1873): 6.

74. *Banner of Light* 34, no. 20 (Feb. 14, 1874): 4.

75. *Banner of Light* 46, no. 18 (Jan. 24, 1870):6.

76. *Banner of Light* 21, no. 16 (July 6, 1867): 6.

77. Ibid.

78. *Banner of Light* 34, no. 1 (Oct. 4, 1873): 6.

79. Coward, 98.

80. Ibid., 102.

81. Ibid., 120.

82. Ibid., 113.

83. Francis Prucha, *The Great Father: The United States Government and the American Indians* (Lincoln: Nebraska University Press, 1984), 1:461.

84. Horatio Wood, *Philosophy of Creation: Unfolding the Laws of the Progressive Development of Nature, and Embracing the Philosophy of Man, Spirit, and the Spirit World* (Boston: Bela Marsh, 1864), 88,99, quoted in Cox, 106.

85. Bennett, 51.

86. Charles Hammond, *Light from the Spirit World: Comprising a Series of Articles on the Conditions of Spirits, and the Development of Mind in the Rudimental and Second Spheres, Written Wholly by the Control of Spirits, without any Volition or Will by the Medium, or any Thought or Care in Regard to the Matter Presented by His Hand,* 2nd ed. (Boston: 1852), 194, quoted in Cox, 193.

87. Cox, 207.

88. Coward, 162.

89. Jeffrey Ostler, *The Plains Sioux and United States Colonialism from Lewis and Clark to Wounded Knee* (Cambridge: Cambridge University Press, 2004), 48.

90. *Banner of Light* 37, no. 9 (May 29, 1875): 4.

91. Ibid.

92. *Banner of Light* 32, no. 16 (Jan. 18, 1873): 6.

93. *Banner of Light* 16, no. 2 (Oct. 1 1864): 6.

94. *Banner of Light* 36, no. 2 (Oct. 10, 1874): 5.

95. McGarry, 66.

96. Ibid., 71.

97. Ibid., 73.

98. Berkhofer, 145.

99. Ibid., 155.

100. Ibid., 152.

101. George Tinker, preface to *Kill the Indian, Save the Man: The Genocidal Impact of American Indian Residential Schools* (San Francisco: City Lights Publishers, 2004), xiii.

102. *Banner of Light* 27, no.26 (Sept. 10, 1870): 4.

103. McGarry, 73.

104. Ibid., 75.

105. *Banner of Light* 14, no. 12 (Dec. 12, 1863): 3.

106. Ibid.

107. *Banner of Light* 16, no. 2 (Oct. 1, 1864): 6.

108. See for example Farmer, 254; Deloria, 4; Berkhofer, 77.

109. *Banner of Light* 21, no. 3 (April 6, 1867): 6.

110. "Narrative of the Life on Earth, and Experience in the Spheres of Chee-wa-tune (Much Strong Brave), with an Introduction on the Mission of the Redman, by Sa-go-ye-wat-ha, (Red Jacket) And a Chapter on Physical Development on Earth, by Edward W. Southwick late of Maine," *Religio-Philosophical Journal* 4, no. 11 (June 6, 1868): 1.

111. McGarry, 67.
112. *Banner of Light* 34, no. 18 (Jan. 31, 1874): 8.
113. Bederman, 25.
114. Greenberg, 3.
115. *Banner of Light* 7, no. 17 (July 21, 1860): 6.
116. *Banner of Light* 12, no. 7 (Nov. 8, 1862): 6.
117. Bederman, 26.
118. Ibid., 18.
119. Ibid., 178.
120. Greenberg, 21.
121. Haller, 98.
122. Morgan and Powell, cited by Haller, 100.
123. For more detailed readings of the history of anthropology and the discipline's development of racial ideologies on the whole, see: Miceala di Leonardo, *Exotics at Home: Anthropologies, Others, and American Modernity* (Chicago: University of Chicago Press, 2000): Lee D. Baker, *From Savage to Negro: Anthropology and the Construction of Race, 1896–1954* (Berkeley: University of California Press, 1998): George. W. Stocking Jr., *Race, Culture, and Evolution: Essays in the History of Anthropology* (Chicago: University of Chicago Press, 1982).
124. Coward, 8.
125. Berkhofer, 76.
126. Greenberg, 19.
127. Ibid.
128. Bederman, 183.
129. Prucha, 458.
130. Ibid., 459.
131. *Banner of Light* 20, no. 24 (March 2, 1867): 6.
132. Ibid.
133. Ibid.
134. Ibid.
135. *Banner of Light* 21, no. 16 (July 6, 1867): 6.
136. *Banner of Light* 21 no. 2 (March 30, 1867): 6.
137. Bederman, 12.
138. Ibid., 13.
139. Berkhofer, 35, 38.
140. Bederman, 181, 183.
141. *Banner of Light* 21, no. 16 (July 6, 1867): 6.

142. *Banner of Light* 31, no. 13 (June 8, 1872): 6.
143. *Banner of Light* 32, no. 1 (Sept. 14, 1872): 6.
144. Braude, 190.
145. Mrs. Mary T. Shelhamer Longly, *Teachings and Illustration as they Emanate from the Spiritual: Methods of Concentration—Application and Demonstration of Spiritual Works—How they Build Homes, Temples, Heal the Soul-Sick who Come to their Worlds from Earth—How Worlds are Made* (Chicago: The Progressive Thinker Publishing House, 1908), 75.
146. *Banner of Light* 14, no. 7 (Nov. 7, 1863): 2.
147. Ibid.
148. *Banner of Light* 51, no. 18 (July 22, 1882): 4.
149. Beaver, 63.
150. Ibid., 68.
151. David Wallace Adams, *Education for Extinction: American Indians and the Boarding School Experience, 1875–1928* (Lawrence: University of Kansas Press, 1995), 8.
152. *Banner of Light* 51, no. 18 (July 22, 1882): 4.
153. Dippie, 96.
154. Conn, 31.
155. Cox, 106.
156. Day, 184.
157. *Banner of Light* 51, no. 18 (July 22, 1882): 4.
158. Prucha, 135.
159. *Banner of Light* 49, no. 1 (March 26, 1881): 6.
160. *Banner of Light* 50, no. 3 (Oct. 8, 1881): 8.
161. *Banner of Light* 53, no. 4 (April 14, 1883): 6.
162. *Banner of Light* 54, no. 20 (Feb. 2, 1884): 6.
163. Ibid.
164. *Banner of Light* 55, no. 9 (May 17, 1884): 6.
165. William Alexander Hammond, *Spiritualism and Allied Causes and Conditions of Nervous Derangement* (New York: G. P. Putnam's Sons, 1876), 225. Dr. Hammond was a professor of Diseases of the Mind and Nervous System in the Medical Department of the University of the City of New York.
166. Day, 152.
167. Deloria, 8.
168. Ibid., 57.
169. Ibid., 175.
170. *Banner of Light* 16, no. 8 (Nov. 12, 1864): 2.

Chapter 4. Spectral Romance

1. Bederman, 25.
2. Ibid., 28.
3. Bennett, 104.
4. Trachtenberg, 192.
5. *Banner of Light* 34, no. 7 (Nov. 15, 1873): 2.
6. *Religio-Philosophical Journal* 17, no. 13 (Dec. 12, 1874): 6.
7. *Religio-Philosophical Journal* 18, no. 3 (April 3, 1875): 1.
8. *Religio-Philosophical Journal* 20, no. 24 (Aug. 26, 1876): 1.
9. "Wonderful Manifestations," *Religio-Philosophical Journal* 21, no. 24 (Feb. 24, 1877): 6.
10. *Religio-Philosophical Journal* 18, no. 3 (April 3, 1875): 1.
11. *Banner of Light* 42, no. 19 (Feb. 2, 1878): 3.
12. *Banner of Light* 47, no. 2 (April 3, 1880): 1.
13. Ibid.
14. *Banner of Light* 49, no. 24 (Sept. 3, 1881): 3.
15. *Banner of Light* 54, no. 1 (Sept. 22, 1883): 2.
16. Haller, 7.
17. *Religio-Philosophical Journal* 18, no. 3 (April 3, 1875): 1.
18. Mary Dana Schindler, *A Southerner Among the Spirits: A Record of Investigations into the Spiritual Phenomena* (Memphis: Tennessee Southern Baptist Publication Society 1877), 61–62.
19. *Religio-Philosophical Journal* 18, no. 21 (Aug. 7, 1875): 168.
20. *Banner of Light* 42, no. 19 (Feb. 2, 1878): 3.
21. *Banner of Light* 54, no. 1 (Sept. 22, 1883): 2.
22. Farmer, 304.
23. *Religio-Philosophical Journal* 18, no. 3 (April 3, 1875): 1.
24. Deloria, 106.
25. Ibid.
26. Hoxie Neale Fairchild, *The Noble Savage: A Study in Romantic Naturalism* (New York: Russell and Russell, 1961), 1.
27. Ibid., 7.
28. *Banner of Light* 45, no. 8 (May 17, 1879): 6.
29. *Banner of Light* 53, no. 7 (May 5, 1883): 6.
30. Deloria, 106.
31. Fairchild, 444.
32. Farmer, 305.

33. Fairchild, 366.
34. Simard, 352.
35. Barnett, 89.
36. *Religio-Philosophical Journal* 6, no. 22 (Aug. 21, 1869): 4.
37. Barnett, 91.
38. *Banner of Light* 1, no. 18 (Aug. 6, 1857): 7.
39. See for example *Banner of Light* 36, no. 2 (Oct. 10, 1874): 5; *Banner of Light* 34, no. 20 (Feb. 14, 1874): 4; and *Banner of Light* 34, no. 23 (March 7, 1874): 6.
40. *Banner of Light* 60, no. 9 (Nov. 13, 1886): 6.
41. *Banner of Light* 19, no. 13 (June 16, 1866): 6.
42. *Banner of Light* 41, no. 13 (June 23, 1877): 6.
43. *Banner of Light* 48, no. 2 (Oct. 2, 1880): 6.
44. *Banner of Light* 49, no. 17 (July 16, 1881): 6.
45. *Flashes of Light from the Spirit Land, through the Mediumship of Mrs. J.H. Conant,* compiled by Allen Putnam (Massachusetts: William White & Co., Banner of Light Office, 1872), 20.
46. *Banner of Light* 34, no. 11 (Dec. 13, 1873): 1.
47. Cora L. V. Richmond, *Ouina's Canoe and Christmas Offering: Filled with Flowers for the Darlings of Earth*, Given through her Medium (Iowa: D. M. and N. P. Fox, 1882), 8.
48. *Flashes,* 22.
49. Farmer, 308, 283, 290.
50. *Banner of Light* 34, no. 11 (Dec. 13, 1873): 1.
51. Richmond, 14.
52. Day, 155.
53. *Banner of Light* 36, no. 18 (Jan. 30, 1875): 6.
54. *Banner of Light* 42, no. 20 (Feb. 9, 1878): 8.
55. *Banner of Light* 57, no. 6 (April 25, 1885): 6.
56. *Banner of Light* 34, no. 11 (Dec. 13, 1873): 1.
57. Andrew Jackson Davis, *The Children's Progressive Lyceum: A Report on its Origin, Rise, Proceedings, Conduct, Lessons, Recitations, and Songs* (Massachusetts: Herald of Progress Office, 1863), 5.
58. McGarry, 85.
59. Mielke, 180.
60. Barnett, 91.
61. McGarry, 170.
62. *Banner of Light* 34, no. 11 (Dec. 13, 1873): 1.

63. Mielke, 125.
64. *Flashes,* 22.
65. Ibid.
66. Fairchild, 368.
67. Cox, 205.
68. *Lifework of Mrs. Cora L. V. Richmond,* ed. Harrison D. Barrett (Illinois: Hack and Anderson, 1895), 88.
69. Day, 183.
70. *Banner of Light* 44, no. 4 (Oct. 19, 1878): 4.
71. *Psychical Research Review* 4, no. 1 (Jan. 1918): 4.
72. Day, 186.
73. Ibid., 193.
74. See for example Fairchild, 368.
75. Day, 158.
76. Ibid., 194.
77. *Banner of Light* 26, no. 14 (Dec. 18, 1869): 4.
78. *Banner of Light* 36, no. 18 (Jan. 30, 1875): 6.
79. Shari Huhndorf, *Going Native: Indians in the American Cultural Imagination* (Ithaca: Cornell University Press, 2001), 5.
80. Ter Ellingson, *The Myth of the Noble Savage* (Berkeley: University of California Press, 2001), 194.
81. *Banner of Light* 50, no. 4 (Oct. 15, 1881): 8.
82. Richmond, 7.
83. Fairchild, 418.
84. *Banner of Light* 5, no. 7 (May 14, 1859): 4.
85. Fairchild, 424.
86. Ibid., 150.
87. Ibid., 426.
88. Ibid., 428.
89. *Banner of Light* 5, no. 7 (May 14, 1859): 5.
90. *Banner of Light* 49, no. 17 (July 16, 1881): 6.
91. Day, 151.
92. Jackson Lears, *No Place of Grace: Antimodernism and the Transformation of American Culture, 1880–1920* (Chicago: University of Chicago Press, 1994).
93. *Banner of Light* 59 no. 1 (March 20, 1886): 2.
94. Ibid.
95. *Lifework,* 94.
96. *Banner of Light* 59, no. 1 (March 20, 1886): 2.

97. *Banner of Light* 50 no. 14 (Dec. 24, 1881): 4.
98. See for example *Banner of Light* 51, no. 17 (July 15, 1882): 4; *Banner of Light* 51, no. 25 (Sept. 9, 1882): 4; *Banner of Light* 54, no. 21 (Feb. 9, 1884): 6; and *Banner of Light* 59, no. 22 (Aug. 14, 1886): 6.
99. *Banner of Light* 57, no. 6 (April 25, 1885): 6.
100. Wolfe.
101. *Banner of Light* 39, no. 8 (May 20, 1876): 6.
102. *Banner of Light* 42, no. 20 (Feb. 9, 1878): 6.
103. *Banner of Light* 48, no. 2 (Oct. 2, 1880): 6.
104. *Banner of Light* 19, no. 13 (June 16, 1866): 6.
105. *Banner of Light* 35, no. 22 (Aug. 29, 1874): 6.
106. *Banner of Light* 48, no. 1 (Sept. 25, 1880): 6.
107. *Banner of Light* 48, no. 21 (Feb. 12, 1881): 6.
108. *Banner of Light* 49, no. 6 (April 30, 1881): 6.
109. *Banner of Light* 49, no. 22 (Aug. 20, 1881): 6.

Chapter 5. Race and Reform Among Spiritualists

1. McGarry, 71.
2. Ibid., 82.
3. William Ramsey, *Spiritualism, A Satanic Delusion, and a Sign of the Times* (Rhode Island: H. L. Hastings, 1856), 67.
4. *Banner of Light* 6, no. 20 (Feb. 11, 1860): 6.
5. Bederman, 25.
6. Berkhofer, 59.
7. Dr. J. M. Peebles, *Seers of the Ages: Embracing Spiritualism Past and Present* (Chicago: Progressive Thinker Publishing House, 1903), 322.
8. Ruth Etnier, "Training Indian Girls," *Indian's Friend* (Feb. 1901): 2; quoted in Peggy Pascoe, *Relations of Rescue: The Search for Female Moral Authority in the American West, 1874–1939* (Oxford: Oxford University Press, 1990), 115.
9. William Jackson Crawford, *Hints and Observations for Those Investigating the Phenomena of Spiritualism* (New York: E. P. Dutton, 1918), 38.
10. C. A. Burgess, ed., *Pictorial Spiritualism* (Illinois: Illinois State Spiritualist Association, 1922).
11. Cox, 192.
12. Shelhamer, 85, quoted in Cox, 195.

13. McGarry, 80.
14. *Banner of Light* 1, no. 5 (May 5, 1857): 6.
15. *Banner of Light* 22, no. 22 (Feb. 15, 1868): 8.
16. Ibid.
17. *Religio-Philosophical Journal* 6, no. 22 (Aug. 21, 1869): 4.
18. Ibid.
19. *Religio-Philosophical Journal* 14, no. 14 (June 21, 1873): 1.
20. *Banner of Light* 36, no. 4 (Oct. 24, 1874): 4.
21. H. A. Giles, "Mesmerism, Planchette, and Spiritualism in China," *Fraser's Magazine* 99 NS19 (1879): 239.
22. Ibid., 244.
23. Ibid., 242.
24. Ibid.
25. Ibid., 243.
26. Ibid., 239.
27. Louis Ebé Boclé, *Future Life: In the Light of Ancient Wisdom and Modern Science* (Chicago: A. C. McClurg, 1906), 33.
28. Ibid.
29. *Seers of the Ages*, 328.
30. Berkhofer, 169.
31. Abraham P. Pierce, *The Revelator: Being an Account of the 21 Days' Entrancement of Abraham P. Pierce, Spirit-Medium of Belfast Maine, together with a Sketch of His Life* (Boston: Adams and Company, 1870), 47.
32. Ibid., 60.
33. Ibid.
34. *Banner of Light* 6, no. 5 (Oct. 29, 1859): 7.
35. *Banner of Light* 26, no. 17 (Jan. 8, 1870): 4.
36. *Banner of Light* 32, no. 4 (Oct. 5, 1872): 4.
37. *Banner of Light* 21, no. 14 (June 22, 1867): 3.
38. *Banner of Light* 27, no. 16 (July 2, 1870): 4.
39. *Banner of Light* 29, no. 19 (July 22, 1871): 4.
40. *Banner of Light* 30, no. 23 (Feb. 17, 1872): 4.
41. *Banner of Light* 41, no. 3 (April 14, 1877): 4.
42. *Banner of Light* 43, no. 24 (Sept. 7, 1878): 4.
43. *Shades of Hiawatha*, 42.
44. *Banner of Light* 48, no. 4 (Oct. 16, 1880): 4.
45. *Banner of Light* 54, no. 26 (March 15, 1884): 4.
46. Ibid.

47. Hayes Peter Mauro, *The Art of Americanization at the Carlisle Indian School* (Albuquerque: New Mexico University Press, 2011), 3.
48. *Banner of Light* 55, no. 13 (June 14, 1884): 4.
49. *Banner of Light* 13, no. 4 (April 18, 1863): 5.
50. *Banner of Light* 25, no. 26 (Sept. 11, 1869): 4.
51. *Banner of Light* 6, no. 5 (Oct. 29, 1859): 7.
52. *Banner of Light* 11, no. 22 (Aug. 23, 1862): 4.
53. Bederman, 21.
54. *Banner of Light* 12, no. 4 (Oct. 18, 1862): 3.
55. Farmer, 312.
56. J. Burns, O.S.T. "What and Where Is Revelation? A Reply to the Rt. Hon. W. E. Gladstone, M.P. Cavendish Rooms, London, Jan. 10, 1886," *Medium and Daybreak* (Jan. 22, 1886): 50.
57. Ibid.
58. Mr. E. W. Wallis at Rochdale, "The Soul: Clairvoyance and Psychometry," *Medium and Daybreak* (Jan. 22, 1886): 49.
59. *Banner of Light* 5, no. 22 (Aug. 27, 1859): 3.
60. *Banner of Light* 21, no. 14 (June 22, 1867): 8.
61. *Banner of Light* 23, no. 21 (Aug. 8, 1868): 8.
62. *Banner of Light* 24, no. 9 (Nov. 14, 1868): 4.
63. *Banner of Light* 26, no. 4 (Oct. 9, 1869): 4.
64. *Banner of Light* 33, no. 12 (June 21, 1873): 8.
65. *Banner of Light* 33, no. 17 (July 26, 1873): 4.
66. *Banner of Light* 50, no. 5 (Oct. 22, 1881): 8.
67. *Banner of Light* 46, no. 5 (Oct. 25, 1879): 4.
68. Ibid.
69. *Banner of Light* 55, no. 16 (July 5, 1884): 4.
70. Adams, 8.
71. Greenberg, 44.
72. Farmer, 311.
73. *Banner of Light* 21, no. 11 (June 1, 1867): 4.
74. *Banner of Light* 21, no. 14 (June 22, 1867): 8.
75. *Banner of Light* 28, no. 22 (Feb. 11, 1871): 4.
76. *Banner of Light* 32, no. 10 (Nov. 16, 1872): 4; Adams, 8.
77. "Gold and Indians," *Banner of Light* 35, no. 26 (Sept. 26, 1874): 4.
78. *Banner of Light* 42, no. 13 (Dec. 22, 1877): 4.
79. *Banner of Light* 44, no. 10 (Nov. 30, 1878): 4.
80. Ibid.

81. *Banner of Light* 48, no. 10 (Nov. 27, 1880): 4.
82. *Banner of Light* 10, no. 2 (Oct. 5, 1861): 5.
83. *Banner of Light* 13, no. 6 (May 2, 1868): 3.
84. *Banner of Light* 23, no. 16 (July 4, 1868): 4.
85. *Banner of Light* 28, no. 16 (Dec. 31, 1870): 4.
86. Ibid.
87. *Banner of Light* 34, no. 17 (Jan. 24, 1874): 4.
88. *Banner of Light* 12, no. 20 (Feb. 7, 1863): 4.
89. *Banner of Light* 36, no. 3 (Oct. 17, 1874): 4.
90. Ibid.
91. *Banner of Light* 46, no. 1 (Sept. 27, 1879): 4.
92. *Banner of Light* 7, no. 4 (April 21, 1860): 4.
93. *Banner of Light* 19, no. 13 (June 16, 1866): 4.
94. *Banner of Light* 21, no. 10 (May 25, 1867): 4.
95. *Banner of Light* 21, no. 14 (June 22, 1867): 8.
96. *Banner of Light* 24, no. 9 (Nov. 14, 1868): 4.
97. *Banner of Light* 54, no. 25 (March 8, 1884): 4.
98. *Herald of Progress* 133, vol. 3 no. 29 (Sept. 6, 1862): 5.
99. *Banner of Light* 21, no. 24 (Aug. 21, 1867): 4.
100. *Banner of Light* 22, no. 4 (Oct. 12, 1867): 4.
101. *Banner of Light* 39, no. 17 (July 22, 1876): 4.
102. *Banner of Light* 42, no. 6 (Nov. 3, 1877): 6.
103. Coward, 197.
104. *Banner of Light* 45, no. 16 (July 12, 1879): 4.
105. *Banner of Light* 16 no. 13 (Dec. 17, 1864): 3.
106. *Banner of Light* 39, no. 12 (June 17, 1876): 4.
107. James Bathurst, *Atomic-Consciousness. An Explanation of Ghosts, Spiritualism, Witchcraft: Occult Phenomena, and All Supernormal Manifestations* (Exeter: Harris and Haddon, 1892), 106.
108. *Banner of Light* 40, no. 10 (Dec. 2, 1876): 5.
109. *Banner of Light* 50, no. 9 (Nov. 19, 1881): 6.
110. Bederman, 181.
111. *Banner of Light* 24, no. 5 (Oct. 17, 1868): 4.
112. *Banner of Light* 24, no. 14 (Dec. 19, 1868): 4.
113. *Banner of Light* 42, no. 14 (Dec. 29, 1877): 2.
114. Ibid.
115. *Banner of Light* 39, no. 18 (July 29, 1876): 5.
116. *Banner of Light* 16, no. 19 (Jan. 28, 1865): 4.

117. McGarry, 79.
118. *Banner of Light* 24, no. 9 (Nov. 14, 1868): 4.
119. *Banner of Light* 35, no. 5 (May 3, 1873): 8.
120. *Banner of Light* 46, no. 3 (Oct. 11, 1879): 4.
121. *Banner of Light* 19, no. 8 (May 12, 1866): 4.
122. *Banner of Light* 24, no. 5 (Oct. 17, 1868): 4.
123. *Banner of Light* 24, no. 19 (Jan. 23, 1869): 4.
124. *Banner of Light* 33, no. 15 (July 12, 1873): 8.
125. *Banner of Light* 37, no. 26 (Sept. 26, 1875): 5.
126. *Banner of Light* 46, no. 1 (Sept. 27, 1879): 4.
127. *Banner of Light* 48, no. 21 (Feb. 12, 1881): 4.
128. *Incorporation of America*, 30.
129. *Banner of Light* 19, no. 20 (Aug. 4, 1866): 4.
130. *Banner of Light* 19, no. 22 (Aug. 18, 1866): 2.
131. Deloria, 91.
132. *Banner of Light* 26, no. 16 (Jan. 1, 1870): 4.
133. *Banner of Light* 30, no. 24 (Feb. 24, 1872): 4.
134. *Banner of Light* 47, no. 15 (July 3, 1880): 4.
135. *Banner of Light* 53, no. 17 (July 14, 1883): 4.
136. Hoxie, xiii.
137. Adams 22.
138. *Banner of Light* 58, no. 6 (Oct. 24, 1885): 4.
139. Deloria, 104; Smith, 7.
140. Hoxie, 36.
141. *Banner of Light* 60, no. 14 (Dec. 18, 1886): 4; Prucha, 629.
142. Adams, 7.
143. *Banner of Light* 48, no. 12 (Dec. 11, 1880): 4.
144. *Banner of Light* 22, no. 8 (Nov. 9, 1867): 4.
145. *Banner of Light* 22, no. 18 (Jan. 18, 1868): 5.
146. *Banner of Light* 36, no. 15 (Jan. 9, 1875): 4.
147. *Banner of Light* 53, no. 9 (May 19, 1883): 4.
148. *Banner of Light* 39, no. 19 (Aug. 7, 1875): 4; see also *Banner of Light* 37, no. 24 (Sept. 11, 1875): 4.
149. *Banner of Light* 42, no. 9 (Nov. 24, 1877): 4.
150. *Banner of Light* 23, no. 18 (July 18, 1868): 4.
151. *Banner of Light* 33, no. 19 (Aug. 9, 1873): 3.
152. *Banner of Light* 52, no. 24 (March 3, 1883): 4.
153. *Banner of Light* 53, no. 4 (April 14, 1883): 4.

154. Ibid; *Banner of Light* 56, no. 15 (Dec. 27, 1884): 4.
155. *Banner of Light* 58, no. 20 (Jan. 30, 1886): 4.
156. Adams, 21.
157. Pascoe, 144.
158. Smith, 5.

BIBLIOGRAPHY

PRIMARY MATERIALS

Abbot, David. *Behind the Scenes with the Mediums.* Chicago: Open Court, 1907.
"Affinities Unchangeable." *The Principle* 2, no. 7 (June 1858): 50–56.
Armstrong, Honorable Perry A. *The Sauks and the Black Hawk War, with Biological Sketches, etc.* Springfield: H. W. Rokker, Printer and Binder, 1887.
Ballou, Adin. *An Exposition of Views Respecting the Principal Facts, Causes, and Peculiarities Involved in Spirit Manifestations: Together with Interesting Phenomenal Statements and Communications.* Boston: Bela Marsh, 1852.
Banner of Light (1857–1905).
Barrett, Harrison D., ed. *Lifework of Mrs. Cora L. V. Richmond.* Chicago: Hack and Anderson, 1895.
Barrett, J. O. *The Spiritual Pilgrim: A Biography of James Peeblees.* Boston: William White, 1872.
Bathurst, James. *Atomic Consciousness. An Explanation of Ghosts, Spiritualism, Witchcraft: Occult Phenomena, and all Supernormal Manifestations.* Exeter: Harris and Haddon, 1892.
Beecher, Charles. *A Review of the Spiritual Manifestations Read before the Congregational Association of New York and Brooklyn.* London: Thomas Bosworth and Clarke, Beeton and Co., 1853.
———. *Spiritual Manifestations.* Boston: Lee and Shepard; New York: Charles T. Dillingham, 1879.

Bertolacci, William Robert. *Christian Spiritualism: Wherein Is Shown the Extension of the Human Faculties, by the Application of Modern Spiritual Phenomena, According to the Doctrine of Christ.* London: Emily Faithfull Victoria Press, 1864.

Billings, F. S. "Spiritualism v. Materialism." *Psychical Review* 2 (1893–94): 317–30.

"Blackfoot's Work." *Mind and Matter* 3, no. 8 M.S. 33 (January 15).

Bliss, James. "A Proposition." *Mind and Matter* 3, no. 8 M.S. 33 (January 15).

———. "Special Notice from 'Bliss' Chief's Band." *Mind and Matter* 3, no. 8 M.S. 33 (January 15).

Boclé, Louis Ebé. *Future Life: In the Light of Ancient Wisdom and Modern Science.* 2nd ed. Chicago: A. C. McClurg, 1906.

The Boston Investigator XLVIII (June 19, 1878): 1.

Britten, Emma Hardinge. *Address Delivered at the Winter Soirees.* London: Thomas Scott, 1865.

———. *Autobiography.* Edited by Mrs. Margaret Wilkinson. London: Deansgate and Ridgefield, 1900.

———. *Modern American Spiritualism: A Twenty Years' Record of the Communion Between Earth and the World of the Spirits. Third Edition.* New York: 1870.

Buchanan, Dr. J. R. "Spirituality and Insanity." *Spiritual Telegraph* (June 11, 1853): 1.

Burns, J., O.S.T. "What and Where is Revelation?: A Reply to the Rt. Hon. W. E. Gladstone, M.P. London January 10, 1886. *The Medium and Daybreak* (January 22, 1886): 49.

Caithness, Countess of. *Old Truths in a New Light, or, An Earnest Endeavor to Reconcile Material Science with Spiritual Science and with Scripture.* London: Chapman and Hall, 1876.

"Cancers Cured by Spirits." *Spiritual Telegraph* 3, no. 35 (December 30, 1854): 3.

Capron, Eliab W., and Henry D. Barron. *Singular Revelations. Explanation and History of the Mysterious Communion with Spirits, Comprehending the Rise and Progress of the Mysterious Noises in Western New York, Generally Received as Spiritual Communications.* 2nd ed. Auburn: Fowlers and Wells, 1850.

Carpenter, Dr. William. *Mesmerism, Spiritualism and Christianity Historically and Scientifically Considered: Two Lectures Delivered at the London Institution.* New York: D. Appleton, 1877.

Carrington, Herewald, PhD. *The Physical Phenomena of Spiritualism, Fradulent and Genuine.* New York: Dodd, Mead, 1907.
Chase, Warren. *The Gist of Spiritualism: Viewed Scientifically, Philosophically, Religiously, Politically, and Socially. In a Course of Five Lectures, Delivered in Washington, D.C. January 1865.* 3rd ed. Boston: William White, 1867.
Clark, Uriah. *Plain Guide to Spiritualism.* Boston: William White, 1868.
Coggshall, William Turner. *The Signs of the Times, Comprising a History of the Spirit-Rappings in Cincinnati and Other Places, with Notes of Clairvoyant Revealments.* Ben Franklin Book and Job Printing Office, 1851.
Coleman, Benjamin. *Spiritualism in America.* London: F. Pitman, 1861.
"A Colored Healing Medium." *The Spiritual Age* 1, no. 35 (August 28, 1858): 3.
Colville, William Juvenal. *Metaphysical Qualities: Answered in His Classes on Mental Healing, Held in Boston, Massachusetts during the Season of 1885–1886.* 6th ed. Cambridgeport: 1898.
"Communing with the Dead: Or, What a Chicago Times Reporter Saw and Heard at Mott's House, Memphis, Missouri." *Spiritualist at Work* 1, no. 12 (January 16, 1875): 113–15.
"Convention of Spiritualists." *Mind and Matter* 3, no. 8 (January 15, 1880).
Cox, J. D. *Modern Spiritualism Compared with Christianity, in a Debate between Joel Tiffany, Esq., of Painesville O. and Rev. Isaac Errett, or Warren, O. upon the Following Questions: I. Are the Phenomena and Teachings of Modern Spiritualism Identical in Character with those of Jesus of Nazareth? II. Is the Denomination Known as Disciples, Anti-christ in Faith and Practice? A Phonographic Report by J. D. Cox.* Warren, O: George Adams, 1855.
Crawford, W. J. *Hints and Observations for Those Investigating the Phenomena of Spiritualism.* New York: E. P. Dutton, 1918.
Crookes, William F. R. S. "Spiritualism Viewed by the Light of Modern Science." *The Quarterly Journal of Science* 7 (1870): 316–21.
Cross, Andrew W. "The Unseen World." *Intelligence or the Metaphysical Magazine* 6 (1897): 81–86.
Crowell, Dr. Eugene. *Spiritualism and Insanity.* Boston: Colby and Rich, 1877.
Daniels, J. W. *Spiritualism versus Christianity, or, Spiritualism Thoroughly Exposed.* New York: Miller, Orton, and Mulligan, 1856.
Davies, M. "Ghosts." *Victoria Magazine* 19 (1872): 256–60.
Davis, Andrew Jackson. *Memoranda of Persons, Places, and Events; Embracing Authentic Facts, Visions, Impressions, Discoveries in Magnetism, Clairvoyance, Spiritualism. Also Quotations from the Opposition.* New York: William White, 1868.

———. *The Philosophy of Special Providences: A Vision.* Boston: Bela Marsh, 1850.

Day, John W. *Biography of Mrs. J. H. Conant, the World's Medium of the Nineteenth Century.* 2nd ed. Boston: William White, 1873.

DeLaCamp, Otto. *A Spiritual Tour of the World. In Search of the Line of Life's Evolution.* Boston: Arena Publishing.

Dewey, Mary E. *Historical Sketch of the Formation and Achievements of the Women's National Indian Association in the United States.* Philadelphia: Women's National Indian Association, 1900.

Discourses through the mediumship of Mrs. Cora L. V. Tappan. The new science. Spiritual Ethics. London: J. Burns, Progressive Library and Spiritual Institution, 1875.

Drake, Samuel G. *Biography and History of the Indians of North America.* 3rd ed. Boston: O. L. Perkins, 1834.

Edgeworth. "Relative Longevity of the Negro and Mulatto." *The Spirit of the Age* 1, no. 23 (December 8, 1849): 355–56.

Edmonds, Judge John Worth. *An Appeal to the Public of Spiritualism: Spiritual Tracts, No. 1.* New York: S. T. Munson, 1858.

———. *Letters and Tracts on Spiritualism. Also Two Inspirational Orations by Cora L. V. Tappan and Particulars Respecting the Personal Career and Passing Away of Judge Edmonds.* Edited by J.Burns, Managing Representative of the Spiritual Institution. London: J. Burns Progressive Library and Spiritual Institution, 1875.

Edwards, Lester C. "Pocahontas Visits England." *The Social World* 1, no. 3 (September 1885): 45.

Evans, Reverend F. W. *Spiritualism on Trial: Containing the Arguments of Revered F. W. Evans in the Debate on Spiritualism between Him and mr. A. J. Fishback, held in Osceola, Iowa November 18 to November 28, 1874.* Cincinnati: Hitchcock and Walden, 1874.

Ferguson, J. B. *Spirit Communion: A Record of Communications Through H. B. Champion.* Parkersburg: Globe Press, 1888.

Fletcher, James Henry. *Spiritualism: Its Truth, Helpfulness, and Danger.* New York: The Occult Book Concern Publishers, 1915.

Franchezzo. *A Wanderer in the Spirit Lands.* Chicago: Progerssive Thinker Publishing House, 1901.

Garrett, Julia. *Mediums Unmasked: An Expose of Medium Spiritualism.* Los Angeles: H. N. Lee and Brothers, 1892.

Giles, H. A. "Mesmerism, Planchette, and Spiritualism in China." *Fraser's Magazine* 99 NS19 (1879): 238–45.

Gordon, William R. D. D. *A Three-fold Test of Modern Spiritualism*. New York: Charles and Scribner, 1856.

Hammond, Charles. *Light from the Spirit World. Comprising a Series of Articles on the Condition of Spirits and the Development of Mind in the Rudimental and Second Spheres, being Written Wholly by the Control of Spirits, without any Volition or Will by the Medium, or any Thought or Care in Regard to the Matter Presented by his Hand*. 2nd ed. Rochester: D. M. Dewey, Arcade Hall, 1852.

Hatch, Benjamin Franklin. *Spiritualists' Iniquities Unmasked, and the Hatch Divorce Case*. New York: B. F. Hatch, 1859.

Hawk, Black. *Autobiography of Ma-Ka-Tai-Me-She-Kia-Kiak or Black Hawk*. Translated by Antoine LeClaire. Edited by J. B. Patterson. 1834. 2007 ed. New York: Cosimo, 2007.

Herald of Progress (1860–64).

Hill, J. Arthur. *Spiritualism: Its History, Phenomena, and Doctrine*. New York: George Doran, 1919.

Hopkins, C. T. "Is Spiritism a Science?" *The Pioneer* 4, no. 4 (1855): 193–204.

Howitt, William. *The History of the Supernatural in all Ages and Nations and in all Churches Christian and Pagan Demonstrating a Universal Faith*. Philadelphia: J. B. Lippincott, 1863.

Hutton, R. H. "The Unspiritual World of Spiritualism." *The Victoria Magazine* 1 (1863): 42–60.

Jackson, Helen Hunt. *A Century of Dishonor: A Sketch of the United States Government's Dealings with Some of the Indian Tribes*. New York: Harper and Brothers, 1881.

Jackson, J. W., Esq. "Table-moving, Rappings, and Spiritual Manifestations." *The Zoist: A Journal of Cerebral Physiology and Mesmerism, and their Applications to Human Welfare* XI (March-January 1853–54): 412–29.

Johnson, Julia H. "Shakerism and Spiritualism." *Mind and Matter* M.S. 33 (October 2, 1880): 3.

Kernahan, Coulson. *Spiritualism: A Personal Experience and a Warning*. New York: Fleming H. Revell, 1920.

Lewes, George Henry. "Spiritualism and Materialism: Part I." *The Fortnightly Review* CVII (April 1876): 480–93.

———. "Spiritualism and Materialism: Part II." *The Fortnightly Review* CXIII (1876): 707–19.

"Lo, the Poor Indian!" *Spiritual Republic* 1, no. 15 (April 13, 1867): 233.
Long, Honorable John D. *Indian Question: Report of the Committee*. Boston: Frank Wood, Book and Job Printer, 1880.
Loveland, J. S., ed. "The Necessity of Scientific Culture." *Present Age* 2, no. 26 (December 11, 1869): 4.
"Materialism and Spiritualism." *Partridge and Brittan's Spiritual Telegraph* 4, no. 49 (April 5, 1856).
Mattison, Reverend H. A. M. *Spirit Rapping Unveiled! An Expose of the Origin, History, Theology and Philosophy of Certain Alleged Communications from the Spirit World, by Means of Spirit Rapping, Medium Writing, Physical Demonstrations, etc. with Illustrations*. New York: Mason Brothers, 1853.
McCabe, John. *Spiritualism: A Popular History from 1847*. New York: Dodd, Mead, 1920.
McIntosh, John. *Origin of the North American Indians*. New York: Nafis and Cornish, 1843.
The Medium and Daybreak (January 22, 1886): 49–53.
The Mirror of Progress 1, no. 3 (July 19, 1879): 2–3.
Myers, Frederick W. H. "Some Fresh Facts Indicating Man's Survival of Death." *National Review* 32 (1898–99): 230–42.
Nevins, J. West. *A Lecture on the Law of Spiritual Development*. Pennsylvania: Thomas Price, 1854.
New England Spiritualist 2, no. 19 (August 9, 1856): 4.
Olive Branch (1876).
Owen, Robert Dale. *Footfalls on the Boundary of Another World, with Narrative Illustrations*. Philadelphia: J. B. Lippincott, 1889.
Pease, A. Kelly. "Shaker Socialism." *Spiritual Telegraph* 4, no. 45 (March 8, 1856): 179.
Peebles, Dr. J. M. *The Conflict between Darwinianism and Spiritualism: Do all Tribes and Races Constitute One Human Species? Did Man Originate from Ascidians, Apes, and Gorillas? Are Animals Immortal?* Boston: Colby and Rich, 1876.
———. *Jesus: Myth, Man, or God; or, the Popular Theology and the Positive Religion Contrasted*. London: J. Burns Progressive Library, 1870.
———. *Seers of the Ages: Embracing Spiritualism Past and Present*. Chicago: Progressive Thinker Publishing House, 1903.
———. *Spiritualism in All Lands and Times: An Address to the International Congress of Spiritualists, held in London, June 1898*. Michigan: Drs. Peebles and Burroughs, 1899.

———. *What Is Spiritualism, Who Are These Spiritualists, and What Has Spiritualism Done for the World?* Peebles Institute Print, 1903.

Pierce, Abraham P. *The Revelator: Being an Account of the Twenty One Days' Entrancement of Abraham P. Pierce, Spirit-Medium at Belfast, Maine, Together with a Sketch of His Life.* Boston: Adams, 1870.

Princess Wahletka's Book of Knowledge.

Putnam, Allen. *Flashes of Light from the Spirit Land, through the Mediumship of Mrs. J. H. Conant.* Boston: William White, 1872.

Ramsey, William D. D. *Spiritualism, a Satanic Delusion, and a Sign of the Times.* Peace Dale: H. L. Hastings, 1856.

The Religio-Philosophical Journal (1865–1905).

Richmond, Cora Linn Victoria. *The Day After Death: A Discourse by Spirit Epes Sargent Delivered in Chicago, January 16, 1881.* Boston: Colby and Rich, 1881.

———. *A Discourse on Faith, Hope and Love: Delivered in New York, Sunday April 23, 1857, to which is added a Report of a Philosophical Investigation of the Nature of Mediumship.* B. F. Hatch, 1858.

———. *Ouina's Canoe and Christmas Offering: Filled with Flowers for the Darlings of Earth, Given through her Medium, "Water Lilly."* Ottumwa: D. M. and N. P. Fox, 1882.

Second Annual Report of the Board of Indian Commissioners to the Secretary of the Interior, for Submission to the President for the Year 1870. Washington: Gov. Printing Office, 1871.

Schindler, Mary Dana. *A Southerner among the Spirits: A Record of Investigations into the Spiritual Phenomena.* Memphis: Southern Baptist Publication Society, 1877.

Shelhamer, Mary Theresa. *Life and Labor in the Spirit World: Being a Description of Locatlities, Employments, Surroundings, and Conditions in the Spheres.* Boston: Colby and Rich, 1885.

———. *Teachings and Illustration as they Emanate from the Spiritual: Methods of Concentration—Application and Demonstration of Spiritual Works—How they Build Homes, Temples, Heal the Soul-Sick Who Come to their Worlds from Earth—How Worlds are Made.* Chicago: The Progressive Thinker Publishing House, 1908.

Shepard, Olivia F. "Notes of Progress." *Mind and Matter* 6, no. 24 (July 11, 1885): 3.

The Soul 1, no. 1 (January 1888).

Smith, H. Arthur. "The Facts and Hypotheses of Spiritualism." *The Wesleyan and Methodist Magazine* 118 (1895): 841–45.
The Spirit Messenger 1, no. 31 (March 8, 1851): 243.
"The Spirit of Samosett: from the New York Sun." *The Spiritualist at Work* 1, no. 5 (October 10, 1874): 63.
Spiritual Clarion 1, no. 35 (August 29, 1857): 1–2.
The Spiritual Offering (March 1879): 288–90.
The Spiritual Offering 1, no. 12 (April 1878): 517–19.
The Spiritual Republic (1867).
Spiritual Scientist (October 15, 1874): 65.
Spiritual Scientist 2, no. 7 (April 22, 1875): 75.
The Spiritualist at Work 2, no. 8 (November 20, 1875): 8.
The Star of Truth 1, no. 2 (July 1852).
Stevens, Frank Everett. *The Black Hawk War, Including a Review of Black Hawk's Life.* Chicago: Illinois Chamber of Commerce, 1903.
Thompson, E. J. "Among the Spirits." *Scot's Magazine* 21 (1897–98): 155–60.
Thwaites, R. G. "War with Black Hawk." *Magazine of Western History* 5 (1886–87): 32–45.
Tiffany, Joel. *Spiritualism Explained: Being a Series of Twelve Lectures Delivered before the New York Conference of Spiritualists in January, 1856 Reported Phonographically by Graham and Ellinwood.* New York: Graham and Ellinwood, 1856.
Truesdell, John W. *The Bottom Facts Concerning the Science of Spiritualism: Delivered from Careful Investigations Covering a Period of Twenty Five Years.* New York: G. W. Dillingham, 1892.
Tuttle, Hudson. "Evidences of Spiritualism." *The Radical* 7 (1870): 373–84.
———. "The Social Aspect of Spiritualism." *Ohio Spiritualist* 1, no. 7 (August 15, 1868): 3–4.
Verner, Alexander. *Success and Happiness: How to Gain Health, Money and Happiness, and to Cure Disease; or, Personal Magnetism and Will Power.* Chicago: The Marlowe Company.
Walton, Samuel B. " 'Friends' Among the Indians: from the Friends Intelligencer." *Present Age* 2 no. 19 (October 23, 1869): 4.
Walker, Francis A. *The Indian Question.* Boston: James R. Osgood, 1874.
Wallis, Mr. E. W. "The Soul: Clairvoyance and Psychometry." *The Medium and Daybreak* (January 22, 1886): 50.
Welsh, Herbert. *The Indian Question Past and Present.* J. N. McClintock, 1890.

Wharton, F. "Spiritualism and Jurisprudence." *Lippincott's Magazine of Popular Literature and Science* 16 (1875): 423–33.
Wilson, Ebenezer V. *The Truths of Spiritualism: Immortality Proved Beyond a Doubt by Living Witnesses.* Chicago: Hazlitt and Reed, 1876.
Wolfe, Dr. Napoleon Bonaparte. *Startling Facts in Modern Spiritualism.* Cincinnati: 1874.
Worden, Marcellus. "Religion a Science." *The Spirit of the Age* no. 9 (September 1, 1849): 159.

Theses

Angelino, Bernadino Rose. "Beckoning the Red Man's Spirits: Exploring the Boundaries of Gender, Race, Sacred and Commercial Spaces at the Wigwam Spiritualist Temple Onset, Massachusetts, 1880–1913." PhD diss., University of Massachusetts, Boston, 2010.
Bednarowski, Mary Farrell. "Nineteenth-Century American Spiritualism: An Attempt at a Scientific Religion." PhD diss., University of Minnesota, 1973.
Brown, Burton Gates Jr. "Spiritualism in Nineteenth-Century America." PhD diss., Boston University Graduate School, 1973.
Burgess, Charles A, ed. *Pictorial Spiritualism.* Illinois State Spiritualist Association, 1922.
Burgess, Larry E. "The Lake Mohonk Conferences on the Indian, 1883–1916." PhD diss., The Claremont Graduate University, 1972.
Carroll, Bret. "Unfree Spirits: Spiritualism and Religious Authority in Antebellum America." PhD diss., Cornell University, 1991.
Coen, Rena. "The Indian as the Noble Savage in Nineteenth-Century American Art." PhD diss., University of Minnesota, 1969.
Gilcreast, Everett Arthur. "Richard Henry Pratt and American Indian Policy, 1877–1906: a Study of the Assimilation Movement." PhD diss., Yale University, 1967.
Glass, Grace Marissa. "Visions for Company: Otherness and the Supernatural in Nineteenth-Century England and America." PhD diss., University of Michigan, 2009.
Keller, Robert H. Jr. "The Protestant Churches and Grant's Peace Policy: A Study in Church-State Relations, 1869–1882." PhD diss., The University of Chicago, 1967.

Lenker, Lisa M. "Haunted Culture and Surrogate Space: A New Historicist Account of Nineteenth-Century American Spiritualism." PhD diss., Stanford University, 1998.
Morita, Sally Jean. "Modern Spiritualism and Reform in America." PhD diss., University of Oregon, 1995.
Nelson, Robert Kent. "Society of Souls: Spirit, Friendship, and the Antebellum Reform Imagination." PhD diss., College of William and Mary, 2006.
Nicklason, Fred Herbert. "The Early Career of Henry L. Dawes, 1816–1871." PhD diss., Yale University, 1967.
Wanken, Helen M. " 'Women's Sphere' and Indian Reform: The Women's National Indian Association, 1879–1901." PhD diss., Marquette University, 1981.

SCHOLARLY BOOKS AND ARTICLES

Abzug, Robert. *Cosmos Crumbling: American Reform and the Religious Imagination*. Oxford: Oxford University Press, 1994.
Adams, David Wallace. *Education for Extinction: American Indians and the Boarding School Experience, 1875–1928*. Lawrence: University Press of Kansas, 1995.
Albanese, Catherine. *A Republic of Mind and Spirit: A Cultural History of American Metaphysical Religion*. New Haven: Yale University Press, 2007.
Athearn, Robert G. *William Tecumseh Sherman and the Settlement of the West*. Norman: University of Oklahoma Press, 1995.
Baer, Hans. *The Black Spiritual Movement: A Religious Response to Racism*. Knoxville: University Press of Tennessee, 1984.
Barnett, Louise K. *The Ignoble Savage: American Literary Racism, 1790–1890*. Westport: Greenwood Press, 1976.
Barrow, L. *Independent Spirits: Spiritualism and the English Plebeians, 1850–1910*. London: Routledge and Kegan Paul, 1986.
Beaver, R. Pierce. *Church, State, and the American Indians: Two and a Half Centuries of Partnership in Missions between Protestant Churches and Government*. Saint Louis: Concordia, 1966.
Bederman, Gail. *Manliness and Civilization: A Cultural History of Gender and Race in the United States, 1880–1917*. Chicago: University of Chicago Press, 1995.

Bell, Michael Davitt. *Hawthorne and the Historical Romance of New England.* Princeton: Princeton University Press, 1971.
Bennett, Bridget. "Sacred Theatres: Shakers, Spiritualists, Theatricality, and the Indian in the 1830s and 1840s." *The Drama Review* 40, no. 3 (T184) (Fall 2005): 114–34.
———. *Transatlantic Spiritualism and Nineteenth-century American Literature.* New York: Palgrave Macmillan, 2007.
Bergland, Renee L. *The National Uncanny: Indian Ghosts and American Subjects.* Hanover: Dartmouth, 2000.
Berkhofer, Robert F. Jr. *Salvation and the Savage.* Cambridge: Atheneum, 1972.
———. *The White Man's Indian: Images of the American Indian from Columbus to the Present.* New York: Alfred A. Knopf, 1978.
Berry, Jason. *The Spirit of Black Hawk: A Mystery of Africans and Indians.* Jackson: University Press of Mississippi, 1995.
Bird, S. Elizabeth. *Dressing in Feathers: The Construction of the Indian in American Popular Culture.* Boulder: Westview, 1996.
Bjorling, Joel. *Consulting Spirits: A Bibliography.* Westport: Greenwood, 1998.
Braude, Ann. *News from the Spirit World: A Checklist of American Spiritualist Periodicals, 1847–1900.* Worcester: American Antiquarian Society, 1990.
———. *Radical Spirits: Spiritualism and Women's Rights in Nineteenth-Century America.* Boston: Beacon Press, 1989.
Brooks, Daphne. *Bodies in Dissent: Spectacular Performances of Race and Freedom, 1850–1910.* Durham: Duke University Press, 2006.
Buescher, John B. *The Other Side of Salvation: Spiritualism and the Nineteenth-Century Religious Experience.* Boston: Skinner House Books, 2004.
Carol Christ, *Diving Deep and Surfacing: Women Writers on Spiritual Quest.* Boston: Beacon Press, 1995.
Carter, Kent. *Dawes Commission: And the Allotment of the Five Civilized Tribes, 1893–1914.* Nashville: Ancestry Publishing, 1999.
Castle, Terry. *The Female Thermometer: Eighteenth-Century Culture and the Invention of the Uncanny.* Oxford: Oxford University Press, 1995.
Churchill, Ward. *Kill the Indian, Save the Man: The Genocidal Impact of American Indian Residential Schools.* San Francisco: City Light Books, 2004.
Clifton, James A., ed. *The Invented Indian: Cultural Fictions and Government Politics.* Piscataway: Transaction Publishers, 1990.

Colbert, Charles. *Haunted Visions: Spiritualism and American Art.* Philadelphia: University of Pennsylvania Press, 2011.

Conn, Steven. *History's Shadow: Native Americans and Historical Consciousness in the Ninteenth Century.* Chicago: University of Chicago Press, 2004.

Coward, John. *The Newspaper Indian: Native American Identity in the Press, 1820–1890.* Urbana: University of Illinois Press, 1999.

Cox, Robert. *Body and Soul: A Sympathetic History of American Spiritualism.* Charlottesville: University of Virginia Press, 2003.

Crow, Charles, and Howard Kerr, eds. *Occult in America.* Urbana: University of Illinois Press, 1986.

Deloria, Philip. *Playing Indian.* New Haven: Yale University Press, 1998.

Delp, Robert W. "Andrew Jackson Davis: Prophet of American Spiritualism." *The Journal of American History* 54, no. 1 (June 1967): 43–56.

Dippie, Brian W. *The Vanishing American: White Attitudes and U.S. Indian Policy.* Lawrence: University Press of Kansas, 1991.

Drinnon, Richard. *Facing West: The Metaphysics of Indian-Hating and Empire-Building.* Norman: University of Oklahoma Press, 1997.

Ellingson, Ter. *The Myth of the Noble Savage.* Berkeley: University of California Press, 2001.

Fabian, Ann. *The Skull Collectors: Race, Science, and America's Unburied Dead.* Chicago: University of Chicago Press, 2010.

Fagaly, William. *Tools of Her Ministry: The Art of Sister Gertrude Morgan.* New York: American Folk Art Museum, 2004.

Farmer, Jared. *On Zion's Mount: Mormons, Indians, and the American Landscape.* Cambridge: Harvard University Press, 2008.

Ferguson, Christine. *Determined Spirits: Eugenics, Heredity, and Racial Regeneration in Anglo-American Spiritualist Writing, 1848–1930.* Edinburgh: Edinburgh University Press, 2012.

Fiedler, Leslie A. *Return of the Vanishing American.* New York: Stein and Day, 1992.

Fritz, Henry Eugene. *The Movement for Indian Assimilation, 1860–1890.* Reprint. Westport: Greenwood Press, 1981.

Genetin-pilawa, C. Joseph. *Crooked Paths to Allotment: The Fight over Federal Indian Policy after the Civil War.* Chapel Hill: University of North Carolina Press, 2012.

Gordon, Avery F. *Ghostly Matters: Haunting the Sociological Imagination.* Minneapolis: University of Minnesota Press, 1997.

Green, Rayna. "The Pocahontas Perplex: The Image of Indian Women in American Culture." *The Massachusetts Review* 16, no. 4 (Autumn 1975): 698–714.

———. "The Tribe Called Wannabee: Playing Indian in America and Europe." *Folklore* 99, no. 1(1988): 30–55.

Greenberg, Amy S. *Manifest Manhood and the Antebellum American Empire.* Cambridge: Cambridge University Press, 2005.

Jacobs, Claude, and Andrew Kaslow. *The Spiritual Churches of New Orleans: Origins, Beliefs, and Rituals of an African-American Religion.* Knoxville: University Press of Tennessee, 1991.

Haller, John S. Jr. *Outcasts from Evolution: Scientific Attitudes of Racial Inferiority, 1859–1900.* Urbana: Illinois University Press, 1971.

Hill, Edward E. *Preliminary Inventory of the Records of the Bureau of Indian Affairs.* Washington, DC: The National Archives, 1965.

Hoig, Stan. *The Sand Creek Massacre.* Norman: University of Oklahoma Press, 1974.

Horowitz, Mitch. *Occult America: White House Séances, Ouija Circles and Masons, and the Secret History of Our Nation* New York: Bantam, 2010.

Hoxie, Frederick E. *A Final Promise: The Campaign to Assimilate the Indians, 1880–1920.* Lincoln: University of Nebraska Press, 2001.

Huhndork, Shari. *Going Native: Indians in the American Cultural Imagination.* Ithaca: Cornell University Press, 2001.

Jung, Patrick. *Black Hawk War of 1832.* Norman: Oklahoma University Press, 2007.

Keller, Robert H. Jr. *American Protestantism and United States Indian Policy, 1869–82.* Lincoln: University of Nebraska Press, 1983.

Kelman, Ari. *A Misplaced Massacre: Struggling over the Memory of Sand Creek.* Cambridge: Harvard University Press, 2013.

Kerber, Linda K. "The Abolitionist Perception of the Indian." *The Journal of American History* 62, no. 2 (September 1975): 271–95.

Kerr, Howard. *Mediums, Spirit Rappers and Roaring Radicals: Spiritualism in American Literature, 1850–1900.* Urbana: University of Illinois Press, 1973.

———, and Charles L. Crow, eds. *The Occult in America: New Historical Perspectives.* Urbana: University of Illinois Press, 1983.

Kucich, John. *Ghostly Communion: Cross-Cultural Spiritualism in Nineteenth-Century American Literature.* Hanover: Dartmouth, 2004.

Kvasnicka, Robert M., and Herman J. Viola, eds. *The Commissioners of Indian Affairs, 1824–1977*. Lincoln: University of Nebraska Press, 1979.

Lawlor, Mary. *Recalling the Wild: Naturalism and the Closing of the America West*. New Brunswick: Rutgers University Press, 2000.

Lears, T. J. Jackson. *No Place of Grace: Antimodernism and the Transformation of American Culture 1880–1920*. New York: Pantheon Books, 1981.

Leonard, Todd. *Talking to the Other Side: A History of Modern Spiritualism and Mediumship: A Study of Religion, Science, Philosophy, and Mediums that Encompass this American-Made Religion*. Bloomington: iUniverse, 2005.

Lindsey, Donal F. *Indians at the Hampton Institute, 1877–1923*. Urbana: University of Illinois Press, 1994.

Loring Priest. *Uncle Sam's Stepchildren: The Reformation of United States Indian Policy, 1865–1887*. Lincoln: University of Nebraska Press, 1975.

Lubbers, Klaus. *Born for the Shade: Stereotypes of the Native American in United States Literature and the Visual Arts, 1776–1894*. Amsterdam: Editions Rodopi, 1994.

Maddox, Lucy. *Citizen Indians: Native American Intellectuals, Race, and Reform*. Ithaca: Cornell University Press, 2006.

Mangan, J. A. *Manliness and Morality: Middle Class Masculinity in Britain and America, 1800–1940*. Edited by James Walvin. Manchester: Manchester University Press, 1991.

Mardock, Robert. *Reformers and the American Indian*. London: Eurospan, 1971.

Mathes, Valeria Sherer. "Helen Hunt Jackson and the Ponca Controversy." *Montana: The Magazine of Western History* 39, no. 1 (Winter 1989): 42–53.

———. "Nineteenth Century Women and Reform: The Women's National Indian Association." *American Quarterly* 14, no. 1 (Winter 1990): 1–18.

McCorristine, Shane. *Spiritualism, Mesmerism, and the Occult, 1800–1920*. London: Pickering and Chatto, 2012.

McGarry, Molly. *Ghosts of Futures Past: Spiritualism and the Cultural Politics of Nineteenth-Century America*. Berkeley: University of California Press, 2008.

Mielke, Laura. *Moving Encounters: Sympathy and the Indian Question in Antebellum Literature*. Amherst: University of Massachusetts Press, 2008.

Milner, Clyde A. II. *With Good Intentions: Quaker Work among the Pawnees, Otos, and Omahas in the 1870s.* Lincoln: University of Nebraska Press, 1982.

Mitchell, Lee Clark. *Witnesses to a Vanishing America: The Nineteenth-Century Response.* Princeton: Princeton University Press, 1981.

"The Modern Spiritualism as Flourishing Condition in the Quaker City." *New York Times,* December 2, 1884, 4.

Moore, Robert Laurence. *In Search of White Crows: Spiritualism, Parapsychology, and American Culture.* Oxford: Oxford University Press, 1977.

Mott, Frank Luther. *History of American Magazines, Volume II & III: 1865–1885.* Cambridge: Belknap Press of Harvard University Press, 1938.

Mullin, Robert Bruce. *Miracles and the Modern Religious Imagination.* New Haven: Yale University Press, 1996.

Olson, James C. *Red Cloud and the Sioux Problem.* Lincoln: University of Nebraska Press, 1965.

Ostler, Jeffrey. *The Plains Sioux and U.S. Colonialism from Lewis and Clark to Wounded Knee.* Cambridge: Cambridge University Press, 2004.

Otis, Delos Sackett. *The Dawes Act and the Allotment of Indians Lands.* Edited by Francis P. Prucha. Norman: University of Oklahoma Press, 1973.

Pascoe, Peggy. *Relations of Rescue: The Search for Female Moral Authority in the American West, 1874–1939.* Oxford: Oxford University Press, 1993.

Pearce, Roy Harvey. *Savagism and Civilization: A Study of the Indian and the American Mind.* Berkeley: University of California Press, 1988.

Perry, Lewis. *Radical Abolitionism: Anarchism and the Government of God in Antislavery Thought.* Knoxville: University of Tennessee Press, 1995.

Peter, Hayes. *The Art of Americanization at the Carlisle Indian School.* Albuquerque: University of New Mexico Press, 2011.

Prucha, Francis Paul. *American Indian Policy in Crisis: Christian Reformers and the Indian, 1865–1900.* Norman: University of Oklahoma Press, 1976.

———, ed. *Americanizing the American Indians: Writings by the "Friends of the Indian" 1880–1900.* Cambridge: Harvard University Press, 1973.

———. *Documents of United States Indian Policy.* 3rd ed. Lincoln: University of Nebraska Press, 2000.

———. *The Great Father: The United States Government and the American Indians.* Lincoln: University of Nebraska Press, 1986.

Quandt, Jean B. "Religion and Social Thought: The Secularization of Postmillenialism." *American Quarterly* 25, no. 4 (October 1973): 390–409.

Richardson, Judith. *Possessions: The History and Uses of Haunting in the Hudson Valley.* Cambridge and London: Harvard University Press, 2005.

Romero, Lora. "Vanishing Americans: Gender, Empire, and New Historicism." *American Literature* 63, no. 3 (September 1991): 385–404.

Scheckel, Susan. *The Insistence of the Indian: Race and Nationalism in Nineteenth-Century American Culture.* Princeton: Princeton University Press, 1998.

Schmidt, Leigh Eric. *Hearing Things: Religion, Illusion, and the American Enlightenment.* Cambridge: Harvard University Press, 2002.

Simard, Jean-Jacques. "White Ghosts, Red Shadows: The Reduction of North American Natives." In *The Invented Indian: Cultural Fictions and Government Policies*, edited by James A. Clifton. New Brunswick: Transaction Publishers, 1990.

Smith, Sherry L. *Reimagining Indians: Native Americans through Anglo Eyes, 1880–1940.* Oxford: Oxford University Press, 2002.

Sollors, Werner. "Dr. Benjamin Franklin's Celestial Telegraph, or Indian Blessings to Gas-Lit American Drawing Rooms." *American Quarterly* 35, no. 5 (Winter 1983): 459–80.

Stuart, Paul. *The Indian Office: Growth and Development of American Institution, 1865–1900.* Ann Arbor: UMI Research Press, 1979.

Taves, Ann. *Fits, Trances, and Visions: Experiencing Religion and Explaining Experience from Wesley to James.* Princeton: Princeton University Press, 1999.

Trachtenberg, Alan. *The Incorporation of America: Culture and Society in the Gilded Age.* New York: Hill and Wang, 1982.

———. *Shades of Hiawatha: Staging Indians, Making Americans, 1880–1930.* New York: Hill and Wang, 2005.

Trask, Kerry. *Black Hawk: The Battle for the Heart of America.* New York: Macmillan, 2007.

Vanderwerth, W. C. *Indian Oratory: Famous Speeches by Noted Indian Chiefs.* Norman: University of Oklahoma Press, 1979.

Vickers, Scott B. *Native American Identities: From Stereotype to Archetype in Art and Literature.* Albuquerque: University of New Mexico Press, 1998.

Washburn, Wilcomb E. *The Assault on Indian Tribalism: The General allotment Law (Dawes Act of 1887).* Malabar: Krieger, 1986.

Weisberg, Barbara. *Talking to the Dead: Kate and Maggie Fox and the Rise of Spiritualism.* New York: HarperOne, 2005.
Wheelan, Joseph. *Terrible Swift Sword: The Life of General Philip H. Sheridan.* Cambridge: Da Capo Press, 2012.
Wolfreys, Julian. *Victorian Hauntings: Spectrality, Gothic, the Uncanny, and Literature.* New York: Palgrave, 2002.
Woodworth, Samuel. *Champions of Freedom.* Charleston: Nabu Press, 2011.

INDEX

Anderson, Leafy, 51–53
Anoka (spirit), 101, 110

Ballou, Adin, 58
Beeson, John, 85, 128, 135–136
Big Beaver (spirit), 60
Big Eagle, xxvii, 48, 74–75, 99
Bilmie, William, 78
Black Hawk, xx, 21–9, 36–9, 50–51, 68, 140 ; (spirit), xvi–xvii, xx, xxiv, 21, 30–53, 69, 102
Bland, Dr. T. A., 147
Bonaparte, Josephine (spirit), 8
Boston Indian Citizenship Association, 148
Bowlegs, Billy (spirit), 85
Bright Star (spirit), 94
Britten, Emma Hardinge, xxv, 2–3, 6, 43, 45, 49–50, 67, 123

Carlisle Institute, xiii, xxi, 13, 126–127, 149
Catlin, George, 26, 44, 101
Celestial Spheres, xii, 2, 7–10, 49, 66, 69, 73–74, 79–83, 93, 97, 99, 110–112, 118–127, 131, 147
Cherokee Indians, xiii, xxvi, 13, 60, 116, 125
Cheyenne Indians, 72, 82, 100–101, 139
Child, Dr. Henry T., 79
Children's Progressive Lyceum, 102
Chivington, General John, 72, 82–84, 116
Christian Science, 14
Civil War, xxii, xxviii, 12, 51
Coleman, Benjamin, 32–34, 40–43
Compton, Mrs., 60–62
Conant, Fannie, xiv, xxi, 57–58, 75, 83, 85, 88, 100–102, 108–109
Cooper, James Fenimore, 34, 102
Custer, General George, 116, 138–40; (spirit), 139

Dakota Wars, 24
Davis, Andrew Jackson, xv, 10, 102
Darwin, Charles, xxix, 12, 41, 65
Dawes, Senator Henry, 147–48

Dawes Severalty Act, xiii, xxi, xxiv, 13, 117, 147–152
Day, John, 87–88, 100
Delano, Columbus, 135–136
Dewdrop (spirit), 101
Dunn, Dr. E. C., 59, 69

Eddy, Horatio, 62, 67, 73, 93, 95
Em-mu-ne-es-ka (spirit). *See* Tappan, Minnie

Field, Dr. John, 69
Forest Flower (spirit), 112
Forest Lily (spirit), 112–13
Flying Arrow (spirit), 61
Fox Sisters, xv, 1, 5, 7, 141
Freemasonry, 5

Ghostliness, xiv, 15–19, 222–23, 27, 70, 129, 133
Grant Peace Policy, xiii, xxii, 4, 12–13
Grant, President Ulysses S., 75, 116, 136
The Great Spirit, xii, 27–9, 56, 59, 70–72, 76–84, 93, 99–100, 105–107, 112, 121

Hampton Institute, xiii, 76, 126, 149
The Happy Hunting Ground, xii, 105, 115, 145
Hatch, Cora. *See* Tappan, Cora
Haunting, xxi, xxviii, 15–19, 51, 133, 143, 151
Hayes, President Rutherford B., 112, 148
Hedges, Mr., 2
Hermeticism, xxviii

Hollis-Billings, Mrs., 60, 63
Honto (spirit), 93–95

Indian Peace Commission, xii, xvi, xxii-xxiii, 58, 102, 135, 148
Indian Problem, 11–13, 69, 77, 111, 145–152
Indian Question. *See* Indian Problem
Indian Removal, xiv, xxi-xxiii, xxvii, 11, 24–27, 37–38, 74, 77, 126, 129, 133–134
Indian Rights Association, xxii

Jackson, President Andrew, 11, 25

Keokuk, 37

LeClaire, Antoine, 22–23, 36
Linnaeus, Carl von, 12
Little Crow (spirit), xxi, 31, 69–77, 83, 102, 131
Logan (spirit), xx, 69, 131
Longley, Mary Teresa. *See* Shelhamer, Mary Teresa
Lord, Annie, 30, 33, 45–46
Lord, Jennie, xiv, xx, xxv, 21, 30–49
Lotela (spirit), 107–110
Luna (spirit), 124

Markee, Mrs. E. J., 64
Martha (spirit), 59
Massachusetts Indian Association, 149
Meskino (spirit), 87
Mesmerism, xxviii, 5, 122
Metoka (spirit), 92, 100
Methodism, 3, 11

Index   201

Minnie (spirit). *See* Tappan, Minnie
Minnehaha (spirit). *See* Tappan, Minnie
Minwaw (spirit), 64
Modoc War, xvi
Moke-ta-va-ta (spirit), 70–72
Morning Star (spirit), 100–101, 112
Morton, Samuel George, 12, 41

Nanamakee, 27, 36
National Indian Association, xxii, 119, 149
National Indian Defense Association, 147
Ne-os-co-le-ta (spirit), 105
New Age, xxvii, 152
New Thought, 14
Ninna (spirit), 101, 106
The Noble Savage, xxi, xxvi, xxix, 3, 45, 81–82, 92, 98–102, 106–108

Old Ski, (spirit). *See* Skiwaukee
Osage Indians, 134, 137
Osceola (spirit), 64, 67, 85
Oskaloosa (spirit), 95
Ouina (spirit), xxi, 92, 100–111
Ounondita (sprit), 70

Parapsychology, 14
Peebles, Dr. James. M., 3, 9, 119
King Philip (spirit), xx–xxi, 82, 85, 102, 116, 144
Phillips, Wendell, 131, 138–139
Phrenology, xxviii, 5
Pierce, Abraham, 10, 124
Plains Indians, 24, 36, 137, 140

Playing Indian, xxv–xxviii, 6, 49, 66, 88–89
Pocahontas, 103; (spirit), 68, 124
Pogonakasheek (spirit), 75
Ponca Affair, xiii, xvi
Ponca Indians, xxvi, 116, 132
Post, Amy & Isaac, 141
Powhatan (spirit), xx–xxi, 59, 69, 131
Pratt, Richard, xxi, 76, 126

Quakerism, xxvii–xxviii, 5–7, 11, 13

Ramsey, William, 7, 118
Red Cloud, 74–77
Red Eagle (spirit), 88
Red Jacket, 34, 58; (spirit), 58, 68, 71, 79, 99
Red Wing (spirit), 60, 86–88
Richmond, Cora. *See* Tappan, Cora
Romanticism, xvi, xxi, xxix, 4, 8, 15, 17, 25, 35, 92, 96–98, 101, 104–108
Ross, Mrs. H. V., 94

Sac Indians, 21, 26–27, 36–37
Samoset (spirit), 68
Sand Creek Massacre, xii, 13, 72, 82, 105, 131–132, 138, 148
Santo (spirit), 64
Sargent, Epes, 42
Schurz, Carl, 146
Seminole Indians, 38, 86, 126, 140
Seneca (spirit), 44, 58–64, 67
Sequoia, 125
Shakerism, xxviii, 6, 30, 39, 66–67
Shawnee Indians, 86

Shelhamer, Mary Teresa, xi, xiv, xx–xxi, 21–23, 35, 46–48, 57, 85, 120
Shenandoah (spirit). *See* Ouina
Sheridan, Colonel Philip, 77, 116, 132, 134
Sherman, General William S., 83–84, 116, 140
Shining Star (spirit), 100, 108, 112
Silver Star (spirit), 112
Sioux Indians, xxvi, 74–75, 101, 105, 110, 116
Skiwaukee (spirit), 60–63, 110
Snowball (spirit), 112
Snowdrop (spirit), 112–113
Speech, Mr. F., 58
Spring Flower (spirit), 92, 101, 105
Star Flower (spirit), 97, 100, 112
Starlight (spirit), 100–101, 113
Steward, Mrs., 95
Summer Blossom (spirit), 94
Summer-Land, 8, 106, 111
Sunbeam (spirit), 92, 94–95, 101, 112
Swedenborgianism, xxviii, 7

Tappan, Colonel Samuel, 58, 102, 105, 121, 148
Tappan, Cora, xiv, xxi, xxv, 58, 72, 100, 102, 107–108, 148
Tappan, Minnie, 102–105, 138, 148; (spirit), 64, 93–94, 100–102, 112
Taylor, Mr., 64
Tecumseh (spirit), 78, 85, 131
Theosophy, 14

Transcendentalism, xxviii
Tuttle, Hudson, 68

The Uncanny, xiv, 1, 14–17, 31, 69
Unitarianism, 107
Universalism, xxviii

Vanishing Rhetoric, xii, xviii, xxvi–xix, 7, 15–17, 26, 37–38, 51, 69, 73–74, 77, 92, 107–108, 127–129, 133, 146, 151

Wahallahee (spirit), 105
Wampanoag Indians, 86
War of 1812, 22, 28
Washtinah (spirit), 67
Wasso (spirit), 87
Webb, Jennie Lord. *See* Lord, Jennie
Week, Mrs. M. E., 95
Welsh, William, 135
White Antelope, (spirit), 71–72, 82–84
White Eagle (spirit), 60, 69, 79, 88
White Fawn (spirit), 97, 101
White Flower (spirit), 112
White Wing (spirit), 59
Wildflower (spirit), 101
Winona (spirit), xxi, 101–104
Wolfe, Napoleon Bonaparte, 4, 60, 63
Women's National Indian Association, xxii, 119, 149
Wounded Knee Massacre, 139

Yellow Wolf, 127

www.ingramcontent.com/pod-product-compliance
Ingram Content Group UK Ltd.
Pitfield, Milton Keynes, MK11 3LW, UK
UKHW041855111225
465990UK00015B/87